A Collection of the Promises of Scripture

Under Their Proper Heads

In Two Parts, Representing
I. The Blessings Promised,
II. The Duties to Which Promises Are Made

By Samuel Clarke

Published by Pantianos Classics

ISBN-13: 978-1-78987-530-0

First published in 1720

This reprint is derived from an edition published in 1895

Contents

The Recommendation iv

Preface vi

The Introduction xv

Part One - The Blessings Promised to the Good 29

Chapter One - Promises *of* Temporal Blessings 29

Chapter Two - Promises *relating to* Troubles *of Life*. 38

Chapter Three - Promises *of* Spiritual Blessings *in this Life* 49

Chapter Four - Promises *of* Blessings *in the* Other World 82

Part Two - Promises to Several Graces and Duties 89

Chapter One - Promises *to* Duties *of the* First Table 89

Chapter Two - Promises *to* Duties *of the* Second Table 110

Chapter Three - Promises *to* Duties *belonging to* Both Tables .. 123

An Appendix of Promises Relating to the State *of the* Church 129

Conclusion - *That* God *will perform all His* Promises 146

"Tis of excellent use to lie on the table
"in a chamber of sickness, and now and
"then to take a sip of the river of life,
"which runs through it in a thousand
"little rills of peace and joy."

Is. Watts.

The Recommendation

THE BIBLE is a Book of such transcendent Worth, and so happily suited to all the Parts and Purposes of the Christian Life, that it can never be too much recommended to the World: Every Thing that allures the World to peruse it, is a Blessing to Mankind. And though it is hard for our narrow Capacities to grasp and take in the several distinguishing Excellencies of it at one View, yet if we take a separate Survey of the Doctrines and Duties, the Promises and Threatnings, the Prophecies and Histories which are contained therein, each of them will afford us an Aweful or a Delightful Prospect, with Lessons for special Improvement.

The worthy Author of this Collection, whom I have long known with Esteem and Honour, has chosen to reduce all the most useful and important Promises of the Word of God into Order, and set them before us here. These are the most powerful Motives to Duty; these are the constant Food of a living: Christian, as well as his highest Cordials in a fainting Hour. And in such a World as this, where Duties perpetually demand our Practice, and Difficulties and Trials are ever surrounding us, what can we do better than to treasure up the Promises in our Hearts, which are the most effectual Persuasives to fulfil the one, and sustain the other? Here are laid up the true Riches of a Christian, and his highest Hopes on this side Heaven.

The Materials which are collected here are all Divine, and the Disposition of them is Elegant and Regular; so that 'tis an easy matter to find something suited to the Frame of our Souls or our present Wants on every Occasion: And that Soul who knows what a suitable Promise is worth in an Hour of Darkness or Temptation, will never think such a Work as this, and such a various Treasure, can have sufficient Value set upon it.

This is such a Piece as I dare put into the Hands of every Christian among all their divided Sects and Parties in the World. Here is no danger of Error or Mistake in point of Orthodoxy, if the *English* be but truly translated from the Sacred Originals. The noisy Controversies of the Age, which eat out the Vitals of true Religion, have no room nor place here; for these Sentences are the pure Word of God, without any Mixtures of the Wit or Reasonings of Man,

'Tis the least Thing that I can do to shew my Gratitude to the pious Author of this Collection, to tell the World how much I esteem it, how often it has given me Consolation and Support in the midst of my long Infirmities and Confinements in former Years, when I was not capable of reading a whole Page together in any writing: and there are Multitudes of Christians that can bear the same Testimony to the Value of this *Collection of Promises*, who have found it an effectual Spur to Duty, and a divine Relief under surrounding Sorrows.

In order to a better Improvement of these *Promises*, it may be very proper to read the *Introduction* first, which will teach even Christians of the lower Rank how to understand and apply all these Discoveries of Divine Mercy. Those who have little Leisure for Reading may find their Account in keeping this Book always near them, and with the Glance of an Eye they may take in the Riches of Grace and Glory, and derive many a sweet Refreshment from hence, amidst their Labours and Travels through this Wilderness. 'Tis of excellent Use to lie on the Table in a Chamber of Sickness, and now and then to take a Sip of the River of Life, which runs through it in a thousand little Rills of Peace and Joy.

May this *Second Edition* which brings it again into the World, be attended with still greater Success: And I shall be glad to see such an Evidence of growing Christianity and living Religion among us, that such an Assemblage of Divine Mercies, which have been showered down from Heaven in different Ages upon this wretched World, ever since the Fall of Man, comes into the Relish and Taste of Mankind, so far as to be perused and prized by them. May the Holy Spirit of God who indited all these *Promises*, and our Blessed Mediator who by his Ministry and by his Blood has seal'd and confirm'd them all, render them every Day more and more powerful and prevalent to draw the Hearts of Men towards God, and to fit them for the Enjoyment of these Words of Grace in their compleat Accomplishment in Glory.   *Amen.*

I. Watts.

Newington,
January 19th, 1737/8

Preface

The small volume known as "The Scripture Promises" has been a very popular, and is still a well-known work. Since its publication in 1720 it has gone through many editions; the second in 1738, equipped with a preface by Dr. Watts; the third in 1750; the fourth in 1760; and the last of many others, in 1863, its popularity having increased, owing to its publication in a cheaper form, in the present century. Its author, Dr. Samuel Clark, came of a race not unknown in the theological literature of the 17th and 18th centuries. His ancestor, in the fourth degree, was Vicar of Wolston. His great grandfather, Samuel Clark, Vicar of Alcester, and afterwards of Bennet Fink in London, was a voluminous and popular writer, whose "Mirror" and "Martyrology" have gone through many editions, still finding a place in the lower shelves of libraries, and whose books of Lives are even now quoted in all dictionaries of biography. His grandfather, a second Samuel, Fellow of Pembroke Hall, and Rector of Grendon-Underwood, was a very learned and industrious biblical scholar, whose Annotations upon both Old and New Testaments were introduced by Baxter, Owen, Bates, and Howe; commended by Tillotson; largely employed by Doddridge; in the later editions praised by Whitfield, and are still quoted by Commentators. They were accompanied by a "Harmony of the Gospels," one of the earliest of the kind, and followed a few years later by an "Analytical Survey of the Bible," and a Concordance; only superseded by the more copious work of Cruden. Both father and son, and some other collateral kinsmen of their name and family, were among those deprived of their benefices by the Bartholomew Act, all of whom remained in faithful though silent communion with the Church in which they had been baptized and ordained, and had long ministered.

The third Samuel, two generations lower down, the author of this Collection of the Promises, was also a man of some classical learning, and a severe student of the Holy Scriptures. Born in 1684, he became pastor of the congregation, then newly formed, at St. Albans, where he served faithfully for 38 years, and dying suddenly while engaged in his ministry, in 1759, at the age of 66, was buried in the churchyard of St. Peter's Church, beneath a stone on which he is described, no doubt by Doddridge, as "learned, candid, and pious."

He was a man of a remarkably modest and unassuming character, the Pastor of a small and in no way distinguished congregation, which however he declined to exchange for others of greater wealth and higher social or intellectual consideration. That his memory has been preserved is due in part to the present volume, and in part to his intimate connection with Dr. Doddridge, to whose success in life he largely contributed.

Philip Doddridge was descended, collaterally, from the well-remembered Judge of that name, and his grandfather, the Rev. John Doddridge, was one of the ejected ministers. At thirteen years old, being an orphan, he was sent to school at St. Albans, and soon afterwards, by the imprudence of an agent, he was reduced to poverty. Dr. Clark, hearing of his necessities, and probably aware of his grave and studious character, took him by the hand, enabled him to carry on his studies, and finally delivered the charge admitting him to the ministry. Of Dr. Clark's care for his concerns, both spiritual and temporal, Doddridge, in after life, frequently expressed his deep sense, and in the sermon preached at his funeral he says, "to him, I may truly say, that, under God, I owe even myself, and all my opportunities of public usefulness in the Church; to him, who was not only the instructor of my childhood and youth in the principles of religion, but my guardian when a helpless orphan, as well as the generous, tender, faithful friend of all my advancing years."

Many of Dr. Clark's letters, mostly of advice and encouragement, together with others addressed to him by Doddridge, have been printed. Samuel Clark, the Doctor's eldest son, was a pupil of Doddridge, and edited his lectures. When Doddridge left for Lisbon, to Mr. Clark he committed the charge of his affairs, accounting it he says, "a singular happiness that God had given to him an assistant to whom he could cheerfully consign the care of his academy and congregation, whose great prudence and wise disposition of affairs made him quite easy as to both." Samuel Clark was injured by a fall from his horse and died 6th December, 1769, in his 42nd year, unmarried. His epitaph was written by Dr. Nathaniel Cotton, of St. Albans, the friend of Cowper, and the closing lines, though highly eulogistic, were in substance true, and seem to deserve preservation here.

> "What tho' such various worth is seldom known,
>   No adulation rears this sacred stone;
>   No partial love this genuine picture draws;
>   No venal pencil prostitutes applause:
>   Justice and truth in artless colours paint
>   The Man, the Friend, the Preacher, and the Saint."

The feeling, antagonistic to the Church of England, which, strongly political, pervades the Dissenters of the present century, was in no degree felt by Dr. Clark, or by his friends Doddridge and Watts, any more than by their successors, on parallel lines, Wesley and Whitfield. Their objections were to the government and discipline, rather than to the doctrines of the episcopal Church, though they disapproved to some extent of the use of formularies other than the actual words of Scripture. Above all they, were implicit believers in the Divinity of our Lord, and rested their hopes solely upon His sufferings, death, and resurrection. As the descendants of the men ejected under the Bartholomew Act have a history peculiar to themselves, and had little in common with the great body of English Dissenters, it will be convenient briefly to explain their origin, conduct, and position. By some they were called Presbyterians, by others Independents, but they do not seem ever to have assumed these or any other names, nor did they, for many years, if at all, act in a body, or acknowledge any common form of Church government.

When, some years ago, the year of Grace 1862 completed the second century from the passing of the celebrated Act of Uniformity, much was spoken and written in commemoration of the two thousand incumbents of the Church of England who left their benefices and accepted poverty rather than subscribe to its conditions. It was indeed a sacrifice for conscience sake of which Englishmen do well to be proud, and the more so that, as with the Huguenots in France, the sufferers had no organization as a party, had not time even to convene a meeting, but each had to act for himself, and upon the dictates of his own conscience.

But what, at the time, was passed by in silence, was the curious fact that nearly the whole body of those called orthodox dissenters spoke and acted as though they, and they only, were the representatives of the ejected ministers, while in truth scarcely any were descended from them either carnally or spiritually, and they had little in common with their ecclesiastical opinions, and still less with their attitude towards the Church of England. Even their appellation was incorrectly assumed. Just as the attorney of the last century is now commonly known as a solicitor, the modern Dissenter assumes the name of Nonconformist. No doubt, etymologically, all who do not conform are nonconformists, as all who not swear allegiance are nonjurors, but technically, the term "nonconformist" was confined to the men who were ejected on St. Bartholomew's day under the Act of Uniformity of 1622, just as the term "nonjuror" is confined to those who on the arrival of William III. left the Church of England for opposite reasons. The subject is not without its interest to both Churchmen and Dissenters, and it is here proposed to shew briefly what was the relation of the Bartholomew men to the Established Church, and how they are really represented at the present day.

A CENTURY ago a frequent appendage to the towns and larger villages of England was a square, or rather an oblong building of red brick, with windows narrow in proportion to their height, the roof, chisel pointed and covered with red tiles, and now and then a carved hood over the door. With little architectural merit, these buildings were not vulgar, for they were not pretentious. Unlike many modern meeting houses, they display no attempts at decorations in the Gothic or Ecclesiastical style, but proclaimed to all their origin and occupation. The bricks were always of good colour, and when a little subdued by time, became agreeable to the eye; the walls were of fair thickness, and the workmanship sound and honest. They rose before the employment of plaster, and when large and smooth slates were scarcely in use. The internal fittings were of the plainest; usually of deal, often unpainted; and designed to accommodate with comfort a moderate congregation, with a pulpit so placed that all might hear and take part in the service. Sometimes the building stood in a burial ground of moderate area, and the memorials of the dead were simple and plain. Minister and congregation had been thrust out with some harshness from the Church, but those who had actually suffered the wrong seldom retained any feeling of animosity; they were baptized, married, and not unfrequently buried with their fathers in and about the Parish Church. Their secession was accomplished with great reluctance, and though debarred from ministerial office in the Church, they continued to regard themselves as among her members. The earlier ministers, including Richard Baxter and his friends, attended parochial worship when the pulpit was unusually well filled, and more frequently to partake of the Holy Communion. The Statute book did not indeed place them on the same level with the members of the National Church, but for some years they availed themselves of some of her privileges, declined to regard themselves as schismatics, and by no means desired her destruction. It is also on record that in those halcyon days their form of dissent did not affect the social position of its professors: their congregations included Russells, Cecils, Knightleys, Houghtons and Copes, and some who "wore a coronet and prayed," The first Pastors or Ministers, as they were called, were almost all members of the old universities, nearly all had held benefices, some of them, as Hildersham, Annesley, and Gatacre, were men of good family, and all the elder men had received Episcopal ordination. The points of difference, though many, scarcely extended to doctrine, and a small concession then, as to the later Wesley, would have restored some of them to the Church's fold.

And first as to their origin. Among the varieties of religious opinion called into existence by the Great Reformation were two main types of belief, the one holding the separation from Rome as too sharp and too wide, and the other being of opinion that too great tenderness had been shewn to the Romish doctrines, and too great toleration, especially in the Cathedral Services, for the Romish Ritual. Both these, differing considerably, were nevertheless honest and loyal members of the National Church; though the high party being opposed to change, was naturally favoured by the ruling powers, while the low party, persecuted to the death by Henry, severely repressed by Elizabeth, and teased and irritated by James, was nevertheless not without its share in the dignities of the Establishment, and was occasionally represented in the Episcopal, and even in the Archiepiscopal chairs.

Under Charles and Laud as his minister, the low party, being persecuted civilly and ecclesiastically, prodigiously increased, but they were imbued with much of the spirit of the gospel, were moderate in their opinions, opposed to violence, and in consequence, much disliked by the Independents and fanatics, and regarded with no favour by Cromwell, of whom Baxter says he "kept as much honesty and godliness as his cause and interest would allow him." They were, like Sir Matthew Hale and other patriotic Englishmen, loyal to the existing governments whether of the Parliament or the Protector, and continued to hold their offices and discharge their parochial duties.

Some of their leaders acted as "Triers" for the examination and ordination of candidates and their induction into benefices and, in the absence of the Prelates, necessarily discharged functions which hitherto had been confined to those who regarded themselves as the spiritual descendants of the Apostles. Though tolerant of most other sects, they held little in common with the Baptists, and nothing with the Unitarians or Socinians, of whom, with the Papists, they were strongly intolerant. They may be said to have held pretty much the same relative position spiritually in the Church that was held long afterwards by the followers of Newton, Scott, and Simeon, under the name of the Evangelical party. On the overthrow of the Established Church, their political opinions became more distinctly pronounced, but their doctrine remained unaltered; and they continued to have no objection, on principle, to either an Episcopacy or a Liturgy, though they wished to revive the popular element in the election of the Bishops, and desired a very moderate alteration in the baptismal and burial services, and in that for the visitation of the sick. They had, indeed, their own views on many points of discipline, and became known as Presbyterians. The name was misleading, since it was already borne by the Kirk of Scotland, from which they differed very materially; but in England it served to distinguish them from the Episcopalian, and from other Puritan sects, especially from the Baptists. It is, however, important that those who, in writing, are obliged to make use of the name, should not forget the qualified sense that appertains to it. It should also be remembered that their opinions were speculative only and did not prevent them from holding preferment in the English Church, from signing its articles, or making use of its liturgical formularies.

They approved of the Restoration, though with some misgivings, from the absence of conditions; and a large body of the London Clergy, though holding the above opinions, joined in the procession to meet the King and were well received, and presented him with a Bible. His Majesty was liberal in promises, as was his wont with what cost him nothing. The Bible, he assured them, should be the rule and government of his life. He had already, at the Hague, promised them comprehension and toleration. Ten of their number, including Baxter and Calamy, were nominated as King's chaplains, of whom five preached at least once in that capacity. Three Deaneries and as many Bishoprics were offered to the leaders, and one of the latter, that of Norwich, was accepted.

They were willing to acknowledge an Episcopal government on the basis of Archbishop Usher's scheme: suffragans to be appointed, and the Bishops' powers to be shared with a synod. They had their grievances, which most of them had suffered for during the late King's reign, but they wished if possible to conform, and whatever their nominal demands, a moderate concession would probably have then been accepted.

With the monarchy was restored the Episcopal Order, and the first differences arose on the refusal of the Bishops to acknowledge the ordination or induction of those who during the interregnum, and in their absence, had accepted Church preferment. Upon this point the Bishops were firm, and there was no disposition in the new government to over-rule their decision. This exclusion did not affect the older men, as Baxter, Samuel Clark, and Calamy, but it reduced some scores of the younger men to poverty, and what they liked as little, to silence. Charles, easy, good-natured, and utterly indifferent, would gladly have consented to a compromise, but the royalists were essentially Episcopalians, and the Bishops evidently desired to exclude the whole of the Presbyterian party, as likely to be less troublesome outside than inside the Church. After meetings, at one of which, that of Worcester House, the King was present, and spoke in a very moderate spirit, it became evident that the Bishops desired nothing so little as a compromise, and were as fully determined to hold their ground on the defensive as Baxter and his friends, now greatly excited, and disposed to rise in their demands, were on the other or aggressive side. The latter wished to ventilate their opinions in public, and to have a personal discussion. To this the Bishops were opposed, but a Conference was finally agreed upon, and a royal commission issued with a summons to assemble in the Savoy, where the Presbyterians had held a meeting in 1659. "The Savoy Conference," by which name it is known in the annals of the Church of England, met in May, 1661, and included twelve Doctors on the one side, and twelve leaders of the Presbyterian party on the other; and to each side were allotted nine assistants all, or very nearly all, of whom, were in the Communion of the Church of England. The Conference having talked much, and after many interruptions and many personal reflections from both sides, broke up, having settled nothing, and leaving each party more embittered than ever, if possible, against the other. The result, as no doubt had been foreseen, was a complete failure, Pearson, one is glad to learn, and Bishop Gauden, were distinguished for their moderation; Morley of Winchester was violent, shewing, it was thought by his adversaries, distinctly Romish tendencies, Baxter, as usual intensely critical, with Calamy, led their party. His original demands were thought, even by his own supporters, impracticable, and Samuel Clark, the Martyrologist, his personal friend, and who had been repeatedly President of Sion College, was appointed to counsel moderation, and to calm that fiery and somewhat overbearing spirit. The Bishops however, from the first, would concede nothing, and called upon their opponents to put in a copy of the liturgy as they wished it to stand. This they agreed to do, though very unwillingly, and with reason, for the proposed reform, in Baxter's hands, was a revolution, and the liturgy he drew up went far to shew the impracticability of any kind of union, and thus to justify the Bishops in their refusal to treat. That they used their victory harshly there can be no doubt, having the royalists, and for the time the royalist feeling of the nation with them, they passed the celebrated "Act of Uniformity" under which those ministers who entered their profession when there were no Bishops forthcoming to admit them, were to be episcopally ordained, and all who did not declare their assent and consent to the book of Common Prayer, and to some other points on which that book was silent, by the 24th of August, 1662, being St. Bartholomew's Day, were to be ejected from all benefices, schools, or other ecclesiastical offices. This was closely followed by a second Act, and all preachers, though holding no ecclesiastical office were to be silenced. This again was followed by the Conventicle Act, making penal an assembly of more than five persons under colour of religion, and in 1665 came the Five Mile Act, under which all ministers who refused to swear not at any time "to endeavour any alteration in Church or State," were forbidden to come within five miles of any city or borough, or any place where they had been ministers; and this again led the way to a renewal of the Conventicle Act with a very strict clause, under which it was forbidden to preach in any private house. Even a bequest of money for the relief of such of the ejected ministers as were in want was adjudged illegal, and the money seized and applied to other uses. Those who refused the new oaths were branded as schismatics, although the point in dispute could not finally be held to constitute a schism, and it was well known that many a conformist held opinions which were of the nature of schism, which does not necessarily apply to a mere separation. The result of this persecution was to unite the moderate with the extreme party, and to deprive the Church of England of a large body of earnest, conscientious, law abiding, and by no means unlearned men, of whom a considerable number, had they simply been permitted to remain undisturbed, would have given no further trouble. As it was, nearly 2,000 ministers and their very numerous followers were permanently alienated from the Church, and after a few years of severe persecution took up so strong a position that on the arrival of William III. they built meeting houses and formed independent congregations.

One of William's first acts, at the instance of Tillotson, was to appoint a Commission to consider the questions of toleration and comprehension. Various and indeed extensive alterations in the Liturgy were proposed, mostly in favour of comprehension, and had the spirit then shewn been displayed at the Savoy Conference, it is possible that many of the ministers would have returned to the Church; but time had brought about many changes, congregations had been collected, connexions formed, and chapels built, and the Commission came to an end having produced, after the manner of Commissions, nothing but a report. Some of the new chapels were endowed, and it is remarkable that the trust deeds seldom if ever specify any distinct form of faith. The Presbyterians and Independents were at that time and long afterwards closely allied; the former leaning somewhat towards the Church, the latter rather from it, but with the latter were some of the ejected ministers.

Their education at home being prohibited, their students had recourse to the Universities of Holland and North Germany, nor was it until the Revolution that they were able to afford instruction in their own country. The first fruit of the new liberty was the formation, by voluntary efforts, of the well-known "Presbyterian Fund," the principal object of which was to encourage the education of students for the Christian Ministry, the success of which was immediate and lasting. Under its influence, great and rapid progress was made in the foundation of schools and places of education, the Presbyterian party being at that time not only very numerous, but high in social position and influence. For degrees in divinity they had recourse to the Scottish Universities, but they took ordination at the hands of their own elders. Of their schools and academies, those of Doddridge at Northampton, Jennings at Kibworth, Ashworth at Daventry, Theophilus Gale at Stoke Newington, were celebrated, as were others at Norwich, Birmingham, Leeds, Warrington, Hackney, Hoxton, and in London. Provision was also made by the King's Head Society, in 1730, for the training of future ministers, and produced some of considerable eminence. They did not compete with the universities in the higher branches of criticism or in the graces of classical composition, but they included many branches of knowledge far better suited to the wants of the lower middle classes, and far more immediately useful to those who had to make their way in the world in trade or commerce. They included eminent merchants among their pupils and members, and were especially strong in the City of London. Sir Humphrey Edwin, then Lord Mayor, came to Pinners Hall in state in 1697, and Sir Thomas Abney, also a Presbyterian, filled that office in 1700.

The question of liturgical forms, for some time set aside, forced its way gradually forward, and in 1719 a meeting was convened at Salters Hall in London to discuss and decide upon this very important question. The meeting was well attended, and when the question of Creed or no Creed was put to the vote it was decided in the negative by fifty-seven voices against fifty-one, and declared that no form of belief other than the very words of Scripture should be adopted, and that it should be left to each congregation to hold what opinions seemed to its members to be right, unshackled by any forms inferred or deduced, however strictly, from the Scriptures. A few, and but a few, objecting, took refuge in the Church of England, and joined what afterwards became the Evangelical party, but the greater number seem to have drifted into Unitarian opinions, more or less strongly pronounced. These also, in politics, took extreme views, and became warm approvers of the French Revolution, at least in its earlier stages. Their opinions, strongly taken up at Birmingham, Norwich, and in London, found their way into the pulpits and among the congregations, each of which elected their own ministers according to the views that at the time happened to prevail, so that Unitarian and Trinitarian doctrines were held by contiguous congregations, and were preached not unfrequently from the same pulpit. Thus it came to pass that men who differed widely from Doddridge and Watts, such for example as Priestly, Belsham, Price, Chandler, Kippis, and Aiken, occupied what had been founded as orthodox chapels. By degrees this state of things, this absence of test or liturgical form, offering no check to or even record of any change of opinion, led to the present state of things, in which by far the greater number of the chapels founded by the ejected ministers are occupied by Unitarian congregations, so that the Unitarian body is really the chief representative of the Bartholomew clergy. This to those who, with the present writer, hold the doctrinal opinions of Baxter and the Author of "The Scripture Promises" is painful, but it is not the less the truth, and strange as it may appear, it is the Unitarian section, and not the great body of English Dissenters, who are really derived from the ejected Ministers.

It has been said, and no doubt with truth, that an indifference to the visible bonds of Church union produces a craving for religious excitement, but in this case the effect was of a reverse character, and the congregations for a long time to come certainly could not be accused of a craving for spiritual religion.

The conclusion to which this gradual and at the time imperceptible change of doctrine seems naturally to lead, is surely in favour of the adoption of some kind of formulary to secure the maintenance of a particular belief, or at any rate to mark any departure from it in practice, and it may, perhaps, be permitted to a member of the Church of England, though of a Bartholomew stock, to express an opinion that for spirituality of tone, moderation and charity of temper, fidelity to Scripture, and purity and elevation of style, there exists no collection of formularies to be compared with the Common Prayer Book of his own Church. Not a few indeed of her most faithful members desire to see the Creed called of St. Athanasius, as unfitted for a public service, relegated to her articles or canons; the form of absolution in her Visitation of the Sick made to conform to her general absolution; and the declaration as to the condition of the dead in her Burial service, made the expression of a pious hope rather than of a positive assertion. No human composition is or can be absolutely perfect, and surely these blemishes, if blemishes they be, are not such as to justify clamour or attack, still less to be pleaded as reasons for departure from her Communion.

The Introduction

CONTAINING

Some Observations *upon the* Excellency *and* Use *of the* Promises, *and* Directions *for the right* Application *of them.*

BESIDES the many other Evidences the Holy Scripture carries in it of a Divine Original, there are especially remarkable the Sublimity, Excellency and Reasonableness of the Doctrines it teaches; the Wisdom, Holiness, and Perfection of the Rules of Life it lays down; and the Strength and Efficacy of those Sanctions, with which it enforces its Precepts. As the *Threatnings* have the greatest Tendency to strike an Awe upon the Mind, and to lay a powerful Restraint upon every irregular Inclination, so the *Promises* are of such a Nature as most strongly to excite to, and give the greatest Encouragement in, a Course of Piety and universal Holiness. It is therefore with the highest Reason the Apostle says of them, *That there are given unto us exceeding great and precious Promises, that by these we might be Partakers of the Divine Nature, having escaped the Corruption that is in the World through Lust,* 2 Pet. i. 4. They are great and excellent; whether we consider the Nature and Variety of the Blessings contained in them, the Manner in which they are expressed, the Certainty with which we may depend upon them, or their happy Influence upon the Mind.

They contain Blessings of all Sorts, of the most excellent Nature, and suited to every Circumstance. As Man is made up of Body as well as Spirit, and the Necessities of this present Life must be provided for, as well as his Happiness secured in the next; in the *Promises* abundant Care is taken of both, and Provision is made for the Peace. Comfort, and Welfare of the Christian, both in this, and in the other World. He is assured of the several Necessaries and Conveniences of this Life, in such a measure, as Infinite Wisdom sees best for him. And since we are exposed to various Troubles and Calamities, there are many *Promises* made with relation to them; either that we shall be preserved from those Afflictions, or, if it be necessary we should be exercised with them, that we shall be powerfully supported under them, and in the best Time and Way, delivered from them, after that they have been made to answer the most excellent Ends upon us. Nor is it easy to say, what a vast Variety of Consolations are provided for our Relief in those Trials. But, however valuable, considering the Circumstances of our present State, the *Promises* relating to Temporal Enjoyments and Afflictions, may be, they are not to be compared with the Excellency and Glory of those Spiritual and Eternal Blessings, with which we are blessed in Christ Jesus, and of which we have the most clear, full and express *Promises* in the Gospel. Therein, how great, how particular a Regard is had to the Condition of fallen, sinful Man! What Care is taken to ease the Conscience under the Burden of Guilt, and the Apprehensions of Divine Wrath, by the most gracious *Promises* of Pardon and Mercy! What Assurances given of Reconciliation and Acceptance with God, through the Blood and Intercession of the Redeemer! To what glorious Privileges and high Honours is the Christian advanced! Such as, The Adoption of Children, A kind Regard to all his Prayers, The Ministry of Angels, and, An Interest in the Grace, Love and Fellowship of God the Father, and of his Eternal Son and Spirit. In the *Promises* is contained all that Grace which is requisite to refine and ennoble our Natures, to inlighten our Understandings, to regulate our Wills, and purify our Affections; to preserve us from Sin, and all the Contrivances and Snares of the Devil and the World, and to exalt us to the highest Perfection of Holiness and Happiness.

The Manner in which these Blessings are promised, still further adds to their Value. They are not expressed in general or ambiguous Terms, but with the greatest Clearness and Perspicuity. God would not leave his People at an Uncertainty, concerning his kind Intentions towards them. If the Meaning of a Promise seems doubtful in one Place, it is abundantly cleared up in several others. Nor is it only here and there in some few Passages, or in a cold and reserved Manner, that God has signified his good Will; but, upon the Account of our Dulness and Slowness to believe what God has promised, he has both made use of the strongest Words and Phrases that Language could furnish out, and has over and over, in great Variety of Expression, often repeated the Assurances of his Favour. He has contrived his *Promises* so as to meet with all our Objections, and remove all our Doubts and Fears: And herein he has been pleased to shew an Affection, Tenderness, and Condescension, which could not be expected from an earthly Prince to his Subjects, much less from the Great and Glorious Majesty of Heaven and Earth to sinful Dust and Ashes.

But what doth in the highest Degree inhance the Worth and Excellency of the Promises, is the Evidences we have that they shall certainly be made good; since, as the Apostle argues, Heb. vi. 17, 18, we have for them both the Word and *Oath of that God who cannot lye,* that *so we might have strong Consolation, who have fled for Refuge, to lay hold upon the Hope set before us.* And of the Covenant thus confirmed, Christ the Son of God is made the Surety, Heb. vii. 22, having ratified it by his own Blood. And that all the Ever-blessed Trinity might concur in establishing our Faith upon the strongest Foundation, the Holy Spirit of God witnesses the Truth of the *Promises,* by his miraculous Operations, when first poured forth upon the Apostles, and by his sanctifying Influences upon the Hearts of all true Christians, both then and ever since. Hereby he inspires into them a lively Hope, and furnishes them with well-grounded Evidences of their Interest in the *Promises;* and *their Hope makes them not ashamed, because the Love of God is shed abroad in their Hearts by the Holy Ghost, which is given unto them,* Rom. v. 5.

The *Promises* therefore of the Gospel being of so excellent a Nature, and confirmed to us by such Authority and Evidence, cannot but have very great and happy Influences upon the Mind, when seriously attended to, and applied with Faith; especially as they are the Means by which the Spirit of God carries on his Work upon the Soul. They are the strongest Arguments to persuade the Sinner to turn to God, the greatest Encouragement to a humble, believing Dependence upon the Grace of Christ in the Gospel, and the most powerful Motives to sincere and universal Obedience: Since by them we are assured, that every penitent Sinner shall find the most gracious Acceptance; that from the Grace of Christ we shall derive sufficient Strength and Capacity for every Duty; and that in keeping God's Commands there is great Reward. So that would we but duly consider the several *Promises* made to every Exercise of Grace, and every Performance of Duty, what a Spur would this be to quicken our slow Pace in the Ways of Holiness! What an Encouragement to be stedfast *and immovable, always abounding in the Work of the Lord, forasmuch as we know that our Labour is not in vain in the Lord,* I Cor. xv. 58.

A Fixed, constant Attention to the *Promises,* and a firm Belief of them, would prevent Solicitude and Anxiety about the Concerns of this Life. It would keep the Mind quiet and compos'd in every Change, and support and keep up our sinking Spirits under the several Troubles of Life. *In the Multitude of my Thoughts within me, thy Comforts delight my Soul, Ps.* xciv. 19. Christians deprive themselves of their most solid Comforts by their Unbelief and Forgetfulness of God's *Promises*. For there is no Extremity so great, but there are *Promises* suitable to it, and abundantly sufficient for our Relief in it.

A THOROUGH Acquaintance with the *Promises* would be of the greatest Advantage in Prayer. With what Comfort may the Christian address himself to God in Christ, when he considers the repeated Assurances that his Prayers shall be heard? With how much Satisfaction may he offer up the several Desires of his Heart, when he reflects upon the Texts wherein those very Mercies are promised? And with what Fervour of Spirit, and Strength of Faith, may he enforce his Prayers, by pleading the several gracious *Promises,* which are expressly to his Case?

Further, Great Assistance and Encouragement may the Christian derive in his Spiritual Warfare, when he takes a View of the many *Promises* of Grace and Strength to mortify Sin, and to resist the Devil; of Success and a final Victory in his Conflicts with the Enemies of his Salvation; and of an incorruptible Crown of Glory, to be given him as the Reward of his Firmness, Constancy and Perseverance. A great deal more may be said, but that I would not too much enlarge this *Introduction,* to shew of what excellent Use the *Promises* would be if duly attended to, to promote all the Exercises of the Divine Life, and to inspire into a good Man Comfort and Joy in every State of Life.

That the Christian might have before him, in one View, the many great and precious *Promises* scattered up and down in Scripture, and in such a Method as easily to find what is suitable to his Case, I have drawn up the following

Collection. The Occasion indeed, of my first entring upon it, was to assist some Young Persons, who very commendably and to their great Advantage, are employ 'd in improving themselves, and one another, in the Knowledge of the Scriptures; one of their Exercises being to treasure up in their Memories, and question one another upon the *Promises,* under their several Heads. At first I intended to put together a small Number, upon some principal Subjects; but, upon searching the Scriptures more and more Texts still offering themselves, which I thought equally to my Purpose, this Collection at length grew so large, that the taking so many Copies as were wanted, would have been a tedious Work; For which Reason, and in hopes it might serve the same useful End to others, I at last gave way to its being made publick. Since I compleated it, I have examin'd some other Collections I have met with, and have added out of them those few Texts, which I had not before observed; So that, I believe, this is the fullest Collection of the kind of any extant, at least that I have seen.

I have endeavour'd to put them together in such a Method as might be easiest and fittest for common Use. I have not increased the Heads to so great a Variety of Particulars as some may expect; both because too many Divisions rather confound than assist the Memory; and also the applying of the *Promises* to Cases too particular, would have too much confin'd their Use, when capable of a more extensive Application. If any therefore want the *Promises* for some Case they don't find there mentioned, they may meet with them under some more general Head, within which that Case is comprehended. And for the same Reason, some of the *Promises* may seem not so properly to belong to the Head under which they are ranged; but as they are near akin to it, I chose rather to put them together, than to multiply Heads. There are also other Texts, which some may think should have been placed elsewhere: For instance, some of the *Promises* under the Head of *Temporal Blessings,* are by some understood in a Figurative Sense of Spiritual, and so on the contrary. I have taken them in the Sense that appeared to me most agreeable to the Design of the Spirit of God; though sometimes, where I thought the Words were capable of both Senses, I have written them in both Places. Many other Texts also might be ranged under different Heads: for Example, either in the First Part, among the Blessings promised; or in the Second, containing the Graces and Duties to which *Promises* are made; and sometimes under either of those Heads, which being nearly related, follow one the other; as the Head of *Sanctifying Grace in general,* and *Converting Grace.* If therefore what you look for be not in one Place, you may expect to find it in the other. For which Purpose the References in the *Table of Contents* will be useful; for I have generally endeavoured to avoid Repetitions. Sometimes, indeed, the same Text may be met with in different Places, but then it is applied to different Purposes; as when several Blessings or Duties are comprised in one, as *Prov.* xxii. 4, in *p.* 13.

Though all the Scriptures here collected under the Name of *Promises* are useful for the Comfort and Encouragement of Christians in the Cases specified; yet they are expressed in different Forms. Some contain direct *Promises* and *Assurances* of such and such Blessings. Of these, some are made to all in general, according to the Rules and Limitations of the Gospel; as *Ps.* lxxxiv. 11, *p.* 1, and *Ps.* xxxiv. 9, 10, *p.* 3. But others are address'd to Particular good Men in Scripture, which yet every Christian may take Comfort in. So that *Promise* made to *Joshua,* Chap. i. 5, *I will not fail thee nor forsake thee,* is by the Apostle apply'd to Christians in general, *Heb.* xiii. 6. In the same manner, *Promises* made to particular Churches, are applicable to the Church of God in general; as those in the Old Testament to the *Jewish* Church, *Is.* xxvii. 3, and Zech. ii. 5, in *p.* 11, and those to the Churches in the New Testament, *Phil.* iv. 19, *p.* 4, *Rom.* xvi. 20, *p.* 80, and many more. The Rule in both these Cases, is That whatsoever *Promises* are made in Scripture to particular Persons, in Cases, and for Reasons, that equally concern other good Men, they are applicable to the Comfort of all, and may be pleaded with Faith in Prayer. The Words of the Apostle afford a sufficient Foundation for this Observation, *Rom.* xv. 4, *Whatsoever Things were written aforetime, were written for our Learning, that we through Patience and Comfort of the Scriptures might have Hope.*

The *Promises* also made in particular Cases to Persons in Scripture, may be applied to the Encouragement of others, so far as the Case and Circumstances agree, though not absolutely, and in their whole Extent. Thus the *Promise* made to Solomon (2 *Chron* i. 11. 13.) of Wisdom, and also of Riches and Honour, beyond all that were before him, because he asked of God Wisdom rather than Riches, &c., is applicable to *Solomon* only, in its whole Extent; but yet gives Encouragement to every good Man to hope, that if he seek of God Wisdom above all other Things, he shall obtain a large Measure of it, according to what his Station requires, and also so much of other worldly Advantages as God sees best for him, according to those more general *Promises, Prov.* viii. 17, 18. In the same manner the *Promises* made by Christ to his Apostles of the Holy Spirit, *to teach them all Things, and bring all Thing's he had said to them to Remembrance,* John xiv. 26, and to *guide* them *into all Truth,* Chap. xvi. 13, though they are not to be apply'd to others in the same degree as to the Apostles, who were by the Spirit extraordinarily inspir'd and instructed in the whole Revelation of the Gospel, and infallibly secured from Error, this being peculiar to their Character as Apostles; yet they encourage all other Christians to expect from the Spirit all that Illumination, Instruction, and Guidance which is necessary for them in their several Circumstances, upon the diligent Use of all appointed Means, so that they shall be preserved from all dangerous and fatal Mistakes and Errors, according to those *Promises*, I *John* ii. 20, 27; *Ps.* xxv. 12, and others; in *p.* 72, 76, made to good Men in general.

Besides those Scriptures that run in the Form of *Promises,* there are others which are Observations or Declarations of the Blessings that generally attend the several Exercises of Piety and Holiness; as *Ps.* cxi. 5, in *p.* 4, and *Prov.* xviii. 10, in *p.* 7, and most of those collected out of the *Proverbs* and *Ecclesiastes.* But as these are Observations made under the Inspiration of the Spirit of God, they give the same Encouragement to expect the Blessings mentioned in them, as if they were in the Form of *Promises.*

Some of the Texts do only express the Experiences of good Men in Scripture, or their Expectations from God; as *Ps.* xvi. 6, in *p.* i, *Ps.* xxiii. throughout, *p.* 3, and *Ps.* lxxi. 20, in *p.* 23. Of which Scriptures the same may be said as of those above, That as Holy Men therein spake under the Direction of the Spirit of God, and what they say of themselves is recorded for our Instruction and Comfort, consequently other good Men may assure themselves, in like Circumstances, of the like Favour and Mercy, Thus, whereas the Psalmist expresses his Confidence in God's Help against all his Enemies, *Ps.* cxviii. 6, the Apostle applies it to all Christians, *Heb.* xiii. 6. *So that we may boldly say, The Lord is my Helper, and I will not fear what Man can do unto me.*

Some of the Texts are Petitions put up by Christ for his Church: as those taken out of *John* xvii. These give the same Encouragement as the *Promises* do; for we are assured that whatever Christ asks for his People, is certainly granted.

The same may be said, in some Degree, of the Prayers put up by other Saints in Scripture, for themselves and others; especially the Prophetical Prayers, *Gen.* xlix., *Deut.* xxxii., and in other Places. Since those Prayers were deliver'd under the Inspiration of the Spirit, we know they were agreeable to the Will of God; and so far as Circumstances are the same, all other good Men may hope to be heard in asking the same Blessings of God. But of this Sort I've taken but few, both because it is more difficult rightly and with Judgment to apply them, and lest I should too much swell this Collection.

The *Blessings promised,* are either of a Temporal, or of a Spiritual and Eternal Nature: It may be necessary to lay down some Rules, to direct the serious Christian in the right Application of these different Sorts of *Promises.*

As to the *Promises* of Temporal Blessings, and those that relate to Temporal Evils, it is acknowledged by all, they are not to be understood Absolutely or Universally, but with the Limitation, as far as may be for God's Glory, and our Good: both which are, in effect. One. Nor will these Limitations lessen their Value, with any thinking, serious Person. For all outward Things are of such a Nature, as to be capable of being either good or evil to us, as Circumstances vary. Riches, though in some Circumstances they may be very useful and valuable, in which case God will bestow them according to the Tenour of his *Promises;* yet in others they may be, and often prove, very pernicious: No wise Man, in that Case, would desire them. Thus Afflictions, in some Instances, may be of the greatest Advantage to us. Then they are Mercies: The inflicting them is a Token of Favour, and the preventing them would be a Judgment, instead of fulfilling a Promise. Now it must be allowed, that of all these Circumstances, the Infinitely Wise and Good God is the best Judge; since he has before him, in one View, the whole Compass of every Case, in all its Circumstances, and is more concern'd and watchful for our Good than we can be ourselves. The *Promises* therefore relating to these Things, should not lie by neglected; but we should fix our Faith upon them for the Mercies we want, with a firm Dependence upon the Power and Faithfulness of God, though with an entire Submission to his superior Wisdom, to chose what is best for us. I verily believe Christians often deprive themselves even of Temporal Favours from God for want of a more frequent, stedfast Exercise of Faith upon the *Promises* relating to these Things. They either ask not, or not *in Faith,* and therefore *receive nothing from God,* Jam. i. 6, 7. Or, they desire and ask but not for right Ends (to take Notice of another Limitation hinted at by the same Apostle, *Jam.* iv. 3,) not for God's Honour, but *to consume it upon their Lusts;* and so *they ask amiss,* and therefore *receive not*. This Collection therefore will give great Assistance to the Faith of Christians when they observe how full and express the *Promises* are, and how suitable to their several Exigencies, even in Things concerning this Life.

It may be objected to many of the Texts that they are taken out of the Old Testament, and were *Promises* made to the *Jews* under a Dispensation, wherein a greater Stress is laid upon Temporal Blessings, than under the Gospel; and consequently, that Christians can't expect so much from those *Promises*.

I ANSWER, That it is true, the Gospel has a much greater Tendency to draw our Affections from, and lessen our Regard to Outward Felicity and Prosperity, than the Law, since it has brought in a better Hope, and gives more clear Discoveries and more full Assurances of Spiritual and Eternal Blessings, and recommends these as our main Concern: And therefore our Desires and Expectations of Temporal Blessings ought to be very moderate, and bear no Proportion with our Concern for Spiritual. But yet, that Christians may take Comfort in, and apply to themselves the *Promises* of the Old Testament, and in Thing's relating to this Life, is evident from that Declaration of the Apostle, I *Tim.* iv. 8, *Godliness is profitable unto all Things, having Promise of the Life that now is, and of that which is to come*. Where the Apostle affirms, not only that Godliness is profitable to this, as well as another Life, but that it has *Promises* relating to both; by which it is probable he meant those of the Old Testament, a great part of the New being not then committed to Writing, or not published among the Churches, Besides, as was observed before, the *Promises* made in the Old Testament the Apostle applies to Christians, and that upon the Principle above-mentioned, *Rom.* xv. 4. An Instance of which we have, among others, in his pressing Obedience to Parents on Christians, Eph. vi, 2, 3, from the Temporal Promise annex'd to the Fifth Commandment, deliver'd to the *Jews*. To which may be added, That there are many *Promises* of Temporal Blessings to be found in the Gospel, as full and as expressive as those in the Old Testament, as will appear upon the Perusal of this Collection.

Nor do I think the Case of Good Men under the Law so different from that of Christians with relation to Outward Blessings as some may apprehend. It is plain, those *Promises* were not to them absolute or universal, but to be understood with the same Limitations as now; and that in those Times, as well as since, the Righteous were frequently exercis'd with severe Afflictions, and the Wicked had many Times a greater Share of Outward Prosperity than even the best of Men: the want of a due Attention to which was the Reason of the heavy Censures *Job* met with from his Friends. The Sentences therefore which in *Job,* in the *Proverbs,* and other Places, express the Earthly Advantages attending Righteousness in its several Branches, and the ill Consequences of Vice are not to be look'd upon as universal Positions, but rather as Observations of the proper Tendency of Virtue, and Vice, and their natural Connection with such and such Benefits and Mischiefs, though liable to some Exceptions in particular Cases, as most general Observations and Maxims are. And there is now the same Connection established by God in the Course of Things between Moral Good and Evil; and several Advantages and Mischiefs, though subject to such Variations as God, in his wise Providence, sees fit to make from his more settled Rules.

As to the *Promises* of Spiritual and Eternal Blessings, they are to be apply'd according to the Tenour of the Gospel. It is to Faith, Repentance, Love, and sincere Obedience, that the *Promises* in general are made of Pardon, Grace, and Glory; as appears from a great Multitude of Texts here collected. And indeed, without these Dispositions, none can justly lay claim to any of the Temporal *Promises*. But because, in many Cases, a serious Person may be doubtful whether he is converted or not, whether there be in him that Faith, Repentance, and Holiness, which may be a Proof that he is in a State of Favour with God, and so entitled to the *Promises,* I observe, That as there is a Difference between Grace begun, in its first Exercises, and when it is arrived to a confirm'd Habit, so many of the *Promises* are made to the first Beginnings and Exercises of Grace, in praying and seeking after God, in the Use of appointed Means, in turning from Sin and coming to Christ. Thus the *Promises* of a new Heart are made to those who enquire after God, Ezek. xxxvi. 26, 37, of Wisdom to them that search for it, *Prov.* ii. 4, 5, of the Spirit to them that ask it, *Luke* xi. 13, and of Rest in Christ to them that being weary, and heavy laden, come to him, *Matt.* xi. 28. Which therefore every one who finds in himself those Beginnings of Grace, may apply them to himself, as an Encouragement to go on.

It is also to be observed, That the other *Promises* of Divine Influences, of the Increase of Grace, of Preservation from Sin, of Grace to persevere to the End, &c., and so of everlasting Life and Glory, tho' every sincere Christian may apply them, and depend upon them, yet they all suppose the diligent Use of all the Means of Grace, Watchfulness, a constant Application to, and Dependance upon, the Strength of Christ, and the Grace of his Holy .Spirit, and a sincere Regard to all the other Duties of the Gospel; as appears from *John* xv. 4, 10, and many other Passages to be found in this Collection, especially in the latter Part.

To obtain the Comfort of the *Promises* in the Second Part, every one must see that they be in a good Degree possess'd of the Graces, and that they diligently perform the Duties, to which the *Promises* are made; and that from a Principle of Faith in Christ, and Love to God, express'd in an habitual Care and Endeavour to please him. For, whatever Duty we do, without a real Regard to God therein, depending upon Christ for Acceptance, *in whom all the Promises are Yea and Amen,* we can expect no Reward from Him, God may justly reject such a Claim, with, *Did ye it at all to me, even to me?* And for the same Reason, the observing of some Duties, while we knowingly allow ourselves in Acts of Disobedience to other Commands, will not support our Claim to the *Promises;* because, if we acted with a sincere Respect to God, we should shew the same Regard to all his known Laws, *Jam.* ii. 10, 11.

As a Christian ought to be concerned not only for himself, but for the whole Church of God, and the Interest of Christ's Kingdom here on Earth, I thought it very necessary to lay before him what the Scripture affords for the raising of his Hopes, and encouraging his Prayers upon those important Subjects. And this is the Design of that Collection of Texts in the *Appendix.* But this I found more difficult than any other Part whatsoever. For, in searching the Scripture upon those Subjects, I met with so many Passages that had a relation to the State of the Church, that a compleat Collection of them was inconsistent with my intended Brevity; and many of the Prophecies were so difficult to be understood, that it could not be expected that the Generality of Christians should know how to make use of them. I have, however, endeavoured to avoid both these Inconveniences, by selecting those Texts which are most full to my Purpose, and most easy to be apprehended by an attentive Reader; hoping that those Scriptures being here laid together, which treat of the same Subject, they would mutually illustrate and explain one another.

I AM sensible that many of the Texts I have brought, which foretell the Enlargement and Glory of the Church, have already had, in some Degree, their Accomplishment, in the Conversion of the *Gentiles* to the Christian Faith; but upon a thorough Consideration of several of the Prophecies concerning the spreading of the Gospel throughout all Nations, the Subjection of all Kings to the Authority of Christ, and the Glorious State of the Church in the latter Days, as *Ps.* lxxxvi. 9, *Is.* lxvi. 18, *Dan.* vii. 27, *Zech.* xiv. 9, &c., it appears to me, there's still to be expected a fuller Accomplishment of them, than has yet been. But which have been already fulfilled, and which still remain to be so, I leave to every one's Judgment, upon considering and comparing the Texts,

Some of the Texts I have applied to the Church in general, are by some Interpreters understood of the Church of the *Jews,* when converted to Christ in the latter Ages of the World; as *Is.* iv. 3, xxvii. 6, lx. and lxii. Nor do I deny, but it is probable, that People is more immediately pointed at in those Prophecies. But as the *Gentile* and *Jewish* Church will then be one, there will be a Communication of Privileges and Glory; and, consequently, in whatever Measures the Spirit of God is poured out, and the Glory of God manifested among the Jews, when converted, the Gentile Church will enjoy their Share of the Benefit: For, *if the Fall of them be the Riches of the World, and the Diminishing of them the Riches of the Gentiles, How much more their Fulness?* Rom. xi. 12.

As to the Conversion of the *Jews,* it has indeed been the Opinion of many learned Men, that nothing more is to be expected, than what has already been done in the several, but especially the first Ages of Christianity; but I don't see what Sense can be made of the Eleventh Chapter to the *Romans,* but upon the Supposition of a further and more general Conversion of the *Jews,* even of that Part of the *Jewish* Nation which were then cut off from the true Church for their Infidelity: And as the Apostle applies to this Purpose a Passage quoted out of one of the Prophets, it seems to me to serve as a Key for the right understanding of a great Number of Places in the Prophets concerning the State of the *Jews* in the latter Days; a great Part of which I have therefore collected, or referr'd to in the last Section. I know, indeed, those Prophecies are suppose! by *Grotius,* and other learned Commentators, to have been fulfill'd by the Return of the Jews from the *Babylonish* Captivity, the Favour they obtain'd from several Princes, and the Victories gain'd by the *Maccabees* over the Enemies of the Jews. And perhaps the Foretelling of those remarkable Events, was in part the Design of at least some of those Prophecies. But they must be allow'd also to have had a further View, if we consider the low, afflicted, and persecuted State of the Jewish Nation most part of the Time after their Return to their own Land, under the *Persian, Grecian,* and at length the *Roman* Empire, and the Corruptions and Disorders that crept into, and at last quite over-run their Church; of which Dr. *Prideaux* has given a very full Account, in his excellent History. Now this no way agrees with those sublime and lively Descriptions of the Peace, Prosperity, Holiness, and flourishing Condition, both of their Church and State, foretold in those Prophecies; as particularly in *Jer.* xxx. 9, 16, *Ezek.* xxxiv. 28, and xxxvi. 11, *Joel* iii. 17, 20, &c. Besides that, in many of those Prophecies, the Latter Days, or the Days of the *Messiah,* are expressly pointed at, as the Time of their Accomplishment. This has therefore led many to apply all those Passages to the *Gentile* Church, which they suppose to be spoken of under Names and Characters proper to the *Jewish* Church as being typified by it. But whoever will carefully observe the Connection of the several Parts of those Prophecies, must acknowledge that the *Jewish* Nation is in some of the Verses plainly spoken of, and that in other Verses of the same Context, the *Promises* of Conversion and Restoration to their own Land, are made to the very same Persons; of which see Instances in the Chapters above-mention'd, and in *Hos.* ii. and iii.

There are many indeed of those who expect a more general Conversion of the *Jews,* that yet will not admit of their Restoration to their own Land, but suppose they shall be, upon their Conversion, imbodied with the several Nations among which they live. But in those Prophecies concerning them, which evidently refer to the Gospel Times, there are several Passages which speak so fully and positively of their Return to their own Country, and that *Jerusalem* shall be rebuilt and reinhabited by them, that it seems to me impossible to understand them in any other than the literal Sense, without doing them great Violence; as *Jer.* xxxii. 41. and xxxiii. 16, *Ezek.* xxxvi. 11, 24, 28, xxxvii. 25, *Zech.* xii. 6, xiv. 11, &c. It is beyond my present Design, and the Compass of this *Introduction,* to give all the Reasons that incline me to these Sentiments: They that please to search further into the Matter, may consult Doctor *Whitby,* and other learned Writers. I shall conclude what I have to say upon this Head, with recommending it to Christians to make use of these Texts to raise their Hopes and Expectations of those future happy Times, when the Gospel shall be preach'd more universally throughout the World, the Christian Church receive a vast Accession by the calling of the *Jews,* and the Coming in of the Fulness of the *Gentiles;* and Holiness, Peace, and Love, shall flourish, probably in a greater measure than ever, at least since the Apostles' Times. Let this be the Subject of their daily and most fervent Prayers, and these *Promises* be made use of as Pleas to inforce their Petitions, and support their Faith.

Though this Collection has cost me not a little Time and Pains, I think it very well bestowed, not only upon the Account of the Advantage I have myself received from the Study of the *Promises,* and the Assistance I still expect from this Book for my private Thoughts and Composures for the Pulpit, by having it continually before me; but also in Hopes it may be useful to others in several Respects, for promoting the Holiness and Comfort of Christians. Here they have before them, in one View, the Riches of the Covenant of Grace: Here are all the strongest Arguments to persuade to real Religion, to recommend every Duty, and to support in every afflicted and perplexed Case. This Book may be very useful to assist in Prayer, both for the Reasons before-mentioned, and also because from hence one may be furnished with Variety of proper Matter, and Expression upon all the Cases we are concerned to represent to God, And as the Study of these *Promises* would be to the Advantage of all sorts of Persons, it might be a very useful and easy Exercise for Children to be employ'd in learning some of the plainest Texts under those Heads which are the most proper for them, and to question one another upon them, being instructed by their Teachers in their Sense and Use. In this Way the Directors of the Education of Children in the Charity Schools, may make this Book serve good Purposes, for the Instruction and Improvement of their Children in the Knowledge of the Scriptures. And I know no better Way of inriching the Minds of Children with useful and solid Knowledge, than by making 'em well acquainted with the Scriptures themselves, those pure unmixed, Fountains of excellent and Divine Wisdom, and treasuring up in their Memories a great Number of select Scriptures most suited to their Capacity and Use. For this End, I have frequently thought of making some proper Collections, particularly for the Benefit of the Charity School at *St. Albans*, and of all other Children, whose Parents or Teachers shall think fit to make use of them; which, perhaps, [1] I may hereafter finish, if this meet with Acceptance.

If we would reap the Comfort and Benefit of these Promises, it is not enough that we have them by us, or now and then look into them; but we must thoroughly acquaint ourselves with 'em, store them up in our Memories, and be often meditating upon them, that they may be ready for Use when we most want them. And whatever Pains we may be at on this Account, the Pleasure and Advantage we shall receive will be a sufficient Recompence: For these are *pleasant Words,* that *are as a Honey-comb; sweet to the Soul, and Health to the Bones, Prov.* xvi. 24, and therefore well deserve to be *bound upon our Fingers, and written upon the Table of our Hearts, Prov.* vii. 3. And would serious Christians make the *Promises* the frequent Subject of their Conversation together, and at the same Time take notice of the several Instances wherein they have been made good to themselves, and others within their Observation, it would both impress them upon their Memories, and very much increase their Force and Influence upon their Hearts.

But Care must be taken to understand them in their true Sense, and rightly to apply them. Mistaken Apprehensions of Scripture, have often been the Cause of People deceiving themselves with ungrounded Comforts and Expectations; or, at least, they have not built their Comforts upon proper Texts, though they may have had sufficient Foundation for them in other Places. The comparing one Scripture with another, as they lie here together, will be, in many Cases of great Use to assist in the right understanding them. And in most Instances, it will be still a further Advantage to turn to the Place quoted and consider the Circumstances of the Text, and its Connection with the Context. This will shew how far there is an Agreement of your Case with that referr'd to in the Text; and, consequently, how far the *Promise* is to be applied, whether absolutely, and in its whole Extent, or only in some Degree, and with Limitations.

In particular Cases, we may draw Comfort, not only from, the *Promises* peculiar to that Case, but also from those that are of a more general Nature. As under Sickness, we may have Relief, not only from those Scriptures which expressly relate to that Circumstance, but also from the *Promises* relating to *Trouble in general,* and the Assurances of God's *Love, Care,* and *Readiness* to *help* his People, &c., which the *Table of Contents* will easily direct to.

That we may have the Comfort of the *Promises,* a steady Exercise of Faith is above all Things necessary. For this Purpose, we must impress upon our Minds the Power, Goodness, and Faithfulness of God, and the Experience of good Men in every Age; and by this Means, and by an attentive Consideration of the *Promises, suck at those Breasts of Consolation till we are satisfied. Is.*

lxvi. ii. But at the same Time our Eyes must be fixed upon the Lord Jesus Christ, as the only Foundation of our Hopes, in and through whom alone all the *Promises* are made good to us; and upon the Holy Spirit the Comforter, that through his powerful Influences we may rightly understand and apply, firmly believe, and clearly discover the Excellency of the *Promises,* and so taste that the Lord is Gracious.

Constantly plead the *Promises* with God in Prayer. He has thereby bound himself to his People, as with a Note under his Hand. Go with it therefore to God, firmly depending upon his Faithfulness; He will acknowledge his own Handwriting, and answer your Demands accordingly. Rest yourself therefore upon God, and wait patiently for him, being assured he'll not be unmindful of his Promise; but leave it to his infinite Wisdom to fulfil it, in that Way, and at that Time, he sees best.

But remember, The *Promises* of God do not discharge from, but encourage and oblige to, the diligent Use of all proper and lawful Means. Christ has promised Food and Raiment; but the Slothful and Careless must not expect the Benefit of that Promise. The same may be said of the Spiritual Blessings promised. *The Soul of the Slothful desireth, and hath nothing: but the Soul of the Diligent shall be made fat, Prov.* xiii. 4.

To conclude: Let the Christian live a Life of Faith upon the *Promises*. A great Part of the Riches of the Nation at this Day, consists in the Credit that is given to Notes, Bonds, Assignments, &c., I am sure that the Riches of the Christian lie chiefly in the Assignments he has under God's Hand, of the most valuable Blessings both of this and a better Life. Let him then know how to value these as the truest Riches, and to make use of them upon all Occasions; he'll find no Want of any good Thing. If he has it not in Hand, he has it in the Promise ready whenever he needs it. So that he may live entirely free from Solicitude and anxious Care, committing himself and all his Concerns, to that God who careth for him.

I AM willing to take this Opportunity of recommending it to those Young Persons, for whose Benefit this Collection was first undertaken, to persevere in their Endeavours to improve themselves and one another, in the Knowledge of the *Promises,* and other Parts of Scripture, which may be most useful to them, that the *Word of Christ may dwell in them richly in all Wisdom;* and to Others, especially of their Age, to imitate their Example in the same commendable Way of employing their Time. To how much better Account will this turn, than the Vanities that ordinarily fill up the Conversation of Youth, or those wrangling Disputes and Controversies, which eat out the Heart of serious, practical Religion! The Advantage which those who have try'd this Course, have reap'd from it, sufficiently encourages their Perseverance in it. May they, and all others, who with them delight in and search after the Treasures of Divine Wisdom in the Scriptures, not only have their Minds beautified and enrich'd with it. but feel its Influence in their Hearts and Lives, May they be *filled with the Knowledge of the Will of God, in all Wisdom and*

Spiritual Understanding, that they may walk worthy of the Lord unto all pleasing, being fruitful in every good Work, and increasing in the Knowledge of God.

[1] I had laid aside this Design upon finding that there was a Variety of such Collections already published. But as some Friends, to whom I have a great Regard, think something of that Nature more suited to the Instruction of Children is wanting, and therefore have put me lately upon it, I am now drawing up a small Collection for the Press.

The Christian's Inheritance Or, a Collection of The Promises

Part One - The Blessings Promised to the Good

Chapter One - Promises *of* Temporal Blessings

I. General Promises *to the Good*.

PSAL. xvi. 6. The Lines are fallen unto me in pleasant Places; I have a good Heritage.

Ps. lxxxiv. 11. The Lord God is a Sun and Shield: The Lord will give Grace and Glory; no good Thing will he withhold from them that walk uprightly.

Eccl. viii. 12. Surely I know that it shall be well with them that fear God, which fear before him.

Is. iii. 10. Say ye to the Righteous, that it shall be well with him, for they shall eat the Fruit of their Doings.

Ps. lviii. 11. Verily there is a Reward for the Righteous.

Ps. v. 12. Thou, Lord, wilt bless the righteous; with Favour wilt thou compass him as with a Shield.

Ps. iii. 8. Salvation belongeth unto the Lord, thy Blessing is upon thy People.

Prov. xxi. 21. He that followeth after Righteousness and Mercy, findeth Life, Righteousness, and Honour.

Prov. x. 6. Blessings are upon the Head of the just. *Ver.* 24. The Desire of the righteous shall be granted. *Ver.* 28. The Hope of the righteous shall be Gladness.

Prov. xi. 18. To him that soweth Righteousness, shall be a sure Reward. *Ver.* 19. Righteousness tendeth to Life. *Ver.* 28. The righteous shall flourish as a Branch.

Prov. iii. 32. His Secret is with the righteous.

Prov. xii. 2. A good Man obtaineth Favour of the Lord.

Prov. xiii. 9. The Light of the righteous rejoiceth. *Ver.* 21. To the righteous good shall be repaid.

Ps. xxiii. 6. Surely Goodness and Mercy shall follow me all the Days of my Life; and I will dwell in the House of the Lord for ever.

Rom. viii. 32. He that spared not his own Son, but delivered him up for us all, how shall he not with him also freely give us all Things?

I *Cor.* iii. 21, 22. All Things are yours, whether Paul, or Apollos, or Cephas, or the World, or Life, or Death, or Things present, or Things to come, all are yours.

I *Tim.* lv. 8. Godliness is profitable unto all Things; having the Promise of the Life that now is, and of that which is to come.

II. Promises *of* Temporal Blessings *in general.*

Ps. xxiii. I. The Lord is my Shepherd, I shall not want. *Ver.* 5. Thou preparest a Table before me, in the Presence of mine Enemies: Thou anointest my Head with Oil, my Cup runneth over.

Ps. xxxiv. 9. There is no Want to them that fear him. *Ver.* 10. They that seek the Lord shall not want any good Thing.

Matt. vi. 33. Seek ye first the Kingdom of God, and his Righteousness, and all these Things shall be added unto you.

Phil. lv. 19. My God shall supply all your Need, according to his Riches in Glory by Christ Jesus.

I *Tim.* vi. 6. Godliness with Contentment is great Gain. *Ver.* 17. Who giveth us richly all Things to enjoy.

III. Particularly *of* Food *and* Raiment.

Ps. xxxvii. 3. Trust in the Lord and do good, so shalt thou dwell in the Land, and verily thou shalt be fed.

Ps. cxi. 5. He hath given Meat unto them that fear him; he will ever be mindful of his Covenant.

Ps. cxxxii. 15. I will abundantly bless her Provision, I will satisfy her Poor with Bread.

Ps. cxlvii. 14. He filleth thee with the finest of the Wheat.

Prov. xiii. 25. The righteous eateth to the satisfying of his Soul.

Matt. vi. 26. Behold the Fowls of the Air, for they sow not, neither do they reap, nor gather into Barns; yet your heavenly Father feedeth them: Are ye not much better than they?

Joel ii. 26. And ye shall eat in Plenty, and be satisfied.

Is. lxv. 13. Behold my Servants shall eat, but ye shall be hungry: Behold my Servants shall drink, but ye shall be thirsty.

Matt. vi, 25. I say unto you, Take no Thought for your Life, what ye shall eat, or what ye shall drink; nor yet for the Body, what ye shall put on: Is not the Life more than Meat, and the Body than Raiment? *Ver.* 30. Wherefore if God so clothe the Grass of the Field, which to Day is, and to Morrow is cast into the Oven, shall he not much more clothe you, O ye of little Faith? *Ver.* 31. Therefore take no Thought, saying, What shall we eat? Or what shall we drink? Or wherewithal shall we be cloathed? *Ver.* 32. For your heavenly Father knoweth that ye have need of all these Things.

IV. Promise *of* Long Life *and* Health.

Deut. v. 33. You shall walk in all the Ways which the Lord your God hath commanded you, that ye may live, and that it may be well with you, and that ye may prolong your Days in the Land which you shall possess.

Deut. vi. 2. That thou mightest fear the Lord thy God, to keep all his Statutes and Commandments, which I command thee; thou, and thy Son, and thy Son's Son, all the Days of thy Life, and that thy Days may be prolonged.

Job. v. 26. Thou shalt come to thy Grave in a full Age, like as a Shock of Corn, Cometh in, in his Season.

Ps. xxxiv. 12. What Man is he that desireth Life, and loveth many Days, that he may see Good. *Ver.* 13. Keep thy Tongue from Evil, and thy Lips from speaking Guile. *Ver.* 14. Depart from Evil and do Good, seek Peace and pursue it.

Ps. xci. 16. With long Life will I satisfy him, and shew him my Salvation.

Prov. iii. 2. Length of Days, and long Life, and Peace, shall they add to thee. *Ver.* 26. Length of Days is in her [Wisdom's] Right Hand.

Prov. ix. 11. By me thy Days shall be multiplied, and the Years of thy Life shall be increased.

Prov. x. 27, The Fear of the Lord prolongeth Days.

Ps. ciii. 3. Who forgiveth all thine Iniquities, who healeth all thy Diseases. *Ver.* 4. Who redeemeth thy Life from Destruction. *Ver.* 5. Who satisfieth thy Mouth with good Things, so that thy Youth is renewed like the Eagles.

Prov. iii. 7. Be not wise in thine own Eyes: Fear the Lord, and depart from Evil. *Ver.* 8. It shall be Health to thy Navel, and Marrow to thy Bones.

Prov. iv. 22. They are Life to them that find them, and Health to all their Flesh.

V. Promises *of* Safety *under the* Divine Protection.

Deut. xxxiii. 12. The beloved of the Lord shall dwell in Safety by him; and the Lord shall cover him all the Day long.

Prov. xviii. 10. The Name of the Lord is a strong Tower; the righteous runneth into it, and is safe.

Ps. cxvi. 8. I have set the Lord always before me: Because he is at my Right Hand, I shall not be moved.

Ps. cxii, 7. He shall not be afraid of evil Tidings; his Heart is fixed, trusting in the Lord.

I *Pet.* iii. 13. And who is he that will harm you, if you be Followers of that which is good?

Job lv. 7. Remember, I pray thee, Who ever perished, being innocent? Or where were the Righteous cut off?

Job xi. 18. Thou shalt be secure, because there is Hope.

Job v. 23. Thou shalt be in league with the Stones of the Field; and the Beasts of the Field shall be at Peace with thee.

Hos. ii. 18. And in that Day will I make a Covenant for them with the Beasts of the Field, and with the Fowls of Heaven, and with the creeping Things of the Ground; and I will break the Bow, and the Sword, and the Battle out of the Earth, and will make them to lie down safely.

Ex. xxxiv. 25. I will make with them a Covenant of Peace, and will cause the evil Beasts to cease out of the Land, and they shall dwell safely in the Wilderness, and sleep in the Woods. *Ver.* 28. And they shall no more be a Prey to the Heathen, neither shall the Beasts of the Land devour them; but they shall dwell safely, and none shall make them afraid.

Gen. ix. 2. And the Fear of you, and the Dread of you shall be upon every Beast of the Earth, and upon every Fowl of the Air, upon all that moveth upon the Earth, and upon all the Fishes of the Sea, into your Hand are they delivered.

Job xi. 18. Thou shalt dig about thee, and thou shalt take thy Rest in Safety. *Ver.* 19. Also thou shalt lie down, and none shall make thee afraid.

Ps. iv. 8. I will both lay me down in Peace, and sleep; for thou Lord only makest me to dwell in Safety.

Ps. cxxvii. 2. He giveth his beloved Sleep.

Prov. iii. 24. When thou liest down, thou shalt not be afraid; yea, thou shalt lie down, and thy Sleep shall be sweet.

I *Sam.* ii. 9. He will keep the Feet of his Saints, and the wicked shall be silent in Darkness, for by Strength shall no Man prevail.

Ps. xxvii. I. The Lord is my Light, and my Salvation, whom shall I fear) The Lord is the Strength of my Life, of whom shall I be afraid?

Ps. xxxiv. 20. He keepeth all his Bones, not one of them is broken.

Ps. xci. I. He that dwelleth in the secret Place of the Most High, shall abide under the Shadow of the Almighty. *Ver.* 2. I will say of the Lord he is my Refuge, and my Fortress; my God, in him will I trust. *Ver.* 4. He shall cover thee with his Feathers, and under his Wings shalt thou trust: His Truth shall be thy Shield and Buckler. *Ver.* 10. There shall no evil befall thee, neither shall any Plague come nigh thy Dwelling.

Ps. cxxi. I. I will lift up mine Eyes unto the Hills, from whence cometh my Help.

Ver. 2. My Help cometh from the Lord, which made Heaven and Earth.

Ver. 3. He will not suffer thy Foot to be moved: he that keepeth thee will not slumber.

Ver. 4. Behold, he that keepeth Israel, shall neither slumber nor sleep.

Ver. 5. The Lord is thy Keeper: The Lord is thy Shade upon thy Right Hand.

Ver. 6. The Sun shall not smite thee by Day, nor the Moon by Night.

Ver. 7. The Lord shall preserve thee from all Evil: He shall preserve thy Soul.

Ver. 8. The Lord shall preserve thy going out, and thy coming in, from this Time forth, and even for evermore.

Ps. cxxiv. 8. Our Help is in the Name of the Lord, who made Heaven and Earth.

Ps. cxxv. 2. As the Mountains are round about *Jerusalem,* so the Lord is round about his People, from henceforth even for ever.

Prov. iii. 23. Then shalt thou walk in thy Way safely, and thy Foot shall not stumble.

Prov. i. 33. But whoso hearkeneth unto me shall dwell safely, and shall be quiet from Fear of Evil.

Is. lv. 5. And the Lord will create upon every Dwelling place of Mount *Sion,* and upon her Assemblies a Cloud, and Smoke by Day, and the shining of a flaming Fire by Night; for upon all the Glory shall be a Defence. *Ver.* 6. And there shall be a Tabernacle for a Shadow in the Day-time from the Heat, and for a Place of Refuge, and for a Covert from Storm and Rain.

Is. xxxiii. 16. He shall dwell on high; his Place of Defence shall be the Munition of Rocks.

Is. xliii. 2. When thou passest through the Waters, I will be with thee; and through the Rivers, they shall not overflow thee: When thou walkest through the Fire, thou shalt not be burnt; neither shall the Flame kindle upon thee. *Ver.* 3. For I am the Lord thy God, the Holy One of *Israel,* thy Saviour.

Is. xxvii. 3. I the Lord do keep it, I will water it every Moment; lest any hurt it, I will keep it Night and Day.

Zech. ii. 5. For I, saith the Lord, will be unto her a Wall of Fire round about, and will be the Glory in the midst of her.

VI. *Promises of* Peace.

Lev. xxvi. 6. And I will give Peace in the Land, and ye shall lie down, and none shall make you afraid; and I will rid evil Beasts out of the Land, neither shall the Sword go through your Land.

Ps. xxix. 11. The Lord will give Strength unto his People, the Lord will bless his People with Peace.

Ps. cxxv. 5. Peace shall be upon *Israel.*

Ps. cxix. 165. Great Peace have they that love thy Law, and nothing shall offend them.

Ps. cxlvii. 14. He maketh Peace in thy Borders.

Is. xxvi. 12. Lord, thou wilt ordain Peace for us; for thou also hast wrought all our Works in us.

Is. xxxvii. 18. My People shall dwell in a peaceable Habitation, and in sure Dwellings, and in quiet Resting-places.

VII. Direction.

Ps. xxxvii. 23. The Steps of a good Man are ordered by the Lord; and he delighteth in his Way.

Ps. xlviii. 14. He will be our Guide, even unto Death.

Ps. lxxiii. 24. Thou shalt guide me with thy Counsel, and afterward receive me to Glory.

Prov. iii. 6. In all thy Ways acknowledge him, and he shall direct thy Paths.

Prov. xi. 5. The Righteousness of the perfect shall direct his Way.

Prov. xvi. 9. A Man's Heart deviseth his Way, but the Lord directeth his Steps.

Is. xxviii. 26. His God doth instruct him to Discretion, and doth teach him.

Is. xlii. 16. And I will bring the Blind by a Way that they know not, I will lead them in Paths that they have not known. I will make Darkness Light before them, and crooked Things strait. These Things will I do unto them, and not forsake them.

VIII. Honour.

Deut. xxviii. 13. And the Lord shall make thee the Head, and not the Tail; and thou shalt be above only, and thou shalt not be beneath; if that thou hearken unto the Commandments of the Lord thy God, which I command thee this Day, to observe and to do them.

Ps. cxii. 6. Surely he shall not be moved for ever: The righteous shall be in everlasting Remembrance. *Ver.* 9. His Horn shall be exalted with Honour.

I *Sam.* ii. 30. Them that Honour me, I will honour.

Prov. xxii. 4. By Humility and the Fear of the Lord, are Riches, and Honour, and Life.

Prov. iii. 16. In her Left Hand are Riches and Honour.

Prov. lv. 8. Exalt her, and she shall promote thee; she shall bring thee to Honour, when thou dost embrace her.

Prov. x. 7. The Memory of the Just is blessed.

Prov. xiv. 19. The Evil bow before the pfood, and the wicked at the Gates of the righteous.

Ps. xci. 14. Because he hath set his Love upon me, therefore will I deliver him; I will set him on high, because he hath known my Name. *Ver.* 15. He shall call upon me, and I will answer him: I will be with him in Trouble, I will deliver him and honour him.

John xii. 26. If any Man serve me, let him follow me: and where I am, there shall also my Servant be: If any Man serve me, him will my Father honour.

Rev. iii. 9. Behold I will make them of the Synagogue of Satan (who say they are *Jews,* and are not, but do lie) to come and worship thee before thy Feet, and to know that I have loved thee.

IX. Success and Prosperity.

Ps. i. 3. He shall be like a Tree planted by the Rivers of Water, that bringeth forth his Fruit in his Season: His Leaf also shall not wither, and whatsoever he doth shall prosper.

Ps. xxxvii. 5. Commit thy Way unto the Lord; trust also in him and he shall bring it to pass.

Ps. cxxviii. 2. Thou shalt eat the Labour of thine Hands: Happy shalt thou be, and it shall be well with thee.

Ps. lvii. 2. I will cry unto God most high; unto God that performeth all Things for me.

Is. lxv. 21. And they shall build Houses, and inhabit them; and they shall plant Vineyards, and eat the Fruit of them.

Ver. 22. They shall not build, and another inhabit; they shall not plant, and another eat: For as the Days of a Tree are the Days of my People, and mine Elect shall long enjoy the Work of their Hands.

Ver. 23. They shall not labour in vain, nor bring forth for Trouble: For they are the Seed of the blessed of the Lord, and their Off-spring with them.

Job xi. 15. Thou shalt be stedfast, and shalt not fear. *Ver.* 17. And thine Age shall be clearer than the Noon-day: Thou shalt shine forth, thou shalt be as the Morning.

Job. xxii. 28. Thou shalt also decree a Thing, and it shall be established unto thee: And the Light shall shine upon thy Ways.

X. Plenty *and* Riches.

Deut. xi. 14. I will give you the Rain of your Land in his due Season; the first Rain and the latter Rain; that thou mayest gather in thy Corn, and thy Wine, and thine Oil. *Ver.* 15. And I will send Grass in thy Fields for thy Cattle, that thou mayest eat and be full.

Deut. xxviii. 12. The Lord shall open unto thee his good Treasure, the Heaven to give the Rain unto thy Land in his Season, and to bless all the Work of thine Hand; and thou shalt lend unto many Nations, and thou shalt not borrow.

Deut. xxx. 9. And the Lord thy God will make thee plenteous in every Work of thine Hand, in the Fruit of thy Body, and in the Fruit of thy Cattle, and in the Fruit of thy Land for good; for the Lord will again rejoice over thee for good, as he rejoiced over thy Fathers, *Deut.* xxviii. ii.

Job. xxii, 24. Thou shalt lay up Gold as Dust, and the Gold of *Ophir* as the Stones of the Brooks.

Ver. 25. And thou shalt have Plenty of Silver.

Ps. cvii. 38. He blesseth them also, so that they are multiplied greatly, and suffereth not their Cattle to decrease.

Ps. cxii. 3. Wealth and Riches shall be in his House, and his Righteousness endureth for ever.

Prov. iii. 16. In her [*i.e.* Wisdom's] Left Hand are Riches and Honour.

Prov. viii. 18. Riches and Honour are with me; yea, durable Riches and Righteousness.

Ver. 19. My Fruit is better than Gold, and my Revenue than choice Silver.

Prov. xv. 6. In the House of the Righteous is much Treasure.

Is. xxx. 23. Then shall he give the Rain of thy Seed, that thou shalt sow the Ground withal, and Bread of the Increase of the Earth, and it shall be fat and plenteous: In that Day shall thy Cattle feed in large Pastures.

XI. Of Children.

Deut. vii. 13. He will love thee, and bless thee, and multiply thee: He will also bless the Fruit of thy Womb.

Deut. xxx. 9. And the Lord thy God will make thee plenteous — in the Fruit of thy Body.

Job. v. 25. Thou shalt know that thy Seed shall be great, and thine off-spring as the Grass of the Earth.

Ps. cxxvii. 3. Lo, Children are an Heritage of the Lord, and the Fruit of the Womb is his Reward.

Ver. 4. As Arrows in the Hands of a mighty Man, so are Children of the Youth. *Ver.* 5. Happy is the Man that hath his Quiver full of them: They shall not be ashamed, but they shall speak with the Enemies in the Gate.

Ps. cxvi. 14. The Lord shall increase you more and more you and your Children.

XII. A Blessing *upon all a good man has.*

Ex. xxiii. 25. And ye shall serve the Lord your God, and he shall bless thy Bread and thy Water.

Deut. xxvi. 11. And thou shalt rejoice in every good Thing, which the Lord thy God hath given unto thee, and unto thine House.

Deut. xxviii. 3. Blessed shalt thou be in the City, and blessed shalt thou be in the Field.

Ver. 4. Blessed shall be the Fruit of thy Body, and the Fruit of thy Ground, and the Fruit of thy Cattle; the Increase of thy Kine, and the Flocks of thy Sheep.

Ver. 5. Blessed shall be thy Basket and thy Store.

Ver. 6. Blessed shalt thou be when thou comest in, and Blessed shalt thou be when thou goest out.

Ver. 8. The Lord shall command a Blessing upon thee in thy Store-Houses, and in all that thou settest thy Hand unto: And he shall bless thee in the Land, which the Lord thy God giveth thee.

Ps. xxxvii. 16. A little that a righteous Man hath, is better than the Riches of many wicked.

Prov. x. 22. The Blessing of the Lord, it maketh rich, and he addeth no Sorrow with it.

Prov. xv. 16. Better is a little with the Fear of the Lord, than great Treasure and Trouble therewith.

Eccl. ii. 26. God doth give to a Man that is good in his Sight, Wisdom, and Knowledge, and Joy: But to the Sinner he giveth Travel, to gather and to heap up, that he may give to him that is good before God.

Eccl. iii. 13. Also that every Man should eat and drink, and enjoy the good of his Labour, it is the Gift of God.

Eccl. v. 19. Every Man, to whom God hath given Riches and Wealth, and hath given him Power to eat thereof, and to take his Portion, and to rejoice in his Labour; this is the Gift of God.

Ver. 20. For he shall not much remember the Days of his Life; because God answereth him in the Joy of his Heart.

XIII. *A Blessing upon the* Children *of the Good.*

Deut. lv. 40. Thou shalt keep his Statutes — that it may go well with thee, and thy Children after thee, *Deut.* v. 29.

Prov. xiii. 22. A good Man leaveth an Inheritance unto his Children's Children; and the Wealth of the Sinner is laid up for the Just.

Prov. xiv. 26. In the Fear of the Lord is strong Confidence; and his Children shall have a Place of Refuge.

Prov. xi. 21. The Seed of the Righteous shall be delivered.

Prov. xix. 7. The just Man walketh in his Integrity: His Children are blessed after him.

Ps. cii. 28. The Children of thy Servants shall continue, and their Seed shall be established before thee.

Ps. cxii. 2. His Seed shall be mighty upon Earth: The Generation of the Upright shall be blessed.

Ps. xxv. 13. His Seed shall inherit the Earth.

Ps. XXX vii. 25. I have been young and now am old, yet have I not seen the Righteous forsaken, nor his Seed begging Bread.

Ver. 26. He is ever merciful and lendeth: And his Seed is blessed.

Ps. cxlvii. 13. He hath blessed thy Children within thee.

Jer. xxxii. 39. I will give them one Heart and one Way, that they may fear me for ever, for the good of them, and of their Children after them.

XIV. A Blessing upon the Families of the Good.

Job v. 24. Thou shalt know also that thy Tabernacle shall be in Peace; and thou shalt visit thy Habitation, and shalt not sin.

Job viii. 6. If thou wert pure and upright, surely now he would awake for thee, and make the Habitation of thy Righteousness prosperous.

Ver. 7. Tho' thy Beginning were small, yet thy latter End should greatly increase.

Ps. cxxviii. 3. Thy Wife shall be as a fruitful Vine by the Sides of thine House; thy Children like Olive-Plants round about thy Table.

Ver. 4. Behold, thus shall the Man be blessed that feareth the Lord.

Ver. 5. The Lord shall bless thee out of Sion; and thou shalt see the Good of *Jerusalem* all the Days of thy Life.

Ver. 6. Yea, thou shalt see thy Children's Children, and Peace upon *Israel*.

Prov. iii. 33. He blesseth the Habitation of the Just.

Prov. xii. 7. The House of the Righteous shall stand.

Prov. xiv. 11. The Tabernacle of the Upright shall flourish.

Chapter Two - Promises *relating to* Troubles *of Life*.

I. In General.

Job v. 19. He shall deliver thee in six Troubles; yea, in seven, there shall no Evil touch thee.

Ps. xxxi. 13. The Lord preserveth the faithful.

Ps. xxxii. 6, For this shall every one that is godly pray unto thee, in a Time when thou mayest be found: Surely in the Floods of great Waters they shall not come nigh unto him.

Ver. 7. Thou art my hiding Place, thou shalt preserve me from Trouble: Thou shalt compass me about with Songs of Deliverance.

Ps. xci. 10. There shall no Evil befall thee, neither shall any Plague come nigh thy Dwelling.

Prov. xii. 21. There shall no Evil happen to the Just.

Prov. xvi, 19. The Way of the Slothful Man is an Hedge of Thorns: But the Way of the Righteous is made plain.

Job viii. 20. Behold, God will not cast away a perfect Man, neither will he help the Evil-doers.

Ver. 21. Till he fill thy Mouth with laughing, and thy lips with rejoicing.

Job xi. 16. Thou shalt forget thy Misery, and remember it as Waters that pass away.

Job xxxvi. 16. Even so would he have removed thee out of the strait into a broad Place, where there is no Straitness; and that which should be set on thy Table, should be full of Fatness.

Ps. xxx. 5. His Anger endureth but a Moment: In his Favour is Life: Weeping may endure for a night, but Joy cometh in the Morning.

Ps. xxxiv. 19. Many are the Afflictions of the righteous, but the Lord delivereth him out of them all.

Ps. xlii. 11. Why art thou cast down, O my Soul? And why art thou disquieted within me? Hope thou in God, for I shall yet praise him, who is the Health of my Countenance, and my God.

Ps. lxviii. 13. Though ye have lien among the Pots, yet shall ye be as the Wings of a Dove covered with Silver, and her Feathers with yellow Gold.

Ps. lxxi. 20. Thou, which hast shewed me great and sore Troubles, shalt quicken me again, and shalt bring me up again from the Depths of the Earth.

Ps. xviii. 27. Thou wilt save the afflicted People, but will bring down high Looks.

Ve7'. 28. For thou wilt light my Candle; The Lord my God will enlighten my Darkness.

Ps. cxlvi. 8. The Lord openeth the Eyes of the Blind, the Lord raiseth them that are bowed down.

Ps. cvii. 19. They cry unto the Lord in their Trouble: he delivereth them out of their Distresses.

Ps. cxxvi, 5. They that sow in Tears, shall reap in Joy.

Ver. 6. He that goeth forth and weepeth, bearing precious Seed, shall doubtless come again with rejoicing, bringing his Sheaves with him.

Prov. xxi. 8. The Righteous is delivered out of Trouble, and the Wicked cometh in his stead.

Prov. xii. 13. The Wicked is snared by the Transgression of his Lips; but the just shall come out of Trouble.

P7^ov. xxvi. 16. A just Man falleth seven times, and riseth up again.

Jer. xxix. 11. I know the Thoughts that I think towards you, saith the Lord; Thoughts of Peace, and not of Evil, to give you an expected End.

Jer. xxxi. 12. Their Soul shall be as a watered Garden, and they shall not sorrow any more.

Ver. 13. I will turn their Mourning into Joy, and will comfort them, and make them rejoice from their Sorrow.

Hos. vi. I. Come and let us return unto the Lord, for he hath torn, and he will heal us; he hath smitten, and he will bind us up.

Ps. ix. 9. The Lord will be a Refuge for the oppressed, a Refuge in times of trouble.

Ps. xxii. 24. He hath not despised nor abhorred the Affliction of the Afflicted; neither hath he hid his Face from him: But when he cried unto him, he heard.

Ps. xxvii. 14. Wait on the Lord; be of good courage, and he shall strengthen thine Heart: Wait, I say, on the Lord.

Ver. 12. When my Father and my Mother forsake me, then the Lord will take me up.

Ps. xxxvii. 24, Though he fall, he shall not be utterly cast down: For the Lord upholdeth him with his Hand,

Ver. 39. The Salvation of the Righteous is of the Lord: He is their Strength in the Time of Trouble.

Ps. xviii. 2. The Lord is my Rock, and my Fortress, and my Deliverer: My God my Strength, in whom I will trust; my Buckler, and the Horn of my Salvation, and my high Tower.

Ps. xlvi. 1. God is our Refuge and Strength, a very present Help in Trouble.

Ver. 2. Therefore will we not fear, tho' the Earth be removed, and tho' the Mountains be carried into the midst of the Sea. *Ver.* 3. Though the Waters thereof roar, and be troubled; though the Mountains shake with the swelling thereof. *Selah.*

Ps. lv. 22. Cast thy Burden upon the Lord, and he shall sustain thee: He shall never suffer the Righteous to be moved.

Ps. xxxi. 7. I will be glad and rejoice in thy Mercy: For thou hast considered my Trouble: thou hast known my Soul in Adversities.

Exod. iii, 7. I have surely seen the Affliction of my People which are in *Egypt*, and have heard their Cry by reason of their Task-masters: For I know their Sorrows.

Ps. xli. 1. Blessed is he that considereth the Poor; the Lord will deliver him in time of Trouble.

Ps. lxxi. 3. Thou hast given Commandment to save me, for thou art my Rock and my Fortress.

Ps. cxii. 4. Unto the Upright there ariseth Light in the Darkness.

Ps. cxxxvi. 23. Who remembered us in our low Estate: For his Mercy endureth for ever.

Ps. cxxxviii. 7. Though I walk in the midst of Trouble, thou wilt revive me; Thou shalt stretch forth thine Hand against the Wrath of mine Enemies, and thy Right Hand shall save me.

Ps. lxxiii. 26. My Flesh and my Heart faileth; but God is the Strength of my Heart.

Ps. cxlv. 14. The Lord upholdeth all that fall, and raiseth up all that are bowed down.

Is. xxv. 4. Thou hast been a Strength to the Poor, a Strength to the Needy in his Distress, a Refuge from the Storm, a Shadow from the Heat, when the Blast of the terrible ones is as a Storm against the Wall,

Is. xxvii. 8. In Measure, when it shooteth forth, thou wilt debate with it: He stayeth his rough Wind in the Day of the East Wind.

Job xxxiv. 23. He will not lay upon Man more than is right, that he should enter into the Judgment with God.

Is. 1. 10. Who is among you that feareth the Lord, that obeyeth the Voice of his Servant, that walketh in Darkness and hath no Light, let him trust in the Name of the Lord, and stay upon his God.

Lam. iii. 31. The Lord will not cast off for ever.

Ver. 32. But though he cause Grief, yet will he have Compassion, according to the multitude of his Mercies.

Ver. 33. For he doth not afflict willingly, nor grieve the Children of Men.

Jer. xxx. 11. I am with thee, saith the Lord, to save thee: I will correct thee in measure, and will not leave thee altogether unpunished.

Jer. xvi. 19. O Lord, my Refuge and my Fortress; and my Refuge in the Day of my Affliction.

Mic. vii. 8. Rejoice not against me, O mine Enemy: When I fall, I shall arise; when I sit in Darkness, the Lord shall be a Light unto me.

Ver. 9. I will bear the Indignation of the Lord, because I have sinned against him, until he plead my Cause, and execute Judgment for me: He will bring me forth to the Light, and I shall behold his Righteousness.

Nah. i. 7. The Lord is good, a strong Hold in the Day of Trouble, and he knoweth them that trust in him.

Matt. xi, 28. Come unto me, all ye that labour, and are heavy laden, and I will give you Rest.

John xvi. 33. These Things I have spoken unto you, that in me ye might have Peace: In the World ye shall have Tribulation; but be of good cheer, I have overcome the World.

2 *Cor.* i. 5. For as the Sufferings of Christ abound in us, so our Consolation also aboundeth by Christ.

2 *Cor.* lv. 8. We are troubled on every side, yet not distressed; we are perplexed, but not in despair.

Ver. 9. Persecuted, but not forsaken; cast down, but not destroyed.

II. *Promises relating to* Sickness, Old Age, &c.

Exod. xxiii. 25. Ye shall serve the Lord your God, and I will take away sickness from the midst of thee.

Exod. xv. 26. If thou wilt diligently hearken to the Voice of the Lord thy God, and wilt do that which is right in his Sight, and wilt give ear to his Commandments, and keep all his Statutes; I will put none of these Diseases upon thee which I have brought upon the *Egyptians:* For I am the Lord that healeth thee.

Job xxxiii. 24. He is gracious unto him, and saith. Deliver him from going down to the Pit, I have found a Ransom.

Ver. 25. His Flesh shall be fresher than a Child's: He shall return to the Days of his Youth.

Ver. 26. He shall pray unto God, and he will be favourable unto him, and he shall see his Face with Joy: For he will render unto Man his Righteousness.

Ver. 28. He will deliver his Soul from going into the Pit, and his Life shall see the Light.

Ps. xci. 3. Surely he shall deliver thee from the Snare of the Fowler, and from the noisome Pestilence.

Jer. 5. Thou shalt not be afraid for the Terror by Night, nor for the Arrow that flieth by Day:

Ver. 6. Nor for the Pestilence that walketh in Darkness; nor for the Destruction that wasteth at Noon-day.

Ps. ciii. 3. Who forgiveth all thine Iniquities; who healeth all thy Diseases.

Deut. vii. 15. The Lord will take away from thee all Sickness, and will put none of the evil Diseases of *Egypt* upon thee.

Jer. xxxiii. 6. Behold I will bring Health and Cure; and I will cure them, and will reveal unto them the Abundance of Peace and Truth,

Ps. xli. 3. The Lord will strengthen him upon the Bed of languishing: Thou wilt make all his Bed in his Sickness.

Ps. cxvi. 6. The Lord preserveth the Simple: I was brought low, and he helped me.

1 *Tim.* ii. 15. Notwithstanding she shall be saved in Child-bearing, if they continue in Faith and Charity, and Holiness with Sobriety.

Deut. vii. 13. He will bless the Fruit of thy Womb.

Gen. xlix. 25. Even by the God of thy Father, who shall help thee; and by the Almighty, who shall bless thee with Blessings of Heaven above, Blessings of the Deep that lieth under, Blessings of the Breasts, and of the Womb.

Ps. lxxi. 9. Cast me not off in the Time of Old Age, forsake me not when my Strength faileth.

Is. xlvi. 4. And even to your Old Age I am he, and even to hoary Hairs will I carry you: I have made, and I will bear; even I will carry and will deliver you.

Prov. xvi. 31. The hoary Head is a Crown of Glory, if it be found in the way of Righteousness.

III. *Of Deliverance from* Famine *and* Want.

Job v. 20. In Famine he shall redeem thee from Death.

Ver. 22. At Destruction and Famine thou shalt laugh.

Ps. xxxiii. 18. Behold the Eye of the Lord is upon them that fear him; upon them that hope in his Mercy:

Ver. 19. To deliver their Souls from Death, and to keep them alive in Famine.

Ps. xxxvii. 19. They shall not be ashamed in the evil Time: And in the Days of Famine they shall be satisfied.

Ps. cxlvi. 7. Which giveth Food to the Hungry.

Is. xli. 17. When the Poor and needy seek Water and there is none, and their Tongue faileth for Thirst; I the Lord will hear them, I the God of Israel will not forsake them.

Ezek. xxxvi. 29. I will call for the Corn, and will increase it, and lay no Famine upon you.

Ver. 30. And I will multiply the Fruit of the Tree, and the Increase of the Field, that ye shall receive no more Reproach of Famine, among the Heathen.

Zech. x. I . Ask ye of the Lord Rain in the Time of the latter Rain, so the Lord shall make bright Clouds, and give them Showers of Rain, to every one Grass in the Field.

Ps. cvii. 9. He satisfieth the longing Soul, and filleth the hungry Soul with Goodness.

Hab. iii. 17. Though the Fig-tree shall not blossom, neither shall Fruit be in the Vines; the Labour of the Olive shall fail, and the Fields shall yield no Meat;

the Flock shall be cut off from the Fold, and there shall be no Herd in the Stall.

Ver. 18. Yet will I rejoice in the Lord: I will joy in the God of my Salvation.

Matt. lv. 4. Man shall not live by Bread alone, but by every Word that proceedeth out of the Mouth of God.

IV. *Deliverance from* War *and* Enemies.

Deut. xx. 4. The Lord your God is he that goeth with you, to fight for you against your Enemies, to save you, *Deut.* xxiii. 14.

Job v. 20. In War he shall redeem thee from the Power of the Sword.

Ps. ix. 12. Through God we shall do valiantly: For he it is that shall tread down our Enemies.

2 *Chron.* xiii. 12. Behold God himself is with us for our Captain.

Prov. iii. 25. Be not afraid of sudden Fear, nor of the Desolation of the Wicked, when it cometh.

Ver. 26. For the Lord shall be thy Confidence, and shall keep thy Foot from being taken.

Is. xli. 11. Behold all they that were incensed against thee, shall be ashamed and confounded: They shall be as nothing; and they that strive with thee shall perish.

Ver. 12. Thou shalt seek them, and shalt not find them, even them that contended with thee: They that war against thee shall be as nothing, and as a Thing of nought.

Jer. xxxii. 17. I will deliver thee in that Day, saith the Lord, and thou shalt not be given into the Hand of the Men of whom thou art. afraid.

Ver. 18. For I will surely deliver thee, and thou shalt not fall by the Sword; but thy Life shall be for a Prey unto thee, because thou hast put thy Trust in me, saith the Lord.

Kings vi. 16. Fear not, for they that be with us are more than they that be with them.

2 *Chron.* xiv. ii. Lord, it is nothing with thee to help, whether with many, or with them that have no Power.

2 *Kings* xvii. 39. The Lord your God ye shall fear, and he shall deliver you out of the Hand of all your Enemies.

Ps. xvii. 7. Shew thy marvellous Loving-Kindness, O thou that savest by thy Right Hand them which put their Trust in thee, from those that rise up against them.

Ps. xxvii. 5. In the Time of Trouble he shall hide me in his Pavilion; in the secret of his Tabernacle shall he hide me: He shall set me up upon a Rock.

Ver. 6. And now shall mine Head be lifted up above mine Enemies round about me: Therefore will I offer in his Tabernacle Sacrifices of Joy; I will sing, yea, I will sing Praises unto the Lord.

Ps. xxxvii. 32. The Wicked watcheth the Righteous, and seeketh to slay him.

Ver. 33. The Lord will not leave him in his Hand, nor condemn him when he is judged.

Ver. 40. And the Lord shall help and deliver them: He will deliver them from the Wicked, and save them, because they trust in him.

Ps. xcvii. 10. He preserveth the Souls of his Saints; he delivereth them out of the Hand of the Wicked.

Ps. cxii. 8. His Heart is established, he shall not be afraid, until he see his Desire, upon his Enemies.

Ps. cxviii. 7. The Lord taketh my part with them that help me: Therefore shall I see my Desire upon my Enemies.

Ps. cxxv. 3. The Rod of the Wicked shall not rest upon the Lot of the Righteous, lest the Righteous put forth their Hands unto Iniquity.

Job viii. 22. They that hate thee shall be clothed with Shame, and the Dwelling-place of the Wicked shall come to nought.

Prov. xvi. 7. When a Man's Ways please the Lord, he maketh even his Enemies to be at Peace with him.

Is. xxv. 5. Thou shalt bring down the Noise of Strangers as the Heat in a dry Place; even the Heat with the Shadow of a Cloud: The Branch of the terrible ones shall be brought low.

Is. liv. 17. No Weapon that is formed against thee shall prosper; and every Tongue that shall rise against thee in Judgment, thou shalt condemn. This is the Heritage of the Servants of the Lord, and their Righteousness is of me, saith the Lord.

Ver. 15. Whosoever shall gather together against thee, shall fall for thy Sake.

Deut. xxviii. 7. The Lord shall cause thine Enemies, that rise up against thee, to be smitten before thy Face: They shall come out against thee one Way, and flee before thee seven Ways.

Luke xviii. 7, 8. Shall not God avenge his own Elect, that cry Day and Night unto him, though he bear long with them? I tell you that he will avenge them speedily.

Acts xviii. 10. I am with thee: And no Man shall set on thee, to hurt thee.

Heb. xiii. 6. So that we may boldly say, the Lord is my Helper, I will not fear what Man shall do unto me. *Ps.* cxviii. 6.

Luke i. 71. That we should be saved from our Enemies, and from the Hand of all that hate us.

Ver. 74. That he would grant unto us, that we being delivered out of the Hands of our Enemies, might serve him without Fear.

Ver. 75. In Holiness and Righteousness before him, all the Days of our Life.

V. *From* Oppression *and* Injustice.

Exod. xxii. 26. If thou at all take thy Neighbour's Raiment to pledge, thou shalt deliver it to him by that the Sun goeth down.

Ver. 27. For that is his Covering only, it is his Raiment for his Skin: Wherein shall he sleep? And it shall come to pass, when he crieth unto me, that I will hear; for I am gracious.

Ps. xii. 5. For the Oppression of the Poor, for the Sighing of the Needy, now will I arise, saith the Lord: I will set him in safety from him that puffeth at him,

Ps. xxxv. 10. All my Bones shall say. Lord, who is like unto thee? which deliverest the Poor from him who is too strong for him; yea, the Poor and the Needy, from him that spoileth him.

Ps. lxxii. 4. He shall judge the Poor of the People, he shall save the Children of the Needy, and shall break in Pieces the Oppressor.

Ver. 14. He shall redeem their Soul from Deceit and Violence: And precious shall their Blood be in his Sight.

Ps. cix. 3 I. He shall stand at the Right Hand of the Poor, to save him from those that condemn his Soul.

Ps. cxlvi. 7. Which executeth Judgment for the Oppressed.

Eccl. v. 8. If thou seest the Oppression of the Poor, and violent perverting of Judgment and Justice in a Province, marvel not at the Matter: For he that is higher than the highest regardeth, and there be higher than they.

Is. liv. 14. In Righteousness shalt thou be established: Thou shalt be far from Oppression, for thou shalt not fear; and from Terror, for it shall not come nigh thee.

VI. *From* Slanders *and* Reproach.

Job v. 21, Thou shalt be hid from the Scourge of the Tongue; neither shalt thou be afraid of the Destruction when it cometh.

Job xi. 15. Thou shall lift up thy Face without Spot.

Ps. xxxvii. 6. He shall bring forth thy Righteousness as the Light, and thy Judgment as the Noon-day.

Ps. xxxi. 20. Thou shalt hide them in the secret of thy Presence from the Pride of Man: Thou shalt keep them secretly in a Pavilion, from the Strife of Tongues.

Ps. lvii. 3. He shall send from Heaven, and save me from the Reproach of him that would swallow me up: Selah. God shall send forth his Mercy and his Truth.

Is. li. 7. Hearken unto me, ye that know Righteousness, the People in whose Heart is my Law: Fear ye not the Reproach of Men, neither be ye afraid of their Revilings.

Ver. 8. For the Moth shall eat them up like a Garment, and the Worm shall eat them like Wool: But my Righteousness shall be for ever, and my Salvation from Generation to Generation.

Matt. v. 11. Blessed are ye when Men shall revile you, and persecute you, and shall say all manner of Evil against you falsly, for my sake.

Ver. 12. Rejoice and be exceeding glad; for great is your Reward in Heaven.

Heb. xi. 26. Esteeming the Reproach of Christ greater Riches than the Treasures in Egypt; for he had respect unto the Recompence of the Reward.

I *Pet.* lv. 14. If ye be reproached for the Name of Christ, happy are ye; for the Spirit of Glory and of Gou resteth upon you: On their Part he is evil spoken of, but on your Part he is glorified.

VII. *From* Witchcraft.

Numb. xxiii. 23. Surely there is no Enchantment against *Jacob*, neither is there any Divination against *Israel*.

VIII. *Promises to the* Stranger.

Deut. x. 18. He loveth the Stranger, in giving him Food and Raiment.

Ps. cxlvi. 9. The Lord preserveth the Strangers.

Ezek. xi. 16. Thus saith the Lord God, Although I have cast them far off among the Heathen, and although I have scattered them among the Countries; yet will I be to them as a little Sanctuary, in the Countries where they shall come.

IX. *To the* Poor *and* Helpless.

Ps. ix. 18. The Needy shall not always be forgotten; the Expectation of the Poor shall not perish for ever.

Ps. lxviii. 10. Thou, O God, hast prepared of thy Goodness for the Poor.

Ps. lxix. 33. The Lord heareth the Poor.

Ps. cxxxii. 15. I will satisfy her Poor with Bread.

Is. xiv. 30. The First-born of the Poor shall feed; and the Needy shall lie down in safety.

Ps. lxxii. 2. He shall judge thy People with Righteousness, and thy Poor with Judgment.

Ver. 12. He shall deliver the Needy, when he crieth; the Poor also, and him that hath no Helper.

Ver. 13. Pie shall spare the Poor and Needy, and shall save the Souls of the Needy.

Ps. cii. 17. He will regard the Prayer of the Destitute, and not despise their Prayer.

Ps. cvii. 41. He setteth the Poor on high from Affliction, and maketh his Families like a Flock.

Ps. cxiii. 7. He raiseth up the Poor out of the Dust, and lifteth the Needy out of the Dunghill.

Jer. xx. 13. Sing unto the Lord, praise ye the Lord, for he hath delivered the Soul of the Poor from the Hand of Evildoers.

Job v. 15. He saveth the Poor from the Sword, from their Mouth, and from the Hand of the Mighty.

Ver. 16. So the Poor hath Hope, and Iniquity stoppeth her Mouth.

Job xxxvi. 15. He delivereth the Poor in his Affliction, and openeth their Ears in Oppression.

Jam. i. 9. Let the Brother of low Degree rejoice, in that he is exalted.

Jam. ii. 5. Hearken my beloved Brethren, Hath not God chosen the Poor of this World, rich in Faith, and Heirs of the Kingdom, which he hath promised to them that love him?

Luke xvi. 25. Abraham said. Son, remember, thou in thy Life-time receivedst thy good Things, and likewise Lazarus evil Things: But now he is comforted, and thou art tormented.

X. *To the* Fatherless *and* Widow.

Exod. xxii. 22. Ye shall not afflict any Widow, or fatherless Child.

Ver. 23. If thou afflict them in any wise, and they cry at all unto me, I will surely hear their Cry.

Ver. 24. And my Wrath shall wax hot, and I will kill you with the Sword: And your Wives shall be Widows, and your Children fatherless.

Deut. x. 18. He doth execute the Judgment of the Fatherless and the Widow.

Ps. x. 14. The Poor committeth himself unto thee: Thou art the Helper of the Fatherless.

Ver. 18. To judge the Fatherless and the Oppressed, that the Man of the Earth may no more oppress.

Ps. lxviii. 5. A Father of the Fatherless, and a Judge of the Widow, is God in his holy Habitation.

Ps. cxlvi. 9. He relieveth the Fatherless and Widow.

Prov. xv. 25. The Lord will destroy the House of the Proud; but he will establish the Border of the Widow.

Prov. xxiii. 10. Remove not the old. Land-mark; and enter not into the Fields of the Fatherless.

Ver. 11. For their Redeemer is mighty: He shall plead their Cause with thee.

Jer. xlix. 11. Leave thy fatherless Children, [1] I will preserve them alive; and let thy Widows trust in me.

Hos. xiv. 3. In thee the Fatherless findeth Mercy.

XI. *To the* Childless.

Ps. lxviii. 6. God setteth the Solitary in Families.

Ps. cxiii. 9. He maketh the barren Woman to keep House, and to be a joyful Mother of Children.

Is. lvi. 4. Thus saith the Lord, unto the Eunuchs that keep my Sabbaths, and chose the Things that please me, and take hold of my Covenant.

Ver. 5. Even unto them will I give in mine House, and within my Walls a Place, and a Name, better than of Sons and of Daughters: I will give them an everlasting Name, that shall not be cut off

XII. *To the* Prisoner *and* Captive.

Ps. lxviii. 6. He bringeth out those which are bound with Chains.
Ps. cxlvi. 7. The Lord looseth the Prisoners.
Deut. xxx. 4. If any of thine be driven out unto the utmost Parts of Heaven, from thence will the Lord thy God gather thee, and from thence will he fetch thee.
Ps. lxix. 33. He despiseth not his Prisoners.
Ps. cvii. 14. He brought them out of Darkness, and the Shadow of Death, and brake their Bands in sunder.
Is. li. 14. The captive Exile hasteneth, that he may be loosed, and that he should not die in the Pit, nor that his Bread should fail.
Is. xlix. 25. Thus saith the Lord. Even the Captives of the mighty shall be taken away, and the Prey of the terrible shall be delivered: For I will contend with him that contendeth with thee, and I will save thy Children.
Jer. xv. 11. Verily it shall be well with thy Remnant; verily I will cause the Enemy to entreat thee well in the Time of Evil, and in the Time of Affliction.

XIII. *Promises of Deliverance from* Death.

Job xxxiii. 28. He will deliver his Soul from going into the Pit, and his Life shall see the Light.
Ps. lxviii. 20. He that is our God, is the God of Salvation; and unto God the Lord belong the Issues from Death.
Ps. lxvi. 8. O bless our God, ye People; and make the Voice of his Praise to be heard.
Ver. 9. Who holdeth our Soul in Life, and suffereth not our Feet to be moved.
Ps. cii. 19. From Heaven did the Lord behold the Earth.
Ver. 20. To hear the groaning of the Prisoner, to loose those who are appointed to Death.
Ps. cvii. 18. Their Soul abhorreth all manner of Meat, and they draw near unto the Gates of Death.
Ver. 19. Then they cry unto the Lord in their Trouble; he saveth them out of their Distresses.
Ps. cxvi. 15. Precious in the Sight of the Lord is the Death of his Saints.
Ps. xci. 7. A thousand shall fall at thy Side, and ten thousand at thy Right Hand; but it shall not come nigh thee.
Ps. ix. 13. Thou that liftest me up from the Gates of Death.
1 *Sam.* ii. 6. The Lord killeth, and maketh alive; he bringeth down to the Grave, and bringeth up.

Deut. xxxii. 39. See now, that I, even I am He, and there is no God with me: I kill, I make alive; I wound, and I heal: Neither is there any that can deliver out of my Hand.

[1] *Though the* Chaldee Paraphrase *understands these Words as a Promise to the Families of the Jews, in their Captivity: others, more agreeably to the Context, look upon them as a Threatning against the Edomites, and thus join them to the* 10*th Verse, and render them:* There is none to *say,* Leave thy fatherless Children, &c.

Chapter Three - Promises *of* Spiritual Blessings *in this Life*

I. In General.

Psal. xxv. 10. All the Paths of the Lord are Mercy and Truth, unto such as keep his Covenant and his Testimonies.
Ver. 14. The Secret of the Lord is with them that fear him, and he will shew them his Covenant.
Eph. i. 3. Blessed be the God and Father of our Lord Jesus Christ, who hath blessed us with all spiritual Blessings in heavenly Places in Christ.
Ver. 4. According as he hath chosen us in him before the Foundation of the World, that we should be Holy, and without Blame before him in Love.
Ver. 7. According to the Riches of his Grace.
Ver. 8. Wherein he hath abounded towards us in all Wisdom and Prudence.
Gal. vi. 16. As many as walk according to this Rule, Peace be on them, and Mercy, and upon the *Israel* of God.
Rom. viii. 30. Whom he did predestinate them he also called: And whom he called, them he also justified: And whom he justified, them he also glorified.
2 *Pet.* i. 3. According to his Divine Power hath he given unto us all Things, that pertain unto Life and Godliness, through the Knowledge of him that hath called us unto Glory and Virtue.
Ver. 4. Whereby are given unto us exceeding great and precious Promises.

II. *Of* Justification, Pardon *and* Reconciliation.

Numb. xxiii. 21. He hath not beheld Iniquity in *Jacob,* neither hath he seen Perverseness in *Israel.*
Is. xlv. 25. In the Lord shall all the Seed of *Israel* be justified, and shall glory.
Is. liii. 11. By his Knowledge shall my righteous Servant justify many; for he shall bear their Iniquities.
Ezek. xxxvi. 25. I will sprinkle clean Water upon you, and ye shall be clean: From all your Filthiness, and from all your Idols, will I cleanse you.

Rom. iii. 24. Being justified freely by his Grace, through the Redemption that is in Jesus Christ.

Rom. v. 1. Being justified by Faith, we have Peace with God, thro' our Lord Jesus Christ.

Ver. 9. Being justified by his Blood, we shall be saved from Wrath through him.

Ver. 18. By the Righteousness of One, the free Gift came upon all Men unto Justification of Life.

Ver. 19. For by the Obedience of One, shall many be made Righteous.

Rom. viii. i. There is therefore now no Condemnation to them which are in Christ Jesus, who walk not after the Flesh, but after the Spirit.

Ver. 33. Who shall lay any thing to the Charge of God's Elect? It is God that justifieth:

Ver. 34. Who is he that condemneth? It is Christ that died; yea, rather is risen again, who is even at the Right Hand of God, who also maketh Intercession for us.

2 *Chron.* v. 21. He hath made him to be Sin for us, who knew no Sin; that we might be made the Righteousness of God, in him.

Acts xiii. 39. By him all that believe are justified from all Things, from which ye could not be justified by the Law of Moses.

Tit. iii. 7. That being justified by his Grace, we should be made Heirs according to the Hope of eternal Life.

Exod. xxxiv. 7. Keeping Mercy for Thousands, forgiving Iniquity, and Transgression, and Sin.

Ps. lxv. 3. As for our Transgressions, thou shalt purge them away.

Ps. ciii. 9. He will not always chide, neither will he keep his Anger for ever.

Ver. 10. He hath not dealt with us after our Sins, nor rewarded us according to our Iniquities.

Ver. 11. As the Heaven is high above the Earth, so great is his Mercy toward them that fear him.

Ver. 12. As far as the East is from the West, so far hath he removed our Transgressions from us.

Ps. cxxx. 4. There is Forgiveness with thee, that thou mayst be feared.

Ver. 8. He shall redeem Israel from all his Iniquities.

Is. xxxiii. 24. The Inhabitant shall not say, I am sick: The People that dwell therein, shall be forgiven their Iniquity.

Is. xliii. 25. I, even I, am he that blotteth out thy Transgressions for mine own sake, and will not remember thy Sins.

Is. xliv. 22. I have blotted out as a thick Cloud thy Transgressions, and as a Cloud thy Sins: Return unto me, for I have redeemed thee.

Hos. xi. 8. My Heart is turned within me, my Repentings are kindled together.

Ver. 9. I will not execute the Fierceness of mine Anger, I will not return to destroy *Ephraim*.

Mic. vii. 18. Who is a God like unto thee, that pardoneth Iniquity, and passeth by the Transgression of the Remnant of his Heritage? He retaineth not his Anger for ever, because he delighteth in Mercy.

Ver. 19. He will turn again, he will have Compassion upon us: He will subdue our Iniquities: And thou wilt cast all our Sins into the Depths of the Sea.

Heb. x. 17, Their Sins and Iniquities will I remember no more.

Ps. xxxii. I. Blessed is he whose Transgression is forgiven, whose Sin is covered.

Ver. 2. Blessed is the Man unto whom the Lord imputeth not Iniquity, and in whose Spirit there is no Guile.

Jer. xxxi. 34. I will forgive thine Iniquity, and I will remember their Sin no more.

Heb. viii. 12. I will be merciful to their Unrighteousness, and their Sins and their Iniquities will I remember no more.

Matt. xii. 31. All Manner of Sin and Blasphemy shall be forgiven unto Men.

Ver. 32. And whosoever speaketh a Word against the Son of Man, it shall be forgiven him.

Luke vii. 47. Her Sins, which are many are forgiven, for she loved much.

Ver. 48. And he said unto her, thy Sins are forgiven,

Ver. 50. Thy Faith hath saved thee: Go in Peace. See *Repentance*, Part II. Ch. I. Sect. II.

Is. i. 18. Though your Sins be as Scarlet, they shall be as white as Snow; though they be red like Crimson, they shall be as Wool.

Ps. ciii. 3. He forgiveth all thine Iniquities: He healeth all thy Diseases.

Jer. xxxiii. 8. I will cleanse them from all their Iniquity, whereby they have sinned against me; and I will pardon all their Iniquities whereby they have sinned, and whereby they have transgressed against me.

Ezek. xxxiii. 16. None of his Sins that he hath committed, shall be mentioned unto him.

Jer. iii. 12. Return, thou backsliding *Israel,* saith the Lord, and I will not cause mine Anger to fall upon you.

Ver. 22. Return, ye backsliding Children, and I will heal your Backslidings.

Hos. xiv. 4. I will heal their Backslidings, I will love them freely.

Is. liii. 5. He was wounded for our Transgressions, he was bruised for our Iniquities: The Chastisement of our Peace was upon him, and with his Stripes we are healed.

Ver. 6, All we like sheep have gone astray, we have turned every one to his own Way, and the Lord hath laid on him the Iniquity of us all.

Zech. xiii. 1. In that Day there shall be a Fountain opened to the House of David, and to the Inhabitants of Jerusalem, for Sin and for Uncleanness.

Matt. i. 21. He shall save his People from their Sins.

Acts xiii. 38. Thro' this Man is preached unto you the Forgiveness of Sins.

Eph. i. 7. In whom we have Redemption through his Blood, the Forgiveness of Sins, according to the Riches of his Grace.

Gal. i. 4. Who gave himself for our Sins.

I *Tim.* i. 15. This is a faithful Saying, and worthy of all Acceptation, that Jesus Christ came into the World to save Sinners.

I *Cor.* xv. 3. Christ died for our Sins, according to the Scriptures.

Heb. i. 3. When he had by himself purged our Sins.

Heb. ix. 26. He hath appeared to put away Sin by the Sacrifice of himself

Ver. 28. Christ was once offered to bear the Sins of many.

Heb. x. 14. By one Offering he hath perfected for ever them that are sanctified.

John i. 29. The Lamb of God, which taketh away the Sins of the World.

Matt. xxvi. 28. This is my Blood, which is shed for many, for the Remission of Sins.

I *John* i. 7. The Blood of Jesus Christ cleanseth us from all Sin.

Ver. 9. If we confess our Sins, he is faithful and just to forgive us our Sins, and to cleanse us from all Unrighteousness.

I *John* ii. I. If any Man sin, we have an Advocate with the Father, Jesus Christ the Righteous.

Ver. 2. He is the Propitiation for our Sins: And not for ours only, but for the Sins of the whole World.

Ver. 12. I write to you, little Children, because your Sins are forgiven you, for his Name's sake.

I *John* iii. 5. He was manifested to take away our Sins.

I *Pet.* ii. 24. Who his own self bare our Sins in his own Body on the Tree, that we being dead to Sin should live unto Righteousness: By whose Stripes ye were healed.

Rev. i. 5. That loved us, and washed us from our Sins in his own Blood.

Is. xxvii, 15. Let him take hold of my Strength, that he may make Peace with me, and he shall make Peace with me.

Rom. v. 9. Being now justified by his Blood, we shall be saved from Wrath through him.

Ver. 10. For if when we were Enemies we were reconciled unto God, much more being reconciled we shall be saved by his Life.

2 *Cor.* v. 18. All things are of God, who hath reconciled us to himself by Jesus Christ, and hath given to us the Ministry of Reconciliation.

Ver. 19. To wit, that God was in Christ reconciling the World to himself, not imputing to them their Trespasses.

Eph. ii. 13. Now in Christ Jesus, ye who sometimes were far off, are made nigh by the Blood of Christ.

Ver. 14. For he is our Peace, who hath made both one, and hath broken down the middle Wall of Partition between us.

Ver. 15. Having abolished in his Flesh, the Enmity, even the Law of Commandments, contained in Ordinances, for to make in himself, of twain, one new Man, so making Peace:

Ver. 16. And that he might reconcile both unto God in one Body by the Cross, having slain the Enmity thereby:

Ver. 17. And came, and preached Peace to you that were afar off, and to them that were nigh.

Col. i. 21. You that were sometime alienated, and Enemies in your Mind by wicked Works, yet now hath he reconciled.

Ver. 22. In the Body of his Flesh, thro' Death, to present you Holy and Unblameable, and Unreproveable in his Sight.

Ver. 23. If ye continue in the Faith, grounded and settled, and be not moved away from the Hope of the Gospel, which ye have heard, and which was preached to every Creature, which is under Heaven.

Heb. ii. 17. That he might be a merciful and faithful High Priest, in Things pertaining to God, to make Reconciliation for the Sins of the People.

III. Adoption.

Jer. xxxi. 9. I am a Father to *Israel,* and *Ephraim* is my First-born.

Is. lxiii. 16. Doubtless thou art our Father, though Abraham be ignorant of us, and Israel acknowledge us not: Thou, O Lord, art our Father, our Redeemer; thy Name is from Everlasting.

Is. lxiv. 8. But now, O Lord, thou art our Father: We are the Clay, and thou our Potter; and we are all the Work of thine Hand.

Rom. viii. 14. As many as are led by the Spirit of God, they are the Sons of God.

Ver. 15. For ye have not received the Spirit of Bondage again to fear; but ye have received the Spirit of Adoption, whereby we cry, Abba, Father.

Rom. ix. 26. And it shall come to pass, that in the Place where it was said unto them, Ye are not my People, there shall they be called the Children of the Living God,

2 *Cor.* vi. 18. I will be a Father unto you, and ye shall be my Sons and Daughters, saith the Lord Almighty.

Gal. iii. 26. Ye are all the Children of God by Faith in Christ Jesus.

Gal. iv. 4. God sent forth his Son ___

Ver. 5. To redeem them that were under the Law, that we might receive the Adoption of Sons.

Ver. 7. Wherefore thou art no more a Servant, but a Son; and if a Son, then an Heir of God through Christ.

Eph. i. 5. Having predestinated us to the Adoption of Children by Jesus Christ to himself, according to the good Pleasure of his Will.

Ver. 6. To the Praise of the Glory of his Grace, wherein he hath made us accepted through the Beloved.

John i. 12. As many as received him, to them gave he Power to become the Sons of God, even to them that believe on his Name,

I *John* iii. 1. Behold what manner of Love hath the Father bestowed upon us, that we should be called the Sons of God?

Ver. 2. Beloved, now are we the Sons of God.

IV. Union and Communion with the Church.

Heb. xii. 22. Ye are come unto Mount *Sion,* and unto the City of the living God, the heavenly *Jerusalem,* and to an innumerable Company of Angels.

Ver. 23. To the general Assembly, and Church of the First-born, which are written in Heaven, and to God the Judge of all, and to the Spirits of just Men made perfect.

Ver. 24. And to Jesus the Mediator of the new Covenant, and to the Blood of sprinkling, that speaketh better Things than that of Abel.

Phil. iii. 3. For we are the Circumcision, which worship God in the Spirit, and rejoice in Jesus Christ.

Gal. iii. 28. There is neither *Jew* nor *Greek,* there is neither Bond nor Free, there is neither Male nor Female: For ye are all one in Jesus Christ.

Ver. 29. And if you be Christ's, then are ye Abrahams Seed, and Heirs according to the Promise.

Gal. iv. 26. *Jerusalem,* which is above, is free, which is the Mother of us all.

Ver. 28. Now we, Brethren, as *Isaac* was, are the Children of the Promise.

I *John* i. 3. That which we have seen and heard, declare we unto you, that ye also may have Fellowship with us: And truly our Fellowship is with the Father, and with his Son Jesus Christ.

Eph. ii. 12. That at that Time ye were without Christ, being Aliens from the Commonwealth of Israel, and Strangers from the Covenants of Promise, having no Hope, and without God in the World.

Ver. 13. But now in Christ Jesus, ye who sometimes were far off, are made nigh by the Blood of Christ.

Ver. 19. Now therefore ye are no more Strangers and Foreigners, but Fellow Citizens with the Saints, and of the Household of God.

Ver. 22. In whom [Christ] you also are builded together for an Habitation of God, through the Spirit.

Rom. xi. 17. Thou being a wild Olive-Tree, wert grafted in amongst them, and with them partakest of the Root and Fatness of the Olive-Tree.

V. Free Access *to* God, *with* Acceptance.

Eph. ii. 18. Through him we both have an Access by one Spirit unto the Father.

Eph. iii. 12. In whom we have Boldness and Access with Confidence by the Faith of him.

I *Pet.* ii. 4. To whom, coming as unto a living Stone, disallowed indeed of Men, but chosen of God, and precious.

Ver. 5. Ye also as lively Stones, are built up a spiritual House, a holy Priesthood, to offer up spiritual Sacrifices, acceptable to God, by Jesus Christ.

Heb. x. 19. Having therefore. Brethren, Boldness to enter into the holiest by the Blood of Jesus.

Ver. 20. By a new and living Way, which he hath consecrated for us, thro' the Vail, that is to say his Flesh.

Eph. i. 6. Wherein he hath made us accepted through the Beloved.

Ezek. xx. 40. In mine holy Mountain — I will accept them, and there will I require your Offerings.

Ver. 41. And I will accept you with your sweet favour.

VI. Of Hearing Prayer.

Job xxii. 27. Thou shalt make thy Prayer unto him, and he shall hear thee.

Ps. iv. 3. But know that the Lord hath set apart him that is godly for himself: The Lord will hear, when I call unto him.

Ps. xxxiv. 6. This poor Man cried, and the Lord heard him, and saved him out of all his Trouble.

Ps. xxxiv. 15. The Eyes of the Lord are upon the Righteous, and his Ears are open unto their Cry.

Ver. 17. The Righteous cry, and the Lord heareth, and delivereth them out of all their Troubles.

Ps. i. 15. Call upon me in the Day of Trouble, I will deliver thee, and thou shalt glorify me.

Ps. lxv. 2. O thou that hearest Prayer, unto thee shall all Flesh come.

Ps. xci. 15. He shall call upon me, and I will answer him.

Ps. cxiv. 19. He will fulfil the Desire of them that fear him: He also will hear their Cry, and will save them.

Prov. xv. 29. The Lord is far from the Wicked: But he heareth the Prayer of the Righteous.

Is. xxx. 19. He will be very Gracious unto thee, at the Voice of thy Cry: When he shall hear it, he will answer thee.

Is. lviii. 9. Then shalt thou call, and the Lord shall answer: Thou shalt cry, and he shall say, Here I am.

Is. lxv. 24. And it shall come to pass, that before they call, I will answer; and whilst they are yet speaking, I will hear.

Jer. xxix. 12. Then shall ye call upon me, and ye shall go and pray unto me, and I will hearken unto you.

Zech. xiii. 9. They shall call on my Name, and I will hear them: I will say, It is my People: And they shall say, the Lord is my God.

Matt. vii. 7. Ask, and it shall be given you: Seek, and ye shall find: Knock, and it shall be opened unto you.

Ver. 8. For every one that asketh, receiveth: And he that seeketh, findeth: And to him that knocketh, it shall be opened.

Ver. 11. If ye then, being evil, knowhow to give good Gifts unto your Children, how much more shall your Father which is in Heaven give good Things to them that ask him?

Matt. xxi. 22. And all Things, whatsoever ye shall ask in Prayer, believing, ye shall receive.

John xv. 7. If ye abide in me, and my Works abide in you, ye shall ask what ye will, and it shall be done unto you.

John xvi. 23. And in that Day ye shall ask me nothing: Verily, verily, I say unto you, whatsoever ye shall ask the Father in my Name, he will give it you.

Ver. 24. Hitherto have ye asked nothing in my Name: Ask, and ye shall receive, that your Joy may be full.

John xiv. 13. And whatsoever ye shall ask in my Name, that will I do, that the Father may be glorified in the Son.

Ver. 14. If ye shall ask any Thing in my Name, I will do it.

James v. 15. And the Prayer of Faith shall save the Sick, and the Lord shall raise him up: And if he have committed Sins, they shall be forgiven him.

Ver. 16. Confess your Faults one to another, and pray one for another, that ye may be healed: The effectual fervent Prayer of a righteous Man availeth much.

1 *John* iii. 22. And whatsover we ask, we receive of him, because we keep his Commandments, and do those Things that are pleasing in his Sight. .

1 *John* v. 14. And this is the Confidence that we have in him, that if we ask any Thing according to his Will, he heareth us.

Ver. 15. And if we know that he hear us, whatsoever we ask, we know that we have the Petitions that we desired of him.

Ver. 16. If any Man see his Brother sin a Sin, which is not unto Death, he shall ask, and he shall give him Life for them that sin not unto Death.

VII. *Of Sanctifying* Grace *in General.*

Ps. lxxxiv. 11. The Lord God is a Sun and Shield: The Lord will give Grace and Glory: No good Thing will he with-hold from them that walk uprightly.

John xvii. 17. Sanctify them through thy Truth: Thy Word is Truth.

Ver. 19. And for their Sakes I sanctify myself, that they also might be sanctified through the Truth.

Eph. ii. 10. We are his Workmanship, created in Christ Jesus unto good Works, which God hath before ordained, that we should walk in them.

Phil. ii. 13. For it is God which worketh in you both to will and to do, of his good Pleasure.

Phil lv. 13. I can do all Things through Christ, which strengtheneth me.

2 *Cor.* iii. 5. Not that we are sufficient of ourselves, to think any Thing as of ourselves; but our Sufficiency is of God.

2 *Thess.* ii. 13. We are bound to give Thanks always to God for you, Brethren, beloved of the Lord, because God hath from the beginning chosen you to Salvation, through Sanctification of the Spirit, and Belief of the Truth.

Col. i. 12. Giving Thanks unto the Father, which hath made us meet to be Partakers of the Inheritance of the Saints in Light.

Ver. 21. Yet now hath he reconciled, in the Body of his Flesh through Death, to present you Holy and Unblameable, and Unreproveable in his Sight.

I *Thess.* v. 23. And the very God of Peace sanctify you wholly. And I pray God your whole Spirit, and Soul and Body, be preserved blameless, unto the coming of our Lord Jesus Christ.

Tit. ii. 14. Who gave himself for us, that he might redeem us from all Iniquity, and purify unto himself a peculiar People, zealous of good Works.

Jer. xxxi. 33. This shall be the Covenant that I will make with the House of Israel, After those Days, saith the Lord, I will put my Law in their inward Parts, and write it in their Hearts; and I will be their God, and they shall be my People.

Jer. xxx. 9. They shall serve the Lord their God, and David their Kino-, whom I will raise up unto them.

Luke i. 74. That he would grant unto us, that we being delivered out of the Hands of our Enemies, might serve him without Fear.

Ver. 75. In Holiness and Righteousness before him. all the Days of our Life.

1 *Cor.* vi. 11. And such were some of you: But ye are washed, but ye are sanctified, but ye are justified in the Name of the Lord Jesus, and by the Spirit of our God.

2 *Cor.* iii. 18. But we all, with open Face, beholding as in a Glass the Glory of the Lord, are changed into the same Image, from Glory to Glory, even as by the Spirit of the Lord.

VIII. *Particularly of Converting* Grace.

Deut. xxx. 6. And the Lord thy God will circumcise thine Heart, and the Heart of thy Seed, to love the Lord thy God with all thine Heart, and with all thy Soul, that thou mayst live.

Jer. xxiv. 7. And I will give them a Heart to know me, that I am the Lord and they shall be my People, and I will be their God: For they shall return unto me with their whole Heart.

Jer. xxxi. 18. Turn thou me, and I shall be turned, for thou art the Lord my God.

Ps. cx. 3. Thy People shall be willing" in the Day of thy Power.

Jer l. 4. In those Days, and at that Time, saith the Lord, the Children of *Israel* shall come, they and the Children of *Judah* together, going and weeping: They shall go, and seek the Lord their God.

Ver. 5. They shall ask the Way to *Zion* with their Faces thitherward, saying. Come, and let us join ourselves to the Lord, in a perpetual Covenant, that shall not be forgotten.

Ezek. xi. 19. And I will give them one Heart, and I will put a new Spirit within you; and I will take the stony Heart out of their Flesh, and will give them an Heart of Flesh.

Ver. 20. That they may walk in my Statutes, and keep mine Ordinances, and do them: And they shall be my People, and I will be their God.

Ezek. xxxvi. 26. A new Heart also will I give you, and a new Spirit will I put within you; and I will take away the stony Heart out of your Flesh, and I will give you a Heart of Flesh.

2 *Tim.* ii. 4. Who hath saved us, and called us with a holy Calling; not according to our Works, but according to his own Purpose and Grace, which was given us in Christ Jesus, before the World began.

Tit. iii. 5. Not by Works of Righteousness which we have done, but according to his Mercy he saved us, by the washing of Regeneration, and renewing of the Holy Ghost.

Ezek. xx. 43. And there shall ye remember your Ways, and all your Doings, wherein ye have been defiled, and ye shall loath yourselves in your own Sight, for all the Evils that ye have committed.

Ezek. xxxvi. 31, Then shall ye remember your own evil Way, and your Doings that were not good, and shall loath yourselves in your own Sight, for your Iniquities, and for your Abominations.

Matt. ix. 13. I am not come to call the Righteous, but Sinners to Repentance.

Acts v. 31. Him hath God exalted with his Right Hand, to be a Prince and Saviour, for to give Repentance to *Israel,* and Forgiveness of Sins.

Acts iii. 26. Unto you first, God having raised up his Son Jesus, sent him to bless you, in turning away every one of you from his Iniquities.

Hos. ii. 6. Behold, I will hedge up thy Way with Thorns, and make a Wall that she shall not find her Paths.

Ver. 7. And she shall follow after her Lovers, but she shall not overtake them; and she shall seek them, but shall not find them: Then shall she say, I will go and return to my first Husband, for then was it better with me than now.

Zech. xii. 10. They shall look upon me whom they have pierced.

John vi. 45. It is written in the Prophets, And they shall be all taught of God. Every Man therefore that hath heard and learned of the Father, cometh unto me.

Phil. i. 29. Unto you it is given to believe in Christ.

Eph. ii. 8. For by Grace ye are saved, through Faith, and that not of yourselves, it is the Gift of God.

Jer. xxxii, 40. I will give them one Heart, and one way, that they may fear me for ever.

IX. Knowledge, Wisdom, &c.

Prov. ii. 5. Then shalt thou Knowledge, understand the Fear of the Lord, and find the Knowledge of God.

Ver. 9. Then shalt thou understand Righteousness, and Judgment, and Equity; yea, every good Path.

Prov. xxxviii. 5. Evil Men understand not Judgment: But they that seek the Lord, understand all Things.

Is. ii. 3. He will teach us of his Ways, and we will walk in his Paths: For out of *Zion* shall go forth the Law, and the Word of the Lord from *Jerusalem.*

Is. xxix. 18. And in that Day shall the Deaf hear the Words of the Book, and the Eyes of the Blind shall see out of Obscurity, and out of Darkness.

Ver. 24. They also that erred in Spirit shall come to Understanding, and they that murmured shall learn Doctrine,

Is. xxxv. 8. And an high Way shall be there, and a Way, and it shall be called the Way of Holiness: The Unclean shall not pass over it. but it shall be for those: The Way-faring Men, though Fools, shall not err therein.

Is. lii. 6. My People shall know my Name: Therefore they shall know in that Day, that I am he that speaketh.

Is. xxxii. 3. And the Eyes of them that see, shall not be dim; and the Elars of them that hear, shall hearken.

Jer. xlii. 7. To open the blind Eyes, to bring out the Prisoners from the Prison, and them that sit in Darkness out of the Prison-house.

Jer. xxxi. 34. And they shall teach no more every Man his Neighbour, and every Man his Brother, saying. Know the Lord: For they shall all know me, from the least of them unto the greatest of them, saith the Lord.

Hos. vi. 3. Then shall we know, if we follow on to know the Lord.

Matt. xi. 25. I thank thee, O Father, Lord of Heaven and Earth, because thou hast hid these Things from the wise and prudent, and hast revealed them unto Babes.

2 *Cor.* lv. 6. God who commanded the Light to shine out of Darkness, hath shined in our Hearts, to give the Light of the Knowledge of the Glory of God, in the Face of Jesus Christ.

I *John* v. 20. And we know that the Son of God is come, and hath given us an Understanding that we may know him that is true, even in his Son Jesus Christ.

Luke iv. 18. He hath sent me to preach — Sight to the Blind.

Luke i. 77. To give Knowledge of Salvation unto his People, by the Remission of their Sins.

Ver. 78. Through the tender Mercy of our God; whereby the Day-spring from on high hath visited us.

Ver. 79. To give light to them that sit in Darkness, and in the Shadow of Death, to guide our Feet in the Way of Peace.

John viii. 12. Then spake Jesus again unto them, saying, I am the Light of the World: He that followeth me, shall not walk in Darkness, but shall have the Light of Life.

I *Cor.* ii. 14. The natural Man receiveth not the Things of the Spirit of God, for they are Foolishness unto him; neither can he know them, because they are spiritually discerned.

Ver. 15, But he that is spiritual judgeth all Things.

Prov. ii. 6. The Lord giveth Wisdom: Out of his Mouth cometh Knowledge, and Understanding.

Ver. 7. He layeth up sound Wisdom for the Righteous.

Ps. xvi. 7. I will bless the Lord, who hath given me Counsel: My Reins also instruct me in the Night Season.

Ps. li. 6. Behold, thou desirest Truth in the inward Parts: And in the hidden Part thou shalt make me to know Wisdom.

James i. 5. If any of you lack Wisdom, let him ask of God, that giveth to all Men liberally, and upbraideth not; and it shall be given him.

Eccl. ii. 26. For God giveth to Man that is good in his Sight, Wisdom and Knowledge.

Ps. xxxii. 8. I will instruct thee, and teach thee in the Way which thou shalt go; I will guide thee with mine Eye.

Ps. xxv. 8. Good and Upright is the Lord; therefore will he teach Sinners in the way.

Ver. 12. What Man is he that feareth the Lord? Him shall he teach in the Way that he shall choose.

John vii. 17. If any Man will do his Will, he shall know of the Doctrine, whether it be of God, or whether I speak of myself.

Ps. xxiii. 3. He restoreth my Soul: He leadeth me in the Paths of Righteousness, for his Name's sake.

Ps. lxxiii. 24. Thou shalt guide me with thy Counsel.

Is. xlix. 10. He that hath Mercy on them shall lead them; even by the Springs of Water shall he guide them.

Is. lvii. 11. And the Lord shall guide thee continually.

Is. lxi. 8. I will direct their Work in Truth.

Deut. xxxii. 10. He led him about, he instructed him, he kept him as the Apple of his Eye.

Ver. 11. As an Eagle stirreth up her Nest, fluttereth over her young ones, spreadeth abroad her Wings, taketh them, beareth them on her Wings, so the Lord alone did lead him.

Is. xxx. 21. Thine Ear shall hear a Word behind thee, saying, This is the Way, walk ye in it, when ye turn unto the Right Hand, and when ye turn to the Left.

Prov. x. 31. The Mouth of the Just bringeth forth Wisdom.

Ver. 32. The Lips of the Righteous know what is acceptable.

Is. xxxii. 4. The Heart of the Rash shall understand Knowledge, and the Tongue of the Stammerers shall be ready to speak plainly.

Prov. xvi. 1. The Preparations of the Heart in Man, and the Answer of the Tongue, is from the Lord.

I *Cor.* xii. 8. To one is given by the Spirit of the Word of Wisdom; to another the Word of Knowledge, by the same Spirit.

Luke xxi. 15. I will give you a Mouth, and Wisdom, which all your Adversaries shall not be able to gainsay or resist.

X. *Of the Means of* Grace.

Is. xxx. 20. And though the Lord give you the Bread of Adversity, and the Water of Affliction, yet shall not thy Teachers be removed into a Corner any more, but thine Eyes shall see thy Teachers.

Is. xlix. 9. They shall feed in the Ways, and their Pastures shall be in all high Places.

Ver. 10. They shall not hunger nor thirst, neither shall the Heat nor Sun smite them.

Ps. xxiii, 2. He maketh me to lie down in green Pastures: He leadeth me beside the still Waters.

Is. Hi. 7. How beautiful upon the Mountains are the Feet of him that bringeth good Tidings, that publisheth Peace, that bringeth good Tidings of Good, that publisheth Salvation, that sayeth unto *Zion,* Thy God reigneth.

Ver. 8. Thy Watchmen shall lift up the Voice, with the Voice together shall they sing: For they shall see Eye to Eye, when the Lord shall bring again *Zion*.

Is. lvi. 7. Them will I bring to my holy Mountain, and make them joyful in my House of Prayer: Their Burnt-offerings and their Sacrifices shall be accepted upon mine Altar; for mine House shall be called an House of Prayer for all. People.

Is. lxii. 6. I have set Watchmen upon thy Walls, O *Jerusalem,* which shall never hold their Peace Day nor Night.

Is. xli. 18. I will open Rivers in high Places, and Fountains in the midst of the Valleys: I will make the Wilderness a Pool of Water, and the dry Land Springs of Water.

Jer. iii. 15. I will give you Pastors according to mine Heart, which shall feed you with Knowledge and Understanding.

Jer. xxxi. 12. Their Souls shall be like a watered Garden.

Ver. 14, And I will satiate the Soul of the Priest with Fatness, and my People shall be satisfied with my Goodness, saith the Lord.

Ezek. xxxiv. 15. I will feed my Flock, and I will cause them to lay down, saith the Lord.

Eph. iv. 11. He gave some, Apostles; and some. Prophets; and some, Evangelists; and some. Pastors and Teachers.

Ver. 12. For the perfecting of the Saints, for the Work of the Ministry, for the edifying of the Body of Christ.

Ver. 13. Till we all come in the Unity of the Faith, and of the Knowledge of the Son of God, unto a perfect Man, unto the Measure of the Stature of the Fulness of Christ.

Ps. xxxvi. 8. They shall be abundantly satisfied with the Fatness of thine House; And thou shalt make them to drink of the River of thy Pleasures.

Ver. 10. For with thee is the Fountain of Life: In thy Light shall we see Light.

Ps. lxiii. 2. To see thy Power and thy Glory, so as I have seen thee in the Sanctuary.

Ver. 3. Because thy Loving-kindness is better than Life: My Lips shall praise thee.

Ver. 4. Thus will I bless thee while I live: I will lift up my Hands in thy Name.

Ver. 5. My Soul shall be satisfied as with Marrow and Fatness: And my Mouth shall praise thee with joyful Lips.

Ps. lxv. 4. Blessed is the Man whom thou choosest, and causest to approach unto thee, that he may dwell in thy Courts: We shall be satisfied with the Goodness of thine House, even of thy holy Temple.

Ps. lxviii. 24. They have seen thy Goings, O God; even the Goings of my God, my King, in the Sanctuary.

Ps. lxxxiv. 4. Blessed are they that dwell in thy House: They will be still praising thee.

Ver. 10. For a Day in thy Courts is better than a thousand: I had rather be a Door-Keeper in the House of my God, than to dwell in the Tents of Wickedness.

Ver. 11. For the Lord is a Sun and Shield; He will give Grace and Glory.

Ps. lxxxix. 15. Blessed is the People that know the joyful Sound: They shall walk, O Lord, in the Light of thy Countenance.

Ver. 16. In thy Name shall they rejoice all the Day: And in thy Righteousness shall they be exalted.

Ps. xcii. 13. Those that be planted in the House of the Lord, shall flourish in the Courts of our God.

Cant. ii. 3. I sat under his Shadow with great Delight, and his Fruit was sweet unto my Taste.

Is. xii. 3. With Joy shall we draw Water out of the Wells of Salvation.

Is. xlviii. 17. I am the Lord which teacheth thee to profit.

Is. ix. 7. They shall come with Acceptance upon mine Altar, and I will glorify the House of my Glory.

Matt, xviii. 20. Where Two or Three are gathered together in my Name, there am I in the midst of them.

XI. Of Grace *against* Sin *and* Temptation.

Hos. xiv. 8. Ephraim shall say, What have I to do any more with Idols?

Rom. vi. 6. Knowing this, that our old Man is crucified with him, that the Body of Sin might be destroyed, that henceforth we should not serve Sin.

Ver. 14. Sin shall not have Dominion over you: For ye are not under the Law, but under Grace.

Rom. vii. 24. O wretched Man that I am, who shall deliver me from the Body of this Death?

Ver. 25. I thank God, through Jesus Christ our Lord. So then with the Mind I myself serve the Law of God; but with the Flesh, the Law of Sin.

Rom. viii. 2. The Law of the Spirit of Life in Christ Jesus has made me free from the Law of Sin and Death.

Ver. 3. For what the Law could not do, in that it was weak through the Flesh, God sending his own Son, in the likeness of sinful Flesh, and for Sin, condemned Sin in the Flesh.

Ver. 4. That the Righteousness of the Law might be fulfilled in us, who walk not after the Flesh, but after the Spirit.

Gal. v. 16. Walk in the Spirit, and ye shall not fulfil the Lusts of the Flesh.

John viii. 32. Ye shall know the Truth, and the Truth shall make you free [i.e. *from Sin,* ver. 34.]

John xv. 2. Every branch that beareth Fruit, he purgeth it, that it may bring forth more Fruit.

Rom. viii. 37. In all these Things we are more than Conquerors, through him that loved us.

1 *Cor.* x. 13. God is faithful, who will not suffer you to be tempted above that ye are able; but will with the Temptation also make a Way to escape, that ye may be able to bear it.

2 *Cor.* xii. 9. My Grace is sufficient for thee; For my Strength is made perfect in Weakness.

Heb. ii. 18. In that he himself has suffered, being Tempted, he is able to succour them that are tempted.

2 *Pet.* ii. 9. The Lord knoweth how to deliver the Godly out of Temptations.

I *John* iv. 4. Ye are of God, little Children, and have overcome them: Because greater is he that is in you, than he that is in the World.

Eccl. vii. 18. He that feareth God shall come forth of them all.

Prov. ii. 12. To deliver thee from the Way of the evil Man, from the Man that speaketh froward Things.

Ver. 16. To deliver me from the strange Woman, even from the Stranger that flattereth with her Words.

Eccl. vii. 26. I find more bitter than Death, the Woman whose Heart is Snares and Nets, and her Hands as Bands: Whoso pleaseth God, shall escape from her, but the Sinner shall be taken by her.

John xvi. 33. Be of good Cheer, I have overcome the World.

John xvii. 15. I pray not that thou shouldest take them out of the World, but that thou shouldest keep them from the Evil.

Gal. i. 4. Who gave himself for our Sins, that he might deliver us from this present evil World.

Gal. vi. 14. By whom [Christ] the World is crucified unto me, and I unto the World.

I *John* v. 4, For whosoever is born of God, overcometh the World: And this is the Victory that overcometh the World, even our Faith.

Ver. 5. Who is he that overcometh the World, but he that believeth that Jesus is the Son of God.

I *John* iv. 4. Ye are of God, little Children, and have overcome them: Because greater is he that is in you, than he that is in the World.

Gen. iii. 15. I will put Enmity between thee and the Woman, and between thy Seed and her Seed: It shall bruise thy Head, and thou shalt bruise his Heel.

Luke xxii. 31. *Simon, Simon,* behold Satan hath desired to have you, that he may sift you as Wheat.

Ver. 32. But I have prayed for thee, that thy Faith fail not.

Rom. xvi. 20. And the God of Peace shall bruise Satan under your Feet shortly.

I *John* ii. 14. I have written unto you, young Men, because you are strong, and the Word of God abideth in you, and ye have overcome the wicked One.

I *John* v. 18. We know that whosoever is born of God sinneth not, but he that is begotten of God keepeth himself, and that wicked One toucheth him not.

James iv. 7. Resist the Devil, and he will flee from you.

XII. Strength, Courage, and Resolution.

Is. xii. 2. Behold God is my Salvation; I will trust, and not be afraid; for the Lord Jehovah is my Strength and my Song, he also is become my Salvation.

Is. xl. 29. He giveth Power to the Faint: And to them that hath no Might, he increaseth Strength.

Ver. 30. Even the Youths shall faint and be weary, and the young Men shall utterly fall.

Ver. 31. But they that wait upon the Lord shall renew their Strength: They shall mount up with Wings as Eagles, they shall run and not be weary, and they shall walk and not faint.

Is. xlii. 3. A bruised Reed shall he not break, and the smoking Flax shall he not quench; he shall bring forth Judgment unto Truth.

Ps. xxix. 11. The Lord will give Strength unto his People, the Lord will bless his People with Peace.

Ps. xxxi. 24. Be of good Courage, and he shall strengthen your Heart, all ye that hope in the Lord.

Ps. lxviii. 35. O God, thou art terrible, out of thy holy Places: The God of *Israel* is he that giveth Strength and Power unto his People.

Zech. xii. 8. In that Day the Lord shall defend the Inhabitants of *Jerusalem,* and he that is feeble among them at that Day, shall be as *David,* and the House of *David* shall be as God, as the Angel of the Lord before them.

Job xi. 15. Thou shalt be stedfast, thou shalt not fear.

Is. xxxv. 3. Strengthen ye the weak Hands, and confirm the feeble Knees.

Ver. 4. Say to them that are of a fearful Heart, be strong, fear not: Behold your God will come with Vengeance, even God with a Recompence, he will come and save you.

Zech. x. 12. I will strengthen them in the Lord, and they shall walk up and down in his Name, saith the Lord.

2 Cor. xii. 9. My Grace is sufficient for thee: For my Strength is made perfect in Weakness.

Joel iii. 16. The Lord will be the Hope of his People, and the Strength of the Children of Israel.

2 Tim. i. 7. God hath not given us the Spirit of Fear, but of Power, and of Love, and of a sound Mind.

XIII. Fruitfulness, *and* Increase *of* Grace.

Ps. i. 3. He shall be like a Tree planted by the Rivers of Water, that bringeth forth his Fruit in his Season: His Leaf also shall not wither, and whatsoever he doth shall prosper.

Jer. xxxi. 12. They shall come and sing in the Height of *Zion,* and shall flow together to the Goodness of the Lord, for Wheat and for Wine, and for Oil, and for the Young of the Flock, and of the Herd: And their Soul shall be as a watered Garden, and they shall not Sorrow any more at all.

Hos. xiv. 5. I will be as the Dew unto Israel: He shall grow as the Lily, and cast forth his Roots as *Lebanon*.

Ver. 8. I am like a green Fir-tree: From me is thy Fruit found.

John xv. I. Every Branch that beareth Fruit, he purgeth it, that he may bring forth more Fruit.

Ver. 5. He that abideth in me, and I in him, the same bringeth forth much Fruit: For without me ye can do nothing.

2 Pet. i. 8. If these Things be in you, and abound, they make you that ye shall neither be barren, nor unfruitful, in the Knowledge of our Lord Jesus Christ.

Ps. xcii. 14. They shall still bring forth Fruit in Old Age: They shall be fat and flourishing.

Job xvii. 9. The Righteous also shall hold on his Way, and he that hath clean Hands shall be stronger and stronger.

Ps. lxxxiv. 7. They go from Strength to Strength, every one of them in *Zion* appeareth before God.

Ps. xcii. 12. The Righteous shall flourish like the Palm-Tree: He shall grow like a Cedar in Lebanon.

Prov. iv. 18. The Path of the Just is as the shining light, that shineth more and more unto the perfect Day.

Mal. iv. 2. But unto you that fear my Name, shall the Sun of Righteousness arise with healing on his Wings: And ye shall go forth, and grow up, as Calves of the Stall.

Matt. xiii. 12. Whosoever hath, to him shall be given, and he shall have more abundance.

Jam. lv. 6. But he giveth more Grace: Wherefore he saith, God resisteth the Proud but he giveth Grace unto the Humble.

Is. xi. 6. The Wolf also shall dwell with the Lamb, and the Leopard shall lie down with the Kid; and the Calf, and the young Lion, and the Fatling together, and a little Child shall lead them.

Ver. 7. The Cow and the Bear shall feed, and their young Ones shall lie down together: And the Lion shall eat Straw like the Ox.

Ver. 8. And the Sucking Child shall play upon the Hole of the Asp, and the weaned Child shall put his Hand on the Cockatrice Den.

Ver. 9. They shall not hurt nor destroy in all my Holy Mountain: For the Earth shall be full of the Knowledge of the Lord, as the Waters cover the Sea.

XIV. Grace *to* Persevere.

John x. 28. And I will give unto them eternal Life, and they shall never perish, neither shall any pluck them out of my Hand.

Ver. 29. My Father that gave them me is greater than all, and no Man is able to pluck them out of my Father's Hand.

John xvii. 11. Holy Father, keep thro' thine own Name those whom thou hast given me, that they may be One, as we are.

Rom. viii. 38. I am persuaded, that neither Death, nor Life, nor Angels, nor Principalities, nor Powers, nor Things present, nor Things to come.

Ver. 39. Nor Height, nor Depth, nor any other Creature, shall be able to separate us from the Love of God, which is in Christ Jesus our Lord.

1 *Cor.* i. 8. Who shall also confirm you unto the End, that ye may be blameless in the Day of our Lord Jesus Christ.

2 *Cor.* i. 21. He which stablisheth us with you in Christ, and hath anointed us, is God.

Phil. i. 6. Being confident of this very Thing, that he which hath begun a good Work in you, will perform it until the Day of Jesus Christ.

1 *Thes.* v. 23. I pray God your whole Spirit and Soul, and Body, be preserved blameless unto the Coming of our Lord Jesus Christ.

Ver. 24. Faithful is he that calleth you, who also will do it.

2 *Thes.* iii. 3. The Lord is faithful, who shall establish you, and keep you from Evil.

2 *Pet.* i. 10. Wherefore the rather. Brethren, give Diligence to make your Calling and Election sure; for if ye do these Things, ye shall never fall.

I *Pet.* i. 5. Who are kept by the Power of God through Faith unto Salvation.

Prov. x. 25. The Righteous is an everlasting Foundation.

Jude 24. Unto him that is able to keep you from falling, and to present you faultless before the Presence of his Glory with exceeding Joy.

I *John* v. 18. We know, that whosoever is born of God, sinneth not; but he that is begotten of God keepeth himself, and that wicked one toucheth him not.

Ps. cxxxviii. 8. The Lord will perfect that which concerneth me: Thy Mercy, O Lord, endureth for ever: Forsake not the Works of thine own Hands.

Ps. xciv. 18. When I said, my Foot slippeth, thy Mercy, O Lord, held me up.

XV. *Sanctified* Afflictions.

Deut. viii. 5. As a Man chasteneth his Son, so the Lord thy God chasteneth thee.

Job. xxxvi. 8. And if they be bound in Fetters, and be holden in Cords of Affliction;

Ver. 9. Then he sheweth them their Work, and their Transgressions, that they have exceeded.

Ver. 10. He openeth also their Ear to Discipline, and commandeth, that they return from Iniquity.

Job v. 17. Happy is the Man whom God correcteth; therefore despise not thou the Chastening of the Almighty.

Ver. 18. For he maketh sore, and bindeth up: He woundeth, and his Hands make whole.

Ps. xciv. 12. Blessed is the Man whom thou chasteneth, O Lord, and teachest him out of thy Law.

Ver. 13. That thou mayst give him Rest from the Days of Adversity, until the Pit be digged for the Wicked.

Ps. cxix. 67. Before I was afflicted I went astray: But now have I kept thy Word.

Ver. 71. It is good for me, that I have been afflicted; that I might learn thy Statutes.

Ver. 75. I know, O Lord, that thy Judgments are right, and that thou in Faithfulness hast afflicted me.

Prov. iii. 12. Whom the Lord loveth, he correcteth, even as a Father the Son in whom he delighteth.

Is. i. 25. I will turn my Hand upon thee, and purely purge away thy Dross, and take away all thy Sin.

Is. xxvii. 9. By this therefore shall the Iniquity of *Jacob* be purged, and this is all the Fruit to take away his Sin.

Is. xlviii. 10. Behold I have refined thee, but not with Silver; I have chosen thee in the Furnace of Affliction.

Hos. ii. 6. I will hedge up thy Way with Thorns, and make a Wall, that she shall not find her Paths.

Ver. 7. And she shall follow after her Lovers, but she shall not overtake them: And she shall seek them, but shall not find them: Then shall she say, I will go and return to my first Husband, for then was it better with me than now.

Rom. v. 3. We glory in Tribulations also, knowing that Tribulation worketh Patience, and Patience Experience, and Experience Hope.

1 *Cor.* xi. 32. When we are judged we are chastened of the Lord, that we should not be condemned with the World.

2 *Cor.* iv. 16. For which Cause we faint not; but though our outward Man perish, yet the inward Man is renewed Day by Day.

Ver. 17. For our light Affliction which is but for a Moment, worketh for us a far more exceeding and eternal Weight of Glory.

Phil. i. 19. I know that this shall turn to my Salvation, through your Prayer, and the Supply of the Spirit of Jesus Christ.

Heb. xii. 6. Whom the Lord loveth he chasteneth, and scourgeth every Son whom he receiveth.

Ver. 7. If ye endure chastening, God dealeth with you as with Sons: For what Son is he whom the Father chasteneth not?

Ver. 10. They verily, for a few Days chastened us after their own Pleasure; but he for our Profit, that we might be Partakers of his Holiness.

Ver. 11. Now no Chastening for the present seemeth to be joyous, but grievous: Nevertheless, afterward it yieldeth the peaceable Fruit of Righteousness, unto them which are exercised thereby.

Rev. iii. 19. As many as I love, I rebuke and chasten.

James i. 3. The trying of your Faith worketh Patience.

Ver. 12. Blessed is the Man that endureth Temptation: For when he is tried, he shall receive the Crown of Life, which the Lord hath promised to them that love him.

I *Pet.* i. 7. That the Trial of your Faith being much more precious than of Gold that perisheth, though it be tried with Fire, might be found unto Praise and Honour, and Glory, at the appearing of Jesus Christ.

Dan. xi. 35. Some of them of Understanding shall fall, to try them, and to purge, and to make them white, even to the Time of the End.

Dan. xii. 10. Many shall be purified, and made white and tried.

Zech. xiii. 9. I will bring the third Part through the Fire, and will refine them as Silver is refined, and will try them as Gold is tried: They shall call on my Name, and I will hear them: I will say, It is my People; and they shall say, The Lord is my God.

XVI. Grace to the Children of Believers.

Gen. xvii. 7. I will establish my Covenant between me and thee, and thy Seed after thee, in their Generations, for an everlasting Covenant, to be a God unto thee, and to thy Seed after thee.

Ver. 9. Thou shalt keep my Covenant therefore; thou, and thy Seed after thee, in their Generations.

Deut. xxx. 6. And the Lord thy God will circumcise thine Heart, and the Heart of thy Seed, to love the Lord thy God with all thine Heart, and with all thy Soul, that thou mayest live.

Is. xliv. 3. I will pour my Spirit upon thy Seed, and my Blessing upon thy Offspring".

Ver. 4. And they shall spring up as among the Grass, as Willows by the Water Courses.

Ver. 5. One shall say, I am the Lord's: And another shall call himself by the Name of *Jacob:* And another shall subscribe with his Hand unto the Lord, and surname himself by the Name of *Israel.*

Is. liv. 18. All thy Children shall be taught of the Lord, and great shall be the Peace of thy Children.

Acts ii. 39. The Promise is unto you, and to your Children.

Acts xvi. 31. Believe on the Lord Jesus Christ, and thou shalt be saved, and thy House.

Mark x. 14. Suffer little Children to come unto me, and forbid them not: for of such is the Kingdom of God.

Ver. 16. And he took them up in his Arms, put his Hands upon them, and blessed them.

I *Cor.* vii. 14. Now are they [*your Children*] Holy.

XVII. *Promises of an* Interest *in* God.

Gen. xvii. 7. I will establish my Covenant — to be a God unto thee.

Lev. xxvi. 12. And I will walk among you, and will be your God, and ye shall be my People.

Ps. xlviii. 14. This God is our God for ever and ever; he will be our Guide, even unto Death.

Is. xli. 10. Fear thou not, for I am with thee; be not dismayed, for I am thy God.

Ezek. xxxiv. 24. I the Lord will be their God, and my Servant *David* a Prince, among them.

Ver. 31. Ye my Flock, the Flock of my Pasture, are Men, and I am your God, saith the Lord,

2 *Cor.* vi. 16. I will be their God, and they shall be my People.

Heb. viii. 10. I will be to them a God, and they shall be to me a People.

Rev. xxi. 3. God himself shall be with them, and be their God.

Heb. xi. 16. God is not ashamed to be called their God. for he hath prepared for them a City.

Is. liv, 5. For thy Maker is thine Husband (the Lord of Hosts is his Name) and thy Redeemer the Holy One of *Israel;* the God of the whole Earth shall he be called.

Jer. xxx. 22. Ye shall be my People, and I will be your God.

Ps. xvi. 5. The Lord is the Portion of mine Inheritance, and of my Cup.

Ps. lxxiii. 26. My Flesh and my Heart faileth, but God is the Strength of my Heart, and my Portion for ever.

Lam. iii. 24. The Lord is my Portion, saith my Soul, therefore will I hope in him.

Gen. xv. I. I am thy Shield, and thy exceeding great Reward.

Is. xxviii. 5. In that Day shall the Lord of Hosts be for a Crown of Glory, and for a Diadem of Beauty unto the Residue of his People.

Exod. xxxiii. 14. My Presence shall go with thee, and I will give thee Rest.

Ps. cxl. 13. The Upright shall dwell in thy Presence.

Numb. xxiii. 21. The Lord his God is with him, and the Shout of a King is among them.

Is. xli. 10. Fear thou not, for I am with thee.

John xiv. 23. If a Man love me, he will keep my Words: And my Father will love him, and we will come unto him, and make our Abode with him.

Deut. xxxi. 8. The Lord, he it is that doth go before thee, he will be with thee, he will not fail thee, neither forsake thee.

2 *Chron.* xv. 2. The Lord is with you while ye be with him; and if ye seek him, he will be found of you.

Joel vi. 27. And ye shall know that I am ill the midst of *Israel,* and that I am the Lord your God, and none else: And my People shall never be ashamed.

Ezek. xxxi v. 30, Thus shall they know that I the Lord their God am with them.

Deut. vii. 13. He will love thee, and bless thee, and multiply thee.

Ps. lv. 3. The Lord hath set apart him that Is godly for himself.

Ps. xlii. 8. He shall command his Loving-kindness in the Day-time.

Ps. cxlvi. 8. The Lord loveth the Righteous.

Prov. xv. 9. He loveth him that followeth after Righteousness.

Is. xliii. 4. Since thou wast precious in my Sight, thou hast been honourable, and I have loved thee.

Is. xlii. 5. As the Bridegroom rejoiceth over the Bride, so shall thy God rejoice over thee.

Jer. xxxi. 3. I have loved thee with an everlasting Love, therefore with Loving-kindness have I drawn thee.

Jer. xxxii. 41. I will rejoice over them to do them good, and I will plant them in this Land, assuredly, with my whole Heart, and with my whole Soul.

Hos. xiv. 4. I will heal their Backsliding, I will love them freely.

Zeph. iii. 17. The Lord thy God in the midst of thee is mighty; he will save, he will rejoice over thee with Joy: He will rest in his Love, he will joy over thee with singing.

Is. lxii. 4. Thou shalt be called Hepzibah - for the Lord delighteth in thee.

John xvi. 27. For the Father himself loveth you, because ye have loved me.

John xvii. 23. That the World may know that thou hast sent me, and hast loved them, as thou hast loved me.

Ver. 26. That the Love wherewith thou hast loved me, may be in them, and I in them.

Rom. ix. 25. I will call her beloved, that was not beloved.

Eph. ii. 4. For his great Love wherewith he loved us.

2 *Thes.* ii. 16. Now our Lord Jesus Christ, and God, even our Father, which hath loved us.

I *John* iv. 10. Herein is Love, not that we loved him, but that he loved us.

Ver. 16. We have known and believed the Love that God hath to us. God is Love, and he that dwelleth in Love dwelleth in God, and God in him.

Ver. 19. We love him because he first loved us.

Ps. ciii. 4. Who crowneth thee with Loving-kindness, and tender Mercies.

Ps. ciii. 13. Like as a Father pitieth his Children, so the Lord pitieth them that fear him.

Ver. 17. The Mercy of the Lord is from Everlasting to Everlasting, upon them that fear him.

Deut. lv. 31. The Lord thy God is a merciful God: He will not destroy thee.

Is. xxx. 18. Therefore will the Lord wait, that he may be gracious unto you; and therefore will he be exalted, that he may have Mercy upon you.

Is. xlviii. 9. For my Name's sake will I defer mine Anger, and for my Praise will I refrain for thee, that I cut thee not off.

Is. ix. 10. In my Wrath I smote thee, but in my Favour have I had Mercy on thee.

Jer. xxxi. 20. My Bowels are troubled for him, and I will surely have Mercy upon him.

Hos. ii. 23. I will sow her unto me in the Earth; And I will have Mercy upon her that had not obtained Mercy.

Hos. xi. 8. How shall I give thee up, *Ephraim?* How shall I deliver thee, *Israel?* How shall I make thee as *Admah?* How shall I set thee as *Zeboim?* Mine Heart is turned within me, my Repentings are kindled together.

Ver. 9. I will not execute the Fierceness of my Anger, I will not return to destroy *Ephraim*.

Exod. xxxiii. 19. I will make all my Goodness pass before thee, and I will proclaim the Name of the Lord before thee, and will be gracious to whom I will be Gracious, and will shew Mercy on whom I will shew Mercy.

Job xi. 6. God exacteth of thee less than thine Iniquity deserveth.

Deut. xxxiii. 27. The eternal God is thy Refuge, and underneath are the everlasting Arms: And he shall thrust out the Enemy from before thee, and shall say, Destroy them.

Ver. 29. Happy art thou, O *Israel!* Who is like unto thee, O People saved by the Lord, the Shield of thy Help, and who is the Sword of thy Excellency! And thine Enemies shall be found Liars unto thee, and thou shalt tread upon their high Places.

Ps. xlvi. 7. The God of *Jacob* is our Refuge. *Selah.*

Ps. xl. 17. Thou art my Help and my Deliverer, make no tarrying, O my God.

Is. xli. 10. I will strengthen thee, yea, I will help thee; yea, I will uphold thee with the Right Hand of my Righteousness.

Ver. 13. I the Lord thy God will hold thy Right Hand, saying unto thee. Fear not, I will help thee.

Ver. 14. Fear not, thou Worm *Jacob,* and ye Men of *Israel:* I will help thee, saith the Lord, and thy Redeemer, the Holy One of Israel.

Hos. xiii. 9. O Israel, thou hast destroyed thyself; but in me is thy Help.

Rom. viii. 31. If God be for us, who can be against us?

Heb. xiii. 6. We may boldly say, The Lord is my Helper, and I will not fear what Man can do unto me.

Deut. xxxii. 11. As an Eagle stirreth up her Nest, fluttereth over her Young, spreadeth abroad her Wings, taketh them, beareth them on her Wings.

Ver. 12. So the Lord alone did lead him, and there was no strange God with him,

Ps. xxxiii. 18. The Eye of the Lord is upon them that fear him: Upon them that hope in his Mercy.

Is. xlvi. 3. Hearken unto me, O House of *Jacob,* and all the Remnant of the House of *Israel,* which are born by me from the Belly, which are carried from the Womb.

Ver. 4. And even to your old Age I am He, and even to hoary Hairs will I carry you, I have made, and I will bear; even I will carry and deliver you.

Is. lxiii. 9. In all their Affliction he was afflicted, and the Angel of his Presence saved them: In his Love and in his Pity he redeemed them, and he bare them, and carried them all the Days of old.

Zech. ii. 8. He that toucheth you, toucheth the Apple of his Eye.

I *Pet.* v. 7. Casting all your Care upon him, for he careth for you.

Matt. x. 30. The very Hairs of your Head are all numbered.

Luke xxi. 18, There shall not an Hair of your Head perish.

2 *Sam.* xxiii. 5. He hath made with me an everlasting Covenant, ordered in all Things, and sure; for this is all my Salvation, and all my Desire.

Is. lv. 3. I will make an everlasting Covenant with you, even the sure Mercies of *David.*

Has. ii. 19. I will betroth thee unto me for ever; yea, I will betroth thee unto me in Righteousness, and in Judgment, and in Loving-kindness, and in Mercies.

Ver. 20. I will even betroth thee unto me in Faithfulness, and thou shalt know the Lord.

Lev. xxvi. 11. I will set my tabernacle amongst you; and my Soul shall not abhor you.

Ps. ix. 10. Thou, Lord, hast not forsaken them that seek thee.

Ps. xxvii, 18. The Lord forsaketh not his Saints, they are preserved for ever.

Ps. xciv. 14. The Lord will not cast off his People, neither will he forsake his Inheritance.

Is. xli. 9. Thou art my Servant, I have chosen thee, and not cast thee away.

Is. xlii, 16. These Things will I do unto them, and not forsake them.

Is. xlix. 14. *Zion* saith, the Lord hath forsaken me, and my Lord hath forgotten me.

Ver. 15. Can a Woman forget her sucking Child, that she should not have Compassion on the Son of her Womb? Yea, they may forget, but I will not forget thee.

Ver. 16. Behold I have graven thee upon the Palms of my Hands, thy Walls are continually before me.

Is. xliv, 21. O *Israel,* thou shalt not be forgotten of me.

Is. liv. 9. As I have sworn that the Waters of *Noah* should no more go over the Earth, so have I sworn that I would no more be wroth with thee, nor rebuke thee.

Ver. 10. For the Mountains shall depart, and the Hills be removed, but my Kindness shall not depart from thee, neither shall the Covenant of my Peace be removed, saith the Lord, that hath Mercy on thee.

Jer. xxxii. 40. I will make an everlasting Covenant with them, that I will not turn away from them to do them good; but I will put my Fear in their Hearts, that they shall not depart from me.

Lam. iii. 31. The Lord will not cast off for ever.

Ver. 32. But though he cause Grief, yet will he have Compassion, according to the Multitude of his Mercies.

Heb. xiii. 5. I will never leave thee nor forsake thee.

XVIII. *Promises of* Christ.

Is. ix. 6. Unto us a Child is born, unto us a Son is given, and the Government shall be upon his Shoulder; and his Name shall be called Wonderful, Counsellor, the Mighty God, the Everlasting Father, the Prince of Peace.

Is. xlii. 6. I, the Lord, have called thee in Righteousness, and will hold thine Hand, and will keep thee, and will give thee for a Covenant of the People, for a Light of the *Gentiles.*

Is. lv. 4. Behold, I have given him for a Witness to the People, a Leader and Commander to the People.

Mal. iv. 2. But unto you that fear my Name, shall the Sun of Righteousness arise with healing in his Wings; and ye shall go forth, and grow up as Calves of the Stall.

John iii. 16. God so loved the World, that he gave his only begotten Son, that whosoever believed on him, should not perish, but have everlasting Life.

John vi. 37. All that the Father giveth me, shall come to me: and him that cometh to me, I will in no wise cast out.

Cant. ii. 16. My beloved is mine, and I am his.

Ezek. xxxiv. 23. I will set up one Shepherd over them, and he shall feed them, even my Servant *David;* he shall feed them, and he shall be their Shepherd.

John i. 16. Of his Fulness have we all received, and Grace for Grace.

Ver. 17. For the Law was given by Moses, but Grace and Truth came by Jesus Christ.

Is. xlv. 24. Surely, shall one say, in the Lord have I Righteousness and Strength.

Eph. i. 23. The Fulness of him that filleth all in all.

I *Cor.* i. 30. Of him are ye in Christ Jesus, who of God is made unto us Wisdom, Righteousness, Sanctification, and Redemption.

Acts v. 31. Him hath God exalted with his Right Hand, to be a Prince and a Saviour, for to give Repentance to *Israel,* and Forgiveness of Sin.

I *Pet.* i. 18. Ye know that ye were not redeemed with corruptible Things, as Silver and Gold, from your vain Conversation, received by Tradition from your Fathers.

Ver. 19. But with the precious Blood of Christ, as of a Lamb without Blemish and without Spot.

Is. xlii. 7. To open the blind Eyes, and to bring out the Prisoners from the Prison, and them that sit in Darkness out of the Prison House.

Is. xlix. 9. That thou mayst say to the Prisoners, Go forth; to them that are in Darkness, shew yourselves.

Mark x. 45. The Son of Man came — to give his Life a Ransom for many.

Eph. i. 7. In whom we have Redemption through his Blood, the Forgiveness of Sins, according to the Riches of his Grace.

Gal. iii. 13. Christ hath redeemed us from the Curse of the Law, being made a Curse for us.

Gal. lv. 4. In the Fulness of Time God sent forth his Son, made of a Woman, made under the Law.

Ver. 5. To redeem them that were under the Law, that we might receive the Adoption of Sons.

Heb. ix. 14. How much more shall the Blood of Christ, who, through the eternal Spirit offered himself without Spot to God, purge your Conscience from dead Works, to serve the living God?

Ver. 15. And for this Cause he is the Mediator of the New Testament, that by means of Death, for the Redemption of the Transgressions that were under the first Testament, they which are called might receive the Promise of eternal Inheritance.

Eph. v. 2. Walk in Love, as Christ also hath loved us, and hath given himself for us, an Offering and Sacrifice to God, for a sweet smelling Savour.

1 *Cor.* v. 7. Christ our Passover is sacrificed for us.

Rev. v. 9. Thou wast slain, and hast redeemed us to God by thy Blood.

John v. 21. As the Father raiseth up the Dead, and quickeneth them, even so the Son quickeneth whom he will,

John vi. 57. He that eateth me, even he shall live by me.

John xiv. 19. Because I live, ye shall live also.

2 *Cor.* xiii. 4. Though he was crucified through Weakness, yet he liveth by the Power of God: For we also are weak in him, but we shall live with him by the Power of God toward you.

Gal. ii. 20. I am crucified with Christ, nevertheless I live; yet not I, but Christ liveth in me: And the Life which I now live in the Flesh, I live by the Faith of the Son of God, who loved me, and gave himself for me.

Eph. ii. 1. You hath he quickened, who were dead in Trespasses and Sins.

Ver. 5. Even when we were dead in Sins, he hath quickened us together with Christ (by Grace ye are saved).

Ver. 6. And hath raised us together, and made us sit together in heavenly Places in Christ Jesus.

Rom. vi. 8. If we be dead with Christ, we believe that we shall also live with him.

Ver. 11. Reckon ye yourselves to be dead indeed unto Sin, but alive unto God, through Jesus Christ our Lord.

Col. iii. 3. For ye are dead, and your Life is hid with Christ in God.

Ver. 4. When Christ who is our Life shall appear, then shall ye also appear with him in Glory.

I *John* v. 12. He that hath the Son, hath Life.

John x. 10. I am come that they might have Life, and that they might have it more abundantly.

2 *Tim.* i. I. The Promise of Life, which is in Christ Jesus.

Is. liii. 12. He made Intercession for the Transgressors.

Rom. viii. 34. It is Christ — who maketh Intercession for us.

Heb. vii. 25. Wherefore he is able also to save them to the uttermost, that come unto God by him, seeing he ever liveth to make Intercession for them.

Heb. ix. 24. Christ is not entered into the holy Place made with Hands, which are the Figures of the true; but into Heaven itself, now to appear in the Presence of God for us.

Heb. lv. 14. Seeing then that we have a great High Priest, that is passed into the Heavens, Jesus the Son of God. let us hold fast our Profession.

Ver. 15. For we have not an High Priest which cannot be touched with the feeling of our Infirmities, but was in all Points tempted like as we are, yet without Sin.

Ver. 16. Let us therefore go boldly unto the Throne of Grace, that we may obtain Mercy, and find Grace to help in Time of need.

John xv. 9. As the Father hath loved me, so have I loved you: Continue ye in my Love.

John xiii. i. Having loved his own which were in the World, he loved them unto the end.

Ver. 34. A new Commandment I give unto you, that ye love one another, as I have loved you, that ye also love one another.

Rom. viii. 37. In all these Things we are more than Conquerors, through him that loved us.

Rev. i. 5. Unto him that loved us, and washed us from our Sins in his own Blood.

Rev. iii. 9. I will make them — to know that I have loved thee.

Ps. xlv. 11. So shall the King greatly desire thy Beauty.

Cant. ii. 4. His Banner over me was Love.

Ver. 6. His Left Hand is under my Head, and his Right Hand doth embrace me.

Cant. lv. 9. Thou hast ravished my Heart, my Sister, my Spouse.

Cant. vii. 10. I am my Beloved's, and his Desire is towards me.

Eph. v. 2. Christ also hath loved us, and hath given himself for us.

Is. xl. 11. He shall feed his Flock like a Shepherd. He shall gather the Lambs with his Arm, and carry them in his Bosom; and shall gently lead those that are with young.

Is. xlii. 2. A bruised Reed shall he not break, and the smoking Flax shall he not quench: He shall bring forth Judgment unto Truth.

Eph. v. 25. Christ also loved the Church, and gave himself for it.

Ver. 26. That he might sanctify and cleanse it with the washing of Water by the Word.

Ver. 27. That he might present it to himself a glorious Church, not having Spot or Wrinkle, or any such Thing.

Ver. 29. For no Man ever yet hated his own Flesh, but nourisheth and cherisheth it, even as the Lord the Church.

Rev. ii. 1. Who walketh in the midst of the seven golden Candlesticks.

John xiv. 18. I will not leave you comfortless; I will come to you.

Ver. 21. I will love him, and will manifest myself to him.

I *John* i. 3. And truly our Fellowship is with the Father, and with his Son Jesus Christ.

Rev. iii. 20. Behold I stand at the Door and knock: If any Man hear my Voice, and open the Door, I will come in to him, and will sup with him, and he with me.

XIX. Promises of the Spirit.

Prov. i. 23. Behold I will pour out my Spirit unto you, and I will make known my Words unto you.

Is. xxxii. 15. Until the Spirit be poured upon us from on high, and the Wilderness be a fruitful Field.

Is. lix. 21. This is my Covenant with them, saith the Lord, My Spirit that is upon thee, and my Words which I have put in thy Mouth, shall not depart out of thy Mouth, nor out of the Mouth of thy Seed, nor out of the Mouth of thy Seed's Seed, saith the Lord, from henceforth and for ever.

Ezek. xxxvi. 27. And I will put my Spirit within you, and cause you to walk in my Statutes, and ye shall keep my Judgments, and do them.

Luke xi. 13. If ye then, being evil, know how to give good Gifts unto your Children, how much more shall your heavenly Father give the Holy Spirit to them that ask him?

John iv. 10. Jesus answered and said unto her, if thou knewest the Gift of God, and who it is that saith to thee. Give me to drink, thou wouldst have asked of him, and he would have given thee living Water.

Ver. 14. Whosoever drinketh of the Water that I shall give him, shall never thirst; but the Water that I shall give him, shall be in him a Well of Water springing up into everlasting Life.

John vii. 38. He that believeth on me, as the Scripture hath said, out of his Belly shall flow Rivers of living Water.

Ver. 39. But this spake he of the Spirit, which they that believe on him should receive.

John xiv. 16. I will pray the Father and he shall give you another Comforter, that he may abide with you for ever.

Ver. 17. Even the Spirit of Truth, whom the World cannot receive, because it seeth him not, neither knoweth him: But ye know him, for he dwelleth with you, and shall be in you.

Gal. iii. 14. That we might receive the Promise of the Spirit through Faith.

2 *Tim.* i. 14. The Holy Ghost which dwelleth in us,

I *Cor.* ii. 12. Now we have received not the Spirit of the World, but the Spirit which is of God, that we might know the Things that are freely given to us of God.

Luke xii. 12. The Holy Ghost shall teach you in the same Hour, what you ought to say.

I *Cor.* ii. 10. God hath revealed them to us by his Spirit, for the Spirit searcheth all Things, yea, the deep Things of God.

John xvi. 13. When he, the Spirit of Truth is come, he will guide you into all Truth.

I *John* ii. 27. But the anointing which you have received of him, abideth in you: And ye need not that any Man teach you: But as the same anointing teacheth you of all Things, and is Truth, and is no Lie, and even as it hath taught you, ye shall abide in him.

Zech. xii. 10. I will pour upon the House of *David,* and upon the Inhabitants of *Jerusalem,* the Spirit of Grace, and of Supplications.

Rom. viii. 15. Ye have received the Spirit of Adoption, whereby we cry, Abba, Father.

Ver. 26. The Spirit helpeth our Infirmities, for we know not what we should pray for as we ought; but the Spirit itself maketh Intercession for us, with Groanings which cannot be uttered.

Ver. 27. And he that searcheth the Heart, knoweth what is the Mind of the Spirit, because he maketh Intercession for the Saints, according to the Will of God.

Gal. iv. 6. And because ye are Sons, God hath sent forth the Spirit of his Son into your Hearts, crying, Abba, Father,

Ps. x. 17. Lord, thou hast heard the Desire of the Humble, thou wilt prepare their Heart, thou wilt cause thine Ear to hear.

Rom. viii. 16. The Spirit beareth witness with our Spirit, that we are the Children of God.

2 *Cor.* i. 22. Who hath also sealed us, and given the Earnest of the Spirit in our Hearts.

2 *Cor.* v. 5. Now he that hath wrought us for the self same Thing is God, who also hath given us the Earnest of the Spirit.

Eph. i. 13. After that ye believed, ye were sealed with the holy Spirit of Promise.

Ver. 14. Which is the Earnest of our Inheritance, until the Redemption of the purchased Possession, unto the Praise of his Glory.

Eph. iv. 30. Grieve not the holy Spirit of God, whereby ye are sealed unto the Day of Redemption.

Rom. v. 5. And Hope maketh not ashamed, because the Love of God is shed abroad in our Hearts by the Holy Ghost, which is given unto us.

John xiv. 16. He shall give To be our you another Comforter, that Comforter, he may abide with you for ever.

Ver. 18. I will not leave you comfortless, I will come to you,

Acts ix. 31. Then had the Churches Rest throughout all *Judea,* and *Galilee,* and *Samaria,* and were edified; and walking in the Fear of the Lord, and in the Comfort of the Holy Ghost, were multiplied.

Rom. xiv. 17. The Kingdom of God is not Meat and Drink, but Righteousness and Peace, and Joy in the Holy Ghost.

XX. Of the Ministry of Angels.

Ps. xxxiv. 7. The Angel of the Lord encampeth round about them that fear him, and delivereth them.

Ps. xci. 11. He shall give his Angels charge over thee, to keep thee in all thy Ways.

Ver. 12. They shall bear thee up in their Hands, lest thou dash thy Foot against a Stone.

Matt. xviii. 10. Take heed that ye despise not one of these little Ones, for I say unto you, that in Heaven their Angels do always behold the Face of my Father, which is in Heaven.

Heb. i. 14. Are they not all ministering Spirits, sent forth to minister for them who shall be Heirs of Salvation?

XXI. That we shall be Kings and Priests unto GOD.

Exod. xix. 6. Ye shall be unto me a Kingdom of Priests, and an holy Nation.

I *Pet.* ii. 9. Ye are a chosen Generation, a royal Priesthood, an holy Nation, a peculiar People, that ye should shew forth the Praises of him who hath called you out of Darkness into his marvellous Light.

Rev. i. 6. And hath made us Kings and Priests unto God and his Father.

Rev. v. 10. And hath made us unto our God Kings and Priests, and we shall reign on the Earth.

XXII. Peace of Conscience, Comfort and Hope.

Is. xxxii. 17. The Work of Righteousness shall be Peace, and the Effect of Righteousness, Quietness, and Assurance for ever.

Is. lvii. 19. I create the Fruit of the Lips; Peace, Peace to him that is far off, and to him that is near, saith the Lord.

Ps. lxxxv. 8. He will speak Peace to his People, and to his Saints.

Luke vii. 50. Thy Faith hath saved thee, go in Peace,

John xiv. 27. Peace I leave with you, my Peace I give unto you: Not as the World giveth, give I unto you.

Phil. iv. 7. The Peace of God which passeth all Understanding, shall keep your Hearts and Minds through Christ Jesus.

Col. iii. 15. Let the Peace of God rule in your Hearts, to the which also ye are called in one Body.

2 *Thes.* iii. 16. Now the Lord of Peace himself give you Peace always, by all means.

Ps. xxv. 15. His Soul shall dwell at ease.

Ps. cxlvii. 3. He healeth the broken in Heart, and bindeth up their Wounds.

Prov. xiv. 14. A good Man shall be satisfied from himself.

Is. xii. 1. And in that Day thou shalt say, O Lord, I will praise thee: Though thou wast angry with me, thine Anger is turned away, and thou comfortedst me.

Is. xlix. 13. God hath comforted his People, and will have Mercy upon his Afflicted.

Is. li. 12. I, even I, am he that comforteth you.

Is. liv. 7. For a small Moment have I forsaken thee: but with great Mercies will I gather thee.

Ver. 8. In a little Wrath I hid my Face from thee for a Moment; but with everlasting Kindness will I have Mercy on thee, saith the Lord thy Redeemer.

Is. lvii. 18. I have seen his Ways, and will heal him: I will lead him also, and restore Comforts unto him, and to his Mourners.

Is. lxi. 1. He hath sent me to bind up the broken hearted;

Ver. 2. To proclaim the acceptable Year of the Lord, and the Day of Vengeance of our God; To comfort all that mourn;

Ver. 3. To appoint unto them that mourn in *Sion,* to give them Beauty for Ashes, the Oil of Joy for Mourning, the Garment of Praise for the Spirit of Heaviness, that they might be called Trees of Righteousness, the planting of the Lord, that he might be glorified.

Is. lxvi. 11. That ye may suck, and be satisfied with the Breasts of her Consolation, that ye may milk out, and be delighted with the Abundance of her Glory.

Ver. 13. As one whom his Mother comforteth, so will I comfort you: And ye shall be comforted in *Jerusalem.*

Jer. vi. 16. Stand ye in the Ways, and see, and ask for the old Paths. Where is the good Way? And walk therein; and ye shall find Rest for your Souls.

John xiv. 18. I will not leave you comfortless: I will come to you.

2 *Cor.* i. 3. Blessed be God, even the Father of our Lord Jesus Christ, the Father of Mercies, and the God of all Comfort:

Ver. 4. Who comforteth us in all our Tribulation, that we may be able to comfort them that are in any Trouble, by the Comfort wherewith we ourselves are comforted of God.

2 *Cor.* vii. 6. God, that comforteth those that are cast down, comforted us by the coming of Titus.

2 *Thes.* ii. 16. Now our Lord Jesus Christ himself, and God, even our Father, which had loved us, and hath given us everlasting Consolation, and good Hope through Grace.

Heb. vi. 18. That by two immutable Things, in which it was impossible for God to lie, we might have a strong Consolation, who have fled for Refuge to lay Hold upon the Hope set before us.

Ver. 19. Which Hope we have as an Anchor of the Soul, both sure and stedfast, and which entereth into that within the Veil.

Ps. xciv. 19. In the Multitude of my Thoughts within me, thy Comforts delight my Soul.

XXIII. Delight and Joy in God.

Neh. viii. 10. The Joy of the Lord is your Strength.

Job xxii. 26. Then shalt thou have thy Delight in the Almighty, and shalt lift up thy Face unto God.

Ps. iv. 7. Thou hast put Gladness in my Heart, more than in the Time that their Corn and their Wine increased.

Ps. lxiii. 5. My Soul shall be satisfied as with Marrow and Fatness, and my Mouth shall praise thee with joyful Lips.

Ps. lxiv. 10. The Righteous shall be glad in the Lord, and shall trust in him: And all the Upright shall glory.

Ps. lxviii. 3. Let the Righteous be glad: Let them rejoice before God; yea, let them exceedingly rejoice.

Ps. lxxxix. 15. Blessed is the People that know the joyful Sound: They shall walk, O Lord, in the Light of thy Countenance.

Ver. 16. In thy Name shall they rejoice all the Day, and in thy Righteousness shall they be exalted.

Ps. xcvii. 11. Light is sown for the Righteous, and Gladness for the Upright in Heart,

Ps. cxviii. 15. The Voice of Rejoicing and Salvation is in the Tabernacles of the Righteous.

Ps. cxxvi. 5. They that sow in Tears shall reap in Joy.

Ver. 6. He that goeth forth and weepeth, bearing precious Seed, shall, doubtless, come again with rejoicing, bringing his Sheaves with him.

Ps. xxxiii. 21, Our Heart shall rejoice in him, because we have trusted in his holy Name,

Cant. i. 4. We will be glad and rejoice in thee; we will remember thy Love more than Wine.

Is. ix. 3. They joy before thee according to the Joy in Harvest, and as Men rejoice when they divide the Spoil.

Is. xli. 16. Thou shalt rejoice in the Lord, and shalt glory in the Holy One of *Israel*.

Is. lv. 12. Ye shall go out with Joy, and be led forth with Peace.

Is. lxi. 7. For Confusion they shall rejoice in their Portion: Therefore in their Land they shall possess the double; everlasting Joy shall be unto them.

Ver. 10. I will greatly rejoice in the Lord; my Soul shall be joyful in my God.

Is. lxv. 14. Behold my Servants shall sing for Joy of Heart.

Is. li. 11. The Redeemed of the Lord shall return, and come with singing unto *Zion,* and everlasting Joy shall be upon their Head: They shall obtain Gladness and Joy, and Sorrow and Mourning shall flee away.

Hab. iii. 18. I will rejoice in the Lord; I will joy in the God of my Salvation.

John xv. 11. These Things have I spoken unto you, that my Joy might remain in you, and that your Joy might be full.

John xvi. 22. I will see you again and your Heart shall rejoice, and your Joy no Man taketh from you.

Rom. v. 2. We rejoice in hope of the Glory of God.

I *Pet.* i. 8. Whom, having not seen, ye love: In whom, though now ye see him not, yet believing, ye rejoice with Joy unspeakable, and full of Glory.

XXIV. Support *in* Death.

Ps. xxiii, 4. Yea, though I walk through the Valley of the Shadow of Death, I will fear no Evil: For thou art with me; thy Rod and thy Staff they comfort me.

Ps. xxxvii. 37. Mark the perfect Man, and behold the Upright; for the End of that Man is Peace.

Ps. xlviii. 14. For this God is our God, for ever and ever: He will be our Guide, even unto Death.

Ps. xlix. 15. God will redeem my Soul from the Power of the Grave; for he shall receive me.

Ps. lxxiii. 26. My Flesh and my Heart faileth; but God is the Strength of my Heart, and my Portion for ever.

Prov. xiv. 32. The Righteous hath Hope in his Death.

Is. xxv. 8. He will swallow up Death in Victory: and the Lord God will wipe away Tears from off all Faces.

Hos. xiii. 14. I will ransom them from the Power of the Grave: I will redeem them from Death. O Death! I will be thy Plagues: O Grave! I will be thy Destruction.

Rom. viii. 38. For I am persuaded, that neither Death, nor Life, nor Angels, nor Principalities, nor Powers, nor Things present, nor Things to come;

Ver. 39. Nor Height, nor Depth, nor any other Creature, shall be able to separate us from the Love of God, which is in Christ Jesus our Lord,

2 *Cor.* iv, 16. For which Cause we faint not; but though our outward Man perish, yet the inward Man is renewed Day by Day.

2 *Tim.* i. 12. I know whom I have believed, and I am persuaded that he is able to keep that which I have committed unto him, against that Day.

Heb. ii. 14. That through Death he might destroy him that had the Power of Death; that is, the Devil.

Ver. 15. And deliver them, who through Fear of Death, were all their Life-time subject to Bondage.

I *Cor.* xv. 55. O Death! where is thy Sting? O Grave! where is thy Victory?

Ver. 56. The Sting of Death is Sin, and the Strength of Sin is the Law.

Ver. 57. But Thanks be to God, which giveth us the Victory, through our Lord Jesus Christ.

Chapter Four - Promises *of* Blessings *in the* Other World

I. *Of* Deliverance *from* Hell.

Psal. lxxxvi. 13. Great is thy Mercy towards me; and thou hast delivered my Soul from the lowest [1] Hell.

Prov. x. 2. Righteousness delivereth from Death. *Chap.* ii. 4.

Prov. xv. 24. The Way of Life is above to the Wise, that he may depart from Hell beneath.

Is. xlv. 17. *Israel* shall be saved in the Lord, with an everlasting Salvation: Ye shall not be ashamed nor confounded. World without End.

Rom. v. 9. Much more being justified by his Blood, we shall be saved from Wrath through him.

I *Thes.* i. 10. Jesus, which delivered us from the Wrath to come.

I *Thes.* v. 9. God hath not appointed us to Wrath, but to obtain Salvation by our Lord Jesus Christ.

John iii. 15. That whosoever believeth in him should not perish, but have eternal Life.

John viii. 51. If a Man keep my Saying, he shall never see Death.

Rev. xx. 6. Blessed and Holy is he that hath part in the first Resurrection; on such the second Death hath no Power.

II. Of Happiness *immediately after* Death.

Ps. lxxiii. 24. Thou shalt guide me with thy Counsel, and afterward receive me to Glory.

Job iii. 17. There the Wicked cease from Troubling: and there the Weary be at Rest.

Ver. 18. There the Prisoners rest together, they hear not the Voice of. the Oppressor.

Is. lvii. 2. He shall enter into Peace: They shall rest in their Beds, each one walking in his Uprightness.

Luke xvi. 25. *Abraham* said, Son remember, that thou in thy Lifetime receivedst thy good Things, and likewise *Lazarus* evil Things; but now he is comforted, and thou art tormented.

Luke xxiii. 43. Jesus said unto him. Verily I say unto thee, This Day shalt thou be with me in Paradise.

Phil. i. 21. For to me to live is Christ, and to die is Gain.

Ver. 23. Having a Desire to depart, and to be with Christ, which is far better.

2 *Cor.* v. 8. We are confident, I say, and willing rather to be absent from the Body, and to be present with the Lord.

Heb. xii. 23. And to the Spirits of just Men made perfect.

Rev. xiv. 13. Blessed are the Dead which die in the Lord, from henceforth: Yea, saith the Spirit, that they may rest from their Labours: and their Works do follow them.

Ps. xlix. 15. God will redeem my Soul from the Power of the Grave; for he shall receive me.

III. A Glorious Resurrection.

Job xix. 26. Tho' after my Skin Worms destroy this Body, yet in my Flesh shall I see God.

Ver. 27. Whom I shall see for myself, and mine Eyes shall behold, and not another, tho' my Reins be consumed within me.

Is. xxvi. 19. Thy dead Men shall live, together with my dead Body shall they arise. Awake and sing, ye that dwell in the Dust: For thy Dew is as the Dew of Herbs; and the Earth shall cast out the Dead.

Dan. xii. 2. Many of them that sleep in the Dust of the Earth, shall awake; some to everlasting Life, and some to Shame, and everlasting Contempt.

Ps. xvi. 9. My Flesh also shall rest in Hope,

Ver. 10. For thou wilt not leave my Soul in Hell, neither wilt thou suffer thine Holy One to see Corruption.

Luke xx. 35. They which shall be accounted worthy to obtain that World, and the Resurrection from the Dead, neither marry, nor are given in Marriage.

Ver. 36. Neither can they die any more; for they are equal unto the Angels, and are the Children of God, being the Children of the Resurrection.

John v. 28. The Hour is coming, in the which all that are in the Graves shall hear his Voice.

Ver. 29. And shall come forth; they that have done Good, unto the Resurrection of Life; and they that have done Evil, unto the Resurrection of Damnation.

John vi. 39. This is the Father's Will which hath sent me. That of all which he hath given me, I shall lose nothing, but should raise it up at the last Day.

Ver. 40. And this is the Will of him that sent me. That every one that seeth the Son, and believeth on him, may have everlasting Life: And I will raise him up at the last Day.

Ver. 54. Whoso eateth my Flesh, and drinketh my Blood, hath eternal Life, and I will raise him up at the last Day.

John xi. 25. I am the Resurrection and the Life; he that believeth in me, though he were dead, yet shall he live.

Rom. viii. 11. If the Spirit of him that raised up Jesus from the Dead, dwell in you, he that raised up Christ from the Dead, shall also quicken your mortal Bodies by his Spirit that dwelleth in you.

I *Cor.* xv. 21. Since by Man came Death, by Man also came the Resurrection of the Dead.

Ver. 22. For as in *Adam* all die, even so in Christ shall all be made alive.

Ver. 42. So also is the Resurrection of the Dead: It is sown in Corruption, it is raised in Incorruption:

Ver. 43. It is sown in Dishonour, it is raised in Glory: It is sown in Weakness, it is raised in Power.

Ver. 44. It is sown a natural Body, it is raised a spiritual Body.

Ver. 49, As we have borne the Image of the Earthy, we shall also bear the Image of the Heavenly.

Ver. 51. Behold, I show you a Mystery: We shall not all sleep, but we shall all be changed;

Ver. 52. In a Moment, in the Twinkling of an Eye, at the last Trump, (for the Trumpet shall sound) and the Dead shall be raised incorruptible, and we shall be changed.

Ver. 53. For this Corruptible must put on Incorruption, and this Mortal must put on Immortality.

Ver. 54. So when this Corruptible shall have put on Incorruption, and this Mortal shall have put on Immortality; then shall be brought to pass the saying that is written, Death is swallowed up in Victory.

1 *Cor.* vi. 2. Do not you know that the Saints shall judge the World?

Ver. 3. Know ye not that we shall judge Angels?

2 *Cor.* v. 1. We know, that if our earthly House of this Tabernacle were dissolved, we have a Building of God, an House not made with Hands, eternal in the Heavens.

Ver. 2. For in this we groan, earnestly desiring to be cloathed upon with our House, which is from Heaven:

Ver. 3. If so be that being cloathed, we shall not be found naked.

Ver. 4. For we that are in this Tabernacle do groan, being burdened; not for that we would be uncloathed, but cloathed upon, that Mortality might be swallowed up of Life.

2 *Cor.* iv. 14. Knowing, that he which hath raised up the Lord Jesus, shall raise up us also by Jesus, and shall present us with you.

Phil. iii. 21, Who shall change our vile Body, that it may be fashioned like unto his glorious Body, according to the working whereby he is able even to subdue all Things to himself.

2 *Thes.* lv. 14. If we believe that Jesus died, and rose again, even so them also which sleep in Jesus, will God bring with him.

Ver. 15. For this we say unto you by the Word of the Lord, That we which are alive, and remain unto the coming of the Lord, shall not prevent them which are asleep.

Ver. 16. For the Lord himself shall descend from Heaven with a Shout, with the Voice of the Archangel, and with the Trump of God: And the Dead in Christ shall rise first.

Ver. 17. Then we which are alive and remain, shall be caught up together with them in the Clouds, to meet the Lord in the Air.

2 *Tim.* i. 10. Jesus Christ hath abolished Death, and hath brought Life and Immortality to Light through the Gospel.

IV. *Of* Everlasting Happiness *in* Heaven.

Ps. xlix. 14. The Upright shall have Dominion over them in the Morning.

1 *Cor.* ii. 9. Eye hath not seen, nor Ear heard, neither have entered into the Heart of Man, the Things which God hath prepared for them that love him.

Rom. ii. 7. To them who by patient Continuance in Well-doing, seek for Glory, and Honour, and Immortality, eternal Life.

Ver. 10. Glory, Honour, and Peace to every Man that worketh Good; to the *Jew* first, and then to the *Gentile*.

Rom. v. 10. We shall be saved by his Life.

Ver. 17. They which receive abundance of Grace, and of the Gift of Righteousness, shall reign in Life by Jesus Christ.

2 *Thes.* i. 5. That ye may be accounted worthy of the Kingdom of God, for which ye also suffer.

Ver. 7. To you who are troubled, rest with us, when the Lord Jesus shall be revealed from Heaven by his mighty Angels.

Ver. 10. He shall come to be glorified in his Saints, and to be admired in all them that believe in that Day.

Ver. 12. That the Name of our Lord Jesus Christ may be glorified in you. and ye in him, according to the Grace of our God, and the Lord Jesus Christ.

Heb. xi. 9. By Faith he sojourned in the Land of Promise as in a strange Country, dwelling in Tabernacles with Isaac and Jacob, the Heirs with him of the same Promise.

Ver. 10. For he looked for a City which hath Foundations, whose Builder and Maker is God.

Ver. 16. They desire a better Country, that is, an heavenly: Wherefore God is not ashamed to be called their God, for he hath prepared for them a City.

John xiv. 2. In my Father's House are many Mansions; if it were not so, I would have told you: I go to prepare a Place for you.

Ver. 3, And if I go and prepare a Place, I will come again and receive you unto myself, that where I am, there ye may be also.

2 *Tim.* iv. 8. There is laid up for me a Crown of Righteousness, which the Lord the righteous Judge shall give me at that Day; and not to me only, but unto all them also that love his appearing.

Heb. iv. 9. There remaineth therefore a Rest for the People of God.

Heb. ix. 15. He is the Mediator of the New Testament, that by means of Death, for the Redemption of the Transgressions that were under the First Testament, they which are called might receive the Promise of eternal Inheritance.

Ver. 28. Unto them that look for him, shall he appear the second Time without Sin unto Salvation.

2 *Pet.* iii. 13. We, according to his Promise, look for new Heavens and a new Earth, wherein dwelleth Righteousness.

I *Pet.* i. 9. Receiving the End of your Faith, even the Salvation of your Souls.

Ver. 13. Gird up the Loins of your Mind, be sober and hope to the End, for the Grace that is to be brought unto you at the Revelation of Jesus Christ.

Rev. ii. 10. Be thou faithful unto Death, and I will give thee a Crown of Life.

Rev. iii. 4. Thou hast a few Names even in *Sardis,* which have not defiled their Garments; and they shall walk with me in white, for they are worthy.

Rev. vii. 15. They are before the Throne of God, and serve him Day and Night in his Temple: And he that sitteth on the Throne shall dwell among them.

Ver. 16. They shall hunger no more, neither thirst any more, neither shall the Sun light on them, nor any Heat.

Ver. 17. For the Lamb which is in the midst of the Throne shall feed them, and shall lead them unto living Fountains of Waters: And God shall wipe away all Tears from their Eyes.

Rev. xi. 18. Thy Wrath is come, and the Time of the Dead, that they should be judged, and that thou shouldst give Reward unto thy Servants the Prophets, and to the Saints, and to them that fear thy Name, small and great.

Rev. xxi. 22. I saw no Temple therein for the Lord God Almighty and the Lamb are the Temple of it.

Ver. 23. The City had no Need of the Sun, neither of the Moon to shine in it; for the Glory of God did lighten it, and the Lamb is the Light thereof.

Rev. xxii. 5. There shall be no Night there, and they need no Candle, neither Light of the Sun; for the Lord God giveth them Light, and they shall reign for ever and ever. *Is.* lx. 19, 20.

I *John* iii. 2. Now we are the Sons of God: And it doth not yet appear what we shall be; but we know, that when he shall appear, we shall be like him, for we shall see him as he is.

John xvii. 22. The Glory which thou gavest me, I have given them, that they may be one, even as we are one.

Ver. 24. Father, I will that they also whom thou hast given me, be with me where I am, that they may behold my Glory, which thou hast given me.

Rev. xxi. 4. God shall Freedom from wipe away all Tears from their Eyes; and there shall be no more Death, neither Sorrow, nor Crying, neither shall there be any more Pain: For the former Things are passed away.

Is. lx. 20. The Lord shall be thine everlasting Light, and the Days of thy Mourning shall be ended.

Matt. vi. 20. Treasures in Heaven, where neither Moth doth corrupt, nor Thieves break through and steal.

Rev. xxii. 3. And there shall be no more Curse.

Ps. xvi. 11. Thou wilt shew me the Path of Life; in thy Presence is Fulness of Joy, at thy Right Hand there are Pleasures for evermore.

Matt. xxv. 21. I will make thee Ruler over many Things: Enter thou into the Joy of thy Lord.

Jude 24. He is able to present you faultless before the Presence of his Glory, with exceeding Joy.

Matt. xiii. 43. The Righteous shall shine forth as the Sun, in the Kingdom of their Father.

Dan. xii. 3. They that be wise shall shine as the Brightness of the Firmament; and they that turn many to Righteousness, as the Stars, for ever and ever.

Rom. viii. 17. If Children, then Heirs; Heirs of God, and joint Heirs with Christ; if so be that we suffer with him, that we also may be glorified together.

Ver. 18. The Sufferings of this present Life are not worthy to be compared with the Glory which shall be revealed in us.

Ver. 30. Whom he justified, them he also glorified.

2 *Cor.* lv. 17. Our light Affliction, which is but for a Moment, worketh for us a far more exceeding and eternal Weight of Glory.

Ver. 18. While we look not at the Things which are seen, but at the Things which are not seen: For the Things which are seen, are Temporal; but the Things which are not seen, are Eternal.

1 *Pet.* iv. 13. That when his Glory shall be revealed, ye may be glad also with exceeding Joy.

Col. iii. 4. When Christ, who is our Life, shall appear, then shall ye also appear with him in Glory.

2 *Tim.* ii. 10. That they [*the Elect*] may obtain the Salvation, which is in Christ Jesus, with eternal Glory.

Matt. xxv. 34. Come, ye blessed of my Father, inherit the Kingdom, prepared for you from the Foundation of the World.

Luke xii. 32. It is your Father's good Pleasure to give you the Kingdom.

2 *Pet.* i. 11. An Entrance shall be ministered unto you abundantly into the everlasting Kingdom of our Lord and Saviour Jesus Christ.

2 *Tim.* iv. 18. The Lord will preserve me unto his heavenly Kingdom.

Luke xxii. 29. I appoint unto you a Kingdom, as my Father hath appointed unto me.

Ver. 30. That ye may eat and drink at my Table in my Kingdom, and sit on Thrones, judging the Twelve Tribes of Israel.

Eph. i. 18. The Eyes of your Understanding being enlightened; that ye may know what is the Hope of his Calling, and what the Riches of his Glory of his Inheritance in the Saints.

I *Pet.* i. 3. Who hath begotten us again unto a lively Hope, by the Resurrection of Jesus Christ from the Dead.

Ver. 4. To an Inheritance incorruptible and undefiled, and that fadeth not away, reserved in Heaven for you.

Ps. xvii. 15. As for me, I will behold thy Face in Righteousness: I shall be satisfied when I awake, with thy Likeness.

Ps. xxxvi. 9. With thee is the Fountain of Life; in thy Light we shall see Light.

I *Thes.* iv. 17. So shall we be ever with the Lord.

Rev. xxii. 3. The Throne of God and the Lamb shall be in it, and his Servants shall serve him.

Ver. 4. And they shall see his Face, and his Name shall be in their Foreheads.

Matt. xx. 46. The Righteous shall go away into Life eternal.

John vi. 47. Verily, verily I say unto you, he that believeth on me, hath everlasting Life. See *Ver.* 51, 54.

Rom. vi. 23. The Gift of God is eternal Life, thro' Jesus Christ our Lord.

I *John* ii. 25. This is the Promise that he hath promised us, even eternal Life.

I *John* v. 11. God hath given to us eternal Life; and this Life is in his Son.

Ver. 13. That ye may know that ye have eternal Life.

[1] *The Word* Hell, *in these Passages, is probably to be understood of Death and the Grave.*

Part Two - Promises to Several Graces and Duties

Chapter One - Promises *to* Duties *of the* First Table

I. *To* Faith *in* Christ

ISAIAH xxviii. 16. Behold I lay in *Sion* for a Foundation a Stone, a tried Stone, a precious Cornerstone, a sure Foundation. He that believeth, shall not make haste.

I *Pet.* ii. 6. He that believeth on him, shall not be confounded.

Is. xlv. 22. Look unto me, and be ye saved, all the Ends of the Earth.

Mark ix. 23. If thou canst believe, all Things are possible to him that believeth.

John i. 12. As many as received him, to them crave he Power to become the Sons of God, even to them that believe on his Name.

John iii. 16. God so loved the World, that he gave his only begotten Son, that whosoever believeth on him, should not perish, but have everlasting Life.

Ver. 18. He that believeth on him, is not condemned.

Ver. 36. He that believeth on the Son, hath everlasting Life. *John* vi. 47.

John xii. 46. I am come a Light into the World, that whosoever believeth on me, should not abide in Darkness.

Luke vii. 50. Thy Faith hath saved thee, go in Peace.

Acts x. 43. To him give all the Prophets Witness, that through his Name whosoever believeth on him, shall receive Remission of Sins.

Acts xvi. 31. Believe on the Lord Jesus Christ, and thou shalt be saved, and thy House.

Rom. ix. 33. Behold, I lay in *Sion* a Stumbling-Stone, and Rock of Offence, and whosoever believeth on him, shall not be ashamed.

Rom. iv. 5. To him that worketh not, but believeth on him that justifieth the Ungodly, his Faith is counted for Righteousness.

Rom. x. 4. Christ is the End of the Law for Righteousness to every one that believeth.

Gal. iii. 9. They which be of Faith, are blessed with faithful *Abraham*.

Ver. 7. They which are of Faith, the same are the Children of *Abraham*.

Ver. 22. The Scripture hath concluded all under Sin, that the Promise by Faith of Jesus Christ might be given to them that believe.

Heb. x. 38. The just shall live by Faith.

Ver. 39. We are of them that believe, to the saving of the Soul.

Eph. ii. 8. By Grace you are saved, thro' Faith.

Heb. vi. 12. That ye be not slothful, but Followers of them, who through Faith and Patience inherit the Promises.

I *Tim.* iv. 10. We trust in the living God, who is the Saviour of all Men, especially of those that believe.

John xx. 29. Blessed are they that have not seen, and yet have believed.

Matt. xi. 28. Come unto me, all ye that labour and are heavy laden, and I will give you Rest.

John vi. 35. And Jesus said unto them, I am the Bread of Life; he that cometh unto me shall never hunger, and he that believeth on me shall never thirst.

Ver. 37. All that the Father giveth me, shall come to me; and him that cometh to me, I will in no wise cast out.

I *Pet.* ii. 4, 5. To whom coming as unto a living Stone, disallowed indeed of Men, but chosen of God, and precious; Ye, also, as lively Stones, are built up a Spiritual House, a holy Priesthood, to offer up spiritual Sacrifices, acceptable to God by Jesus Christ. See *Justification,* Part I. Chap. III. Sect. II.

Matt. x. 32. Whosoever shall confess me before Men, him will I confess also before my Father which is in Heaven.

Rom. x. 9. If thou shalt confess with thy Mouth the Lord Jesus, and shalt believe in thine Heart, that God hath raised him from the Dead, thou shalt be saved.

Ver. 10. For with the Heart Man believeth unto Righteousness, and with the Mouth Confession is made unto Salvation.

I *John* lv. 15. Whosoever shall confess that Jesus is the Son of God, God dwelleth in him, and he in Him.

II. *To* Repentance.

2 *Chron.* vii. 14. If my People, which are called by my Name, shall humble themselves, and pray, and seek my Face, and turn from their wicked Ways; then will I hear from Heaven, and will forgive their Sin.

2 *Chron.* xxx. 9. The Lord your God is gracious and merciful, and will not turn away his Face from you, if ye return unto him.

Ps. xxxvii. 27. Depart from Evil and do good, and dwell for evermore.

Prov. i. 23. Turn ye at my Reproof: Behold, I will pour out my Spirit upon you: I will make known my Words unto you.

Jer. iv. 14, O *Jerusalem,* wash thine Heart from Wickedness, that thou mayest be saved. How long shall vain Thoughts lodge within thee?

Is. lv. 7. Let the Wicked forsake his Way, and the Unrighteous Man his Thoughts, and let him return unto the Lord, and he will have Mercy upon him; and to our God, for he will abundantly pardon.

Jer. xviii. 8. If that Nation against whom I have pronounced, turn from their Evil, I will repent of the Evil that I thought to do unto them.

Jer. xxvi. 3. If so be they will hearken, and turn every Man from his Evil Way. that I may repent me of the Evil which I purpose to do unto them, because of the Evil of their Doings.

Ver. 13. Amend your Ways and your Doings, and obey the Voice of the Lord your God, and the Lord will repent him of the Evil that he hath pronounced against you.

Jer. xxxvi. 3. That they may return every Man from his evil Way, that I may forgive their Iniquity and their Sin.

Ezek. xviii. 21. If the Wicked will turn from all his Sins that he hath committed, and keep all my Statutes, and do that which is lawful and right, he shall surely live, he shall not die.

Ver. 22. All his Transgressions that he hath committed, they shall not be once mentioned unto him: In his Righteousness that he hath done, he shall live.

Ver. 23. Have I any Pleasure at all that the wicked should die, saith the Lord God, and not that he should return from his Ways and live?

Ver. 30. Repent, and turn yourselves from all your Transgressions; so Iniquity shall not prove your Ruin.

Ver. 31. Cast away from you all your Transgressions, whereby ye have transgressed, and make you a new Heart, and a new Spirit: For why will ye die, O House of *Israel?*

Ver. 32. For I have no Pleasure in the Death of him that dieth, saith the Lord God: Wherefore turn yourselves, and live

Ezek. xxxiii. 14. When I say unto the Wicked, Thou shalt surely die: If he turn from his Sin, and do that which is lawful and right:

Ver. 15. If the Wicked restore the Pledge, give again that he had robbed, walk in the Statutes of Life without committing Iniquity; he shall surely live, he shall not die.

Ver. 16. None of his Sins that he hath committed, shall be mentioned unto him; he hath done that which is lawful and right.

Ver. 19. If the Wicked turn from his Wickedness, and do that which is lawful and right, he shall live thereby.

Joel ii. 12. Turn ye 'even to me with all your Heart, and with Fasting, and with Weeping, and Mourning.

Ver. 13. And rend your Heart, and not your Garments, and turn unto the Lord your God; for he is gracious and merciful, slow to Anger, and of great Kindness, and repenteth him of the Evil.

Ver. 14. Who knoweth, if he will return and repent, and leave a Blessing behind him, even a Meat-Offering and a Drink-Offering, unto the Lord your God?

Zech. i. 3. Turn ye unto me, saith the Lord of Hosts, and I will turn unto you saith the Lord of Hosts. *Mal.* iii. 7.

Job xxii. 23. If thou return to the Almighty, thou shalt be built up; thou shalt put away Iniquity far from thy Tabernacles.

Eph. v. 14. Awake, thou that sleepest, and arise from the Dead, and Christ shall give thee Light.

Acts ii. 38. Repent, and be baptized, every one of you, in the Name of Jesus Christ, for the Remission of Sins, and ye shall receive the Holy Ghost.

Acts iii. 19. Repent ye therefore, and be comforted, that your Sins may be blotted out, when the Times of refreshing shall come from the Presence of the Lord.

Ezek. ix. 4. Go through the Midst of the City, and set a Mark upon the Foreheads of them that sigh, and that cry for all the Abominations that be done in the Midst of it.

Ver. 6. Slay utterly old and young ___ But come not near any Man upon whom is the Mark.

Deut. iv. 30. When thou art in Tribulation, and all these Things are come upon thee, even in the latter Days, if thou turn to the Lord thy God, and shalt be obedient to his Voice;

Ver. 31. (For the Lord thy God is a merciful God) he will not forsake thee, neither destroy thee, nor forget the Covenant of thy Fathers, which he sware unto them.

Deut. xxx. 2. If thou shalt return unto the Lord thy God, and shalt obey his Voice, according to all that I command thee this Day, thou and thy Children, with all thine Heart, and with all thy Soul;

Ver. 3. Then the Lord thy God will turn thy Captivity, and have Compassion upon thee, and will return and gather thee from all the Nations whither the Lord thy God hath scattered thee.

Ver. 8. And thou shalt return, and obey the Voice of the Lord, and do all his Commandments, which I command thee this Day.

Job xxxiii. 27. He looketh upon Men, and if any say, I have sinned and perverted that which was right, and it profited me not;

Ver. 28. He will deliver his Soul from going into the Pit, and his Life shall see the Light.

Hos. vi. I. Come, and let us return unto the Lord; for he hath torn, and he will heal us: He hath smitten, and he will bind us up.

Ps. xxxii. 5. I said, I will confess my Transgressions unto the Lord; and thou forgavest the Iniquity of my Sin.

Prov. xxviii. 13. Whoso confesseth and forsaketh his Sins, shall have Mercy.

I *John* i. 9. If we confess our Sins, he is faithful and just to forgive us our Sins, and to cleanse us from all Unrighteousness.

Lev. xxvi. 40. If they shall confess their Iniquity, and the Iniquity of their Fathers, with their Trespass which they trespassed against me; and that also they have walked contrary unto me;

Ver. 41. And that I have also walked contrary unto them, and have brought them into the Land of their Enemies; If then their uncircumcised Hearts be humbled, and they then accept of the Punishment of their Iniquity;

Ver. 42. Then will I remember my Covenant with *Jacob,* and also my Covenant with *Isaac,* and also my Covenant with *Abraham* will I remember; and I will remember the Land.

Jer. iii, 12. Return, thou backsliding *Israel,* saith the Lord, and I will not cause mine Anger to fall upon you; for I am merciful saith the Lord, and I will not keep Anger for ever.

Ver. 13. Only acknowledge thine Iniquity, that thou hast transgressed against the Lord thy God, and hast scattered thy Ways to the Strangers under every green Tree, and ye have not obeyed my Voice, saith the Lord.

Luke xv. 21. The Son said unto him, Father, I have sinned against Heaven, and in thy Sight, and am no more worthy to be called thy Son.

Ver. 22. But the Father said to his Servants, Bring forth the best Robe, and put it on him, and put a Ring on his Hand, and Shoes on his Feet.

III. Obedience.

Exod. xix. 5. If ye will obey my Voice indeed, and keep my Covenant, then ye shall be a peculiar Treasure unto me above all People.

Lev. xxv. 18. Ye shall do my Statutes, and keep my Judgments, and do them; ye shall dwell in the Land in Safety.

Ver. 19. And the Land shall yield her Fruit, and ye shall eat your Fill, and dwell therein in Safety.

Deut. iv. 1. Hearken, O *Israel,* unto the Statutes, and unto the Judgments which I teach you, for to do them, that ye may live, and go in and possess the Land which the Lord God of your Fathers giveth you.

Ver. 6. Keep therefore and do them, for this is your Wisdom, and your Understanding in the Sight of the Nations, which shall hear all these Statutes, and say. Surely this great Nation is a wise and understanding People.

Deut. v. 29. O that there were such an Heart in them, that they would fear me and keep all my Commandments always, that it might be well with them, and with their Children for ever.

Deut. vi. 3. Hear therefore, O *Israel,* and observe to do it; that it may be well with thee, and that ye may increase mightily, as the Lord God of thy Fathers hath promised thee, in the Land which floweth with Milk and Honey.

Ver. 18. Thou shalt do that which is good and right in the Sight of the Lord, that it may be well with thee, and that thou mayest go in and possess the good Land, which the Lord sware unto thy Fathers;

Ver. 19. To cast out all thine Enemies from before thee, as the Lord hath spoken.

Deut. vii. 12. It shall come to pass, if ye hearken unto these Judgments, and keep and do them, that the Lord thy God shall keep unto thee the Covenant which he sware unto thy Fathers.

Deut. xi. 27. A Blessing, if ye obey the Commandments of the Lord your God, which I command you this Day.

Deut. xiii. 17. That the Lord may turn from the Fierceness of his Anger, and shew thee Mercy, and have Compassion upon thee, and multiply thee, as he hath sworn unto thy Fathers.

Ver. 18. When thou shalt hearken to the Voice of the Lord thy God, to keep all his Commandments, which I command thee this Day, to do that which is right in the Eyes of the Lord thy God.

Deut. xxix. 9. Keep therefore the Words of this Covenant, and do them, that ye may prosper in all that ye do.

Deut. xxx. 15. See, I have set before thee this Day good and Evil:

Ver. 16. In that I command thee this Day to love the Lord thy God, to walk in his Ways, and to keep his Commandments, and his Statutes, and his Judgment, that thou mayest live and multiply; And the Lord thy God shall bless thee in the Land, whither thou goest to possess it.

Deut. xxxii. 46. Set your Hearts unto all the Words which I testify unto you this Day; which he shall command your Children to observe to do all the Words of this Law.

Ver. 47. For it is not a vain Thing for you, because it is your Life; and through this Thing ye shall prolong your Days in the Land whither you go over *Jordan* to possess it.

I *Sam.* xii. 14. If ye will fear the Lord and serve him, and obey his Voice, and not rebel against the Commandment of the Lord, then shall both ye, and also the King that reigneth over you, continue following the Lord your God.

I *Kings* ii. 3. Keep the Charge of the Lord thy God, to walk in his Ways, to keep his Statutes, and his Commandments, and his Judgments, and his Testimonies, that thou mayest prosper in all that thou doest, and withersoever thou turnest thyself.

1 *Chron.* xxii. 12. The Lord give thee Wisdom and Understanding, and give thee Charge concerning *Israel,* that thou mayest keep the Law of the Lord thy God;

Ver. 13. Then shalt thou prosper, if thou takest heed to fulfil the Statutes and Judgments which the Lord charged *Moses* with concerning *Israel.*

2 *Chron.* xv. 7. Be strong; let not your Hands be weak, for your Work shall be rewarded.

Job xxxvi. 11. If they obey and serve him, they shall spend their Days in Prosperity, and their Years in Pleasure.

Ps. xxv. 10. All the Paths of the Lord are Mercy and Truth, unto such as keep his Covenant and his Testimonies.

Ps. l. 23, To him that ordereth his Conversation aright, will I shew the Salvation of God.

Ps. cvi. 3. Blessed are they that keep Judgment, and he that doth Righteousness at all Times.

Ps. cxix. 1. Blessed are the Undefiled in the Way, who walk in the Law of the Lord.

Ver. 2. Blessed are they that keep his Testimonies, that seek him with the whole Heart.

Ver. 6. I shall not be ashamed, when I have respect unto all thy Commandments.

Prov. xix. 16. He that keepeth the Commandment, keepeth his own Soul.

Prov. xxix. 18. He that keepeth the Law, happy is he.

Is. i. 19. If ye be willing and obedient, ye shall eat the Good of the Land.

Is. xlviii. 18. O that thou hadst hearkened to my Commandments! Then had my Peace been as a River, and thy Righteousness as the Waves of the Sea.

Jer. vii. 23. Obey my Voice, and I will be your God, and ye shall be my People; and walk ye in all the Ways that I have commanded you, that it may be well unto you.

Matt. v. 19. Whosoever shall do and teach these Commandments, the same shall be called Great in the Kingdom of Heaven.

Matt. vii. 21. Not every one that saith unto me, Lord, Lord, shall enter into the Kingdom of Heaven: But he that doeth the Will of my Father which is in Heaven.

Matt. xii. 50. Whosoever shall do the Will of my Father which is in Heaven, the same is my Brother, and Sister, and Mother.

John vii. 17. If any Man will do his Will, he shall know of the Doctrine, whether it be of God, or whether I speak of myself.

John xiii. 17. If ye know these Things, happy are ye if ye do them.

James i. 25. Whoso looketh into the perfect Law of Liberty, and continueth therein, he being not a forgetful Hearer, but a Doer of the Word, this Man shall be blessed in his Deed.

I *John.* ii. 17. He that doeth the Will of God, abideth for ever.

I *John* iii. 22. Whatsoever we ask, we receive of him, because we keep his Commandments, and do those Things that are pleasing in his Sight.

Rev. xxii. 14. Blessed are they that do his Commandments, that they may have Right to the Tree of Life, and may enter through the Gates into the City.

Phil. lv. 9. Those Things which ye have both learned and received, and heard and seen in me, do; and the God of Peace shall be with you.

Rom. ii. 13. The Doers of the Law shall be justified.

Exod. xxiii. 22. If thou shalt indeed obey his [*the Angel's*] Voice, and do all that I speak; then will I be an Enemy unto thine Enemies, and an Adversary to thine Adversaries.

Is. l. 10. Who is among you that feareth the Lord, that obeyeth the Voice of his Servant, that walketh in Darkness, and hath no Light? Let him trust in the Name of the Lord, and stay upon his God.

Matt. vii. 24. Whosoever heareth these Sayings of mine, and doeth them, I will liken him unto a wise Man, which built his House upon a Rock.

Ver. 25. And the Rain descended, and the Floods came, and the Winds blew, and beat upon that House; and it fell not, for it was founded upon a Rock.

Heb. v. 9. He became the Author of eternal Salvation to all them that obey him.

John v. 24. He that heareth my Word, and believeth on him that sent me, hath everlasting Life, and shall not come into Condemnation, but is passed from Death unto Life.

John viii. 51. If a Man keep my Saying, he shall never see Death.

John xv. 10. If ye keep my Commandments, ye shall abide in my Love.

IV. *To* Sincerity *and* Uprightness.

1 *Chron.* xxix. 17. I know also, my God, that thou hast Pleasure in Uprightness.

2 *Chron.* xvi. 9. The Eyes of the Lord run to and fro throughout the whole Earth, to shew himself strong in behalf of those whose Heart is perfect towards him.

Job viii. 6. If thou wert pure and upright, surely now he would awake for thee, and make the Habitation of thy Righteousness prosperous.

Ps. xi. 7. The righteous Lord loveth Righteousness; his Countenance doth behold the Upright.

Ps. xv. 1. Lord, who shall abide in thy Tabernacle? Who shall dwell in thy holy Hill?

Ver. 2. He that walketh uprightly, and worketh Righteousness.

Ps. xviii. 25. With an upright Man thou wilt shew thyself upright.

Ps. xxxvii. 18. The Lord knoweth the Days of the Upright; and their Inheritance shall be for ever.

Ps. cxix. 80. Let my Heart be found in thy Statutes, that I be not ashamed.

Ps. cxxv. 4. Do good, O Lord, unto those that be good, and to them that are upright in their Hearts.

Prov. ii. 7. He layeth up sound Wisdom for the Righteous; he is a Buckler to them that walk uprightly.

Ver. 21. The Upright shall dwell in the Land, and the Perfect shall remain in it.

Prov. x. 29. The Way of the Lord is Strength to the Upright.

Prov. xi. 3. The Integrity of the Upright shall guide them.

Ver. 6. The Righteousness of the Upright shall deliver them.

Ver. 20. Such as are upright in their Way are his Delight.

Prov. xiii. 6. Righteousness keepeth him that is upright in the Way.

Prov. xii, 22. They that deal truly, are his Delight.

Prov. xv. 8. The Prayer of the Upright is his Delight.

Prov. xxi. 18. The Wicked shall be a Ransom for the Righteous, and the Transgressor for the Upright.

Prov. xxviii. 10. Whoso causeth the Righteous to ^o astray in an evil Way, he shall fall himself into his own Pit; but the Upright shall have good Things in Possession.

Ver. 18. Whoso walketh uprightly shall be saved.

Ver. 20. A faithful Man shall abound with Blessings.

1 *John* iii. 21. If our Heart condemn us not, then have we Confidence towards God.

Rom. xiv. 22. Happy is he that condemneth not himself in that Thing which he alloweth.

Mic. ii. 7. Do not my Words do good to him that walketh uprightly?

V. To the Love of God.

Exod. xx. 6. Shewing Mercy unto Thousands of them that love me, and keep my Commandments.

Deut. vii. 9. God keepeth Covenant and Mercy with them that love him, unto a thousand Generations.

Judg. v. 31. Let them that love him be as the Sun, when he goeth forth in his Might.

Neh. i. 5. God keepeth Covenant and Mercy for them that love him.

Ps. xxxvii. 4. Delight thyself in the Lord, and he shall give thee the Desire of thine Heart.

Ps. xci. 14. Because he hath set his Love upon me, therefore will I deliver him.

Ps. cxlv. 20. The Lord preserveth all them that love him.

Rom. viii. 28. All Things work together for Good to them that love God.

I *Cor.* ii. 9. Eye hath not seen, nor Ear heard, neither have entered into the Heart of Man, the Things which God hath prepared for them that love him.

I *Cor.* viii, 3. If any Man love God, the same is known of him.

Jam. ii. 5. Heirs of the Kingdom, which he hath promised them that love him.

Deut. xi. 13. And it shall come to pass, if you hearken diligently to my Commandments, which I command you this Day, to love the Lord your God, and to serve him with all your Heart, and with all your Soul;

Ver. 14. That I will give you the Rain of your Land in his due Season, the first Rain, and the latter Rain, that thou mayest gather in thy Corn, and thy Wine, and thine Oil.

Dan. ix. 4. O Lord, the great and dreadful God, keeping the Covenant, and Mercy to them that love him, and to them that keep his Commandments.

Prov. viii. 17. I love them that love me.

Ver. 21. That I may cause those that love me to inherit Substance, and I will fill their Treasures.

John. xiv. 21. He that loveth me, shall be loved of my Father; and I will love him, and will manifest myself to him.

Eph. vi. 24. Grace be with all them that love our Lord Jesus Christ in Sincerity.

Jam. i. 12. The Crown of Life, which he hath promised to them that love him.

2 *Tim.* iv. 8. The Crown of Righteousness, which the Lord the righteous Judge shall give— to them that love his appearing.

VI. *To* Trusting, *and* Hoping *in, and patiently* Waiting *on* God.

Ps. ii. 12. Blessed are all they that put their Trust in him.

Ps. xxvii. 14. Wait on the Lord; be of good Courage, and he will strengthen thy Heart: Wait, I say, on the Lord.

Ps. xxvi. 1. I have trusted in the Lord, therefore I shall not slide.

Ps. xviii. 30. He is a Buckler to all those that trust in him.

Ps. xxxi. 19. O how great is thy Goodness, which thou hast laid up for them that fear thee! which thou hast wrought for them that trust in thee, before the Sons of Men!

Ver. 24. Be of good Courage, and he shall strengthen your Heart, all ye that hope in the Lord.

Ps. xxxii. 10. He that trusteth in the Lord, Mercy shall compass him about.

Ps. xxxiv. 8. O taste and see that the Lord is good: Blessed is the Man that trusteth in him, *Ps.* lxxxiv. 12.

Ps. xxxiv. 22. The Lord redeemeth the Soul of his Servants, and none of them that trust in him shall be desolate.

Ps. xxxvii, 3. Trust in the Lord, and do good: So shalt thou dwell in the Land; and verily thou shalt be fed.

Ver. 9. Those that wait upon the Lord. they shall inherit the Earth.

Ver. 40. The Lord shall help and deliver them: He will deliver them from the Wicked, and save them, because they trust in him.

Ps. xl. 4. Blessed is the Man that maketh the Lord his Trust, and respecteth not the Proud, nor such as turn aside to Lies.

Ps. lvi. 4. In God will I praise his Word; in God I have put my Trust: I will not fear what Flesh can do unto me.

Ps. cxii. 7. He shall not be afraid of evil Tidings; his Heart is fixed, trusting in the Lord.

Ver. 8. His Heart is established, he shall not be afraid, till he see his Desire upon his Enemies.

Ps. cxxv. I. They that trust in the Lord shall be as Mount *Zion,* which cannot be removed for ever.

Ps. cxlvi. 5. Happy is he that hath the God of *Jacob* for his Help, whose Hope is in the Lord his God.

Prov. xvi. 3. Commit thy Works unto the Lord, and thy thoughts shall be established.

Ver. 20. Whoso trusteth in the Lord, happy is he.

Prov. xxviii. 25. He that putteth his Trust in the Lord, shall be made fat.

Prov. xxix. 25. Whoso putteth his Trust in the Lord, shall be safe.

Is. xxv. 9. Lo! this is our God, we have waited for him, and he will save us: This is the Lord, we have waited for him, we will be glad, and rejoice in his Salvation.

Is. xxvi. 3. Thou wilt keep him in perfect Peace, whose Mind is stayed on thee; because he trusteth in thee.

Ver. 4. Trust ye in the Lord for ever; for in the Lord Jehovah is everlasting Strength.

Is. xxx. 15. In Returning and Rest shall ye be saved; in Quietness and in Confidence shall be your Strength.

Ver. 18. Blessed are all they that wait for him.

Is. xlix. 23. They shall not be ashamed that wait for me.

Is. lvii. 13. He that putteth his Trust in me, shall possess the Land, and inherit my holy Mountain,

Jer. xvii. 7. Blessed is the Man that trusteth in the Lord, and whose Hope the Lord *Is.*

Ver. 8. For he shall be as a Tree planted by the Waters, and that spreadeth out her Roots by the River, and shall not see when Heat Cometh, but her Leaf shall be green; and shall not be careful in the Year of Drought, neither shall cease from yielding Fruit.

Neh. i. 7. The Lord knoweth them that trust in him.

Lam. iii. 25. The Lord is good unto them that wait for him, to the Soul that seeketh him.

Ver. 26. It is good that a Man should both hope, and quietly wait for the Salvation of the Lord.

Mic. vii. 7. I will look unto the Lord, I will wait for the God of my Salvation; my God will hear me.

I *Pet.* v. 7. Cast all your Care upon him, for he careth for you.

Rom. viii. 24. We are saved by Hope.

VII. *To the* Fear *of* God.

Ps. xxv. 14. The Secret of the Lord is with them that fear him, and he will shew them his Covenant.

Ps. xxxi. 19. O how great is thy Goodness, which thou hast laid up for them that fear thee!

Ps. lxxxv. 9. Surely his Salvation is nigh them that fear him.

Ps. ciii. 11. As the Heaven is high above the Earth, so great is his Mercy toward them that fear him.

Ps. cxv. 13. He will bless them that fear the Lord, both small and great.

Ps. cxxviii. 1. Blessed is every one that feareth the Lord, that walketh in his Ways.

Ps. cxlvii. 11. The Lord taketh Pleasure in them that fear him.

Prov. xiv. 27. The Fear of the Lord is a Fountain of Life, to depart from the Snares of Death.

Ver. 26. In the Fear of the Lord is strong Confidence, and his Children shall have a Place of Refuge.

Prov. xvi. 6. By the Fear of the Lord Men depart from Evil.

Prov. iii. 7. Be not wise in thine own Eyes: Fear the Lord, and depart from Evil.

Ver. 8. It shall be Health to thy Navel, and Marrow to thy Bones.

Prov. xix. 23. The Fear of the Lord tendeth to Life, and he that hath it shall abide satisfied: He shall not be visited with Evil.

Eccl. viii. 12. It shall be well with them that fear God, which fear before him.

Mal. iv. 2. Unto you that fear my Name, shall the Sun of Righteousness arise with Healing" in his Wings.

Luke i. 50. His Mercy is on them that fear him, from Generation to Generation.

Acts x. 35. In every Nation, he that feareth him, and worketh Righteousness, is accepted with him.

Acts xiii. 26. Whosoever among you feareth God, to you is the Word of this Salvation sent.

I *Sam.* ii. 30. Them that honour me I will honour.

Prov. iii. 9. Honour the Lord with thy Substance, and with the First-Fruits of all thine Increase.

Ver. 10. So shall thy Barns be filled with Plenty, and thy Presses shall burst out with new Wine.

VIII. *To* Prayer.

Job xxxiii. 26. He shall pray unto God, and he shall be favourable unto him, and he shall see his Face with Joy.

Exod. xxxiv. 24. Neither shall any Man desire thy Land, when thou shalt go up to appear before the Lord thy God, thrice in the Year.

Deut. lv. 7. What Nation is there so great, who hath God so nigh unto them, as the Lord our God is in all Things that we call upon him for?

Ps. x. 17. Lord, thou hast heard the Desire of the Humble: Thou wilt prepare thine Heart; thou wilt cause thine Ear to hear.

Ps. vi. 9. The Lord hath heard my Supplication; the Lord will receive my Prayer.

Ps. xviii. 3. I will call upon the Lord, who is worthy to be praised; so shall I be saved from mine enemies.

Ps. lv. 17. Evening, Morning, and at Noon will I pray, and cry aloud, and he shall hear my voice.

Ps. lxxiii, 28. It is good for me to draw near to God.

Ps. lxxxvi. 5. Thou, Lord, art good, and ready to forgive, and plenteous in Mercy to all them that call upon thee.

Ver. 7. In the day of my Trouble, I will call upon thee, for thou wilt answer me.

Ps. cxlv. 18. The Lord is nigh unto all them that call upon him; to all that call upon him in Truth.

Jer. xxxiii. 3. Call unto me, and I will answer thee, and shew thee great and mighty Things, which thou knowest not.

Joel ii. 32. Whosoever shall call upon the Name of the Lord, shall be delivered.

Rom. x. 12. The same Lord over all, is rich unto all that call upon him.

Ver. 13. For whosoever shall call upon the Name of the Lord shall be saved.

Jam. iv. 8. Draw nigh to God, and he will draw nigh to you.

Job xxii. 21. Acquaint thyself with him, and be at Peace; for thereby Good shall come unto thee.

Ezek. xxxvi. 37. I will yet for this be enquired of by the House of *Israel,* to do it for them; I will increase them with Men like a Flock.

Heb. iv. 14. Seeing then that we have a great High Priest, that is passed into the Heavens, Jesus the Son of God, let us hold fast our Profession.

Ver. 15. For we have not an High Priest which cannot be touched with the Feeling of our Infirmities; but was in all Points tempted like as we are, yet without Sin.

Ver. 16. Let us therefore come boldly unto the Throne of Grace, that we may obtain Mercy, and find Grace to help in Time of Need. See *Promises* of *Hearing Prayer,* Part I. Chap. III. Sect. VI.

Deut. iv. 29. If thou shalt seek the Lord thy God, thou shalt find him; if thou seek him with all thy Heart, and with all thy Soul.

I *Chron.* xxviii. 9. If thou seek him, he will be found of thee.

Job viii. 5. If thou wouldst seek unto God betimes, and make thy Supplication unto the Almighty;

Ver. 6. If thou wert pure and upright, surely now he would awake for thee, and make the Habitation of thy Righteousness prosperous.

Ps. ix. 10. Thou, Lord, hast not forsaken them that seek thee.

Ps. lxix. 32. Your Heart shall live, that seek God.

Is. xlv. 19, I said not unto the Seed of Jacob, Seek ye me in vain.

Jer. xxix. 13. Ye shall seek me, and find me, when ye shall search for me with all your Heart.

Hos. x. 12. Seek the Lord till he come, and rain Righteousness upon you.

Amos v. 4. Seek ye me, and ye shall live.

Lam. iii. 25. The Lord is good unto them that wait for him: unto the Soul that seeketh him.

Acts xvii. 27. That they should seek the Lord, if haply they might feel after him, and find him.

Heb. xi. 6. He that cometh to God, must believe that he is; and that he is a Rewarder of all them that diligently seek him.

2 *Chron.* xv. 2. The Lord is with you, while ye be with him; if ye seek him, he will be found of you.

Ezra viii. 22. The Hand of our God is upon all them for Good that seek him.

Matt. vi. 6. Thou, when Secret Prayer, thou prayest, enter into thy Closet, and when thou hast shut the Door pray to thy Father, which is in secret; and thy Father which seeth in secret, shall reward thee openly.

Ps. lxix. 30. I will praise the Name of God with a Song, and will magnify him with Thanksgiving.

Ver. 31. This also shall please the Lord better than an Ox or Bullock, that hath Horns and Hoofs.

Ps. xcii. 1. It is a good Thing to give Thanks unto the Lord, and to sing Praises unto thy Name, O Most High!

Ver. 2. To shew forth thy Loving-kindness in the Morning, and thy Faithfulness every Night.

Ps. cxxxv. 3. Praise ye the Lord, for the Lord is good: Sing Praises unto his Name, for it is pleasant.

Matt. v. 6. Blessed are they which do hunger and thirst after Righteousness; for they shall be filled.

Is. lv. 1. Ho, every one that thirsteth, come ye to the Waters, and he that hath no Money, Come ye, buy and eat; yea, come, buy Wine and Milk, without Money, and without Price.

John vii. 37. Jesus stood, and cried, saying. If any Man thirst, let him come unto me, and drink.

Ver. 38. He that believeth on me, as the Scripture hath said, out of his Belly shall flow Rivers of Water.

Rev. xxi. 6. I am Alpha and Omega, the Beginning and the End: I will give unto him that is athirst, of the Fountain of the Water of Life freely.

Rev. xxii. 17. And let him that is athirst, come; and whosoever will, let him take the Water of Life freely.

Ps. lxxxi. 10. Open thy Mouth wide, and I will fill it.

IX. To Wisdom and Knowledge, and the Study of it.

Prov. iii. 13. Happy is the Man that findeth Wisdom; and the Man that getteth Understanding.

Ver. 14. For the Merchandize of it is better than the Merchandize of Silver, and the Gain thereof than fine Gold.

Ver. 15. She is more precious than Rubies: and all the Things thou canst desire, are not to be compared unto her.

Ver. 16. Length of Days is in her Right Hand; and in her Left Hand Riches and Honour.

Ver. 17. Her Ways are Ways of Pleasantness, and all her Paths are Peace.

Ver. 18. She is a Tree of Life to them that lay hold upon her; and happy is every one that retaineth her.

Ver. 35. The Wise shall inherit Glory.

Prov. iv. 6. Forsake her not, and she shall preserve thee: Love her, and she shall keep thee.

Ver. 8. Exalt her, and she shall promote thee: She shall bring thee to Honour, when thou dost embrace her.

Ver. 9. She shall give to thine Head an Ornament of Grace; a crown of Glory shall she deliver to thee.

Prov. i. 5. A wise Man will hear, and will increase Learning; and a Man of Understanding shall attain unto wise Counsels:

Ver. 6. To understand a Proverb, and the Interpretation; the Words of the Wise, and their dark Sayings.

Prov. viii. 35. Whoso findeth me, [*Wisdom*] findeth Life, and shall obtain Favour of the Lord.

Prov. ix. 12. If thou be wise, thou shalt be wise for thyself.

Prov. x. 17. He is in the Way of Life, that keepeth Instruction; but he that refuseth Reproof, erreth.

Prov. xii. 8. A Man shall be commended according to his Wisdom.

Prov. xiii. 15. Good Understanding gives Favour.

Prov. xv. 24. The Way of Life is above to the Wise, that he may depart from Hell beneath.

Prov. xix. 8. He that getteth Wisdom, loveth his own Soul: He that keepeth Understanding, shall find Good.

Prov. xvi. 20. He that handleth a Matter wisely, shall find Good.

Ver. 22. Understanding is a Well-spring of Life to him that hath it.

Prov. xi. 29. The Fool shall be Servant to the Wise in Heart.

Prov. xxi. 20. There is a Treasure to be desired, and Oil in the Dwelling of the Wise.

Prov. xxiv. 3. Through Wisdom is an House builded, and by Understanding it is established:

Ver. 4. And by Knowledge shall the Chambers be filled with all precious and pleasant Riches.

Ver. 5. A wise Man is strong; yea, a Man of Knowledge increaseth Strength.

Ver. 13. My Son, eat thou Honey, because it is good; and the Honey-comb, which is sweet to thy Taste.

Ver. 14. So shall the Knowledge of Wisdom be unto thy Soul: When thou hast found it, then there shall be a Reward, and thy Expectation shall not be cut off.

Prov. xxviii. 26. Whoso walketh wisely, shall be delivered.

Eccl. viii. I. A Man's Wisdom maketh his Face to shine, and the Boldness of his Face shall be changed.

Eccl. vii. 12. Wisdom is a Defence, and Money is a Defence; but the Excellency of Knowledge is, that Wisdom giveth Life to them that have it.

Dan. ii, 21. He giveth Wisdom unto the Wise, and Knowledge to them that know Understanding.

Dan. xii. 3. They that be wise shall shine as the Brightness of the Firmament.

Ver. 10. The Wise shall understand.

Hos. xiv. 9. Who is wise, and he shall understand these Things? Prudent, and he shall know them?

Ps. cvii. 43. Whoso is wise, and will observe these Things, even they shall understand the Loving-kindness of the Lord.

Eccl. x. 10. Wisdom is profitable to direct.

Prov. ii. 3. If thou criest after Knowledge, and liftest up thy Voice for Understanding;

Ver. 4. If thou seekest her as Silver, and searchest for her as for hid Treasures;

Ver. 5. Then shalt thou understand the Fear of the Lord, and find the Knowledge of God.

Prov. iv. 13. Take fast hold of Instruction, let her not go, keep her, for she is thy Life.

Prov. viii. 17. I love them that love me, and those that seek me early shall find me.

Prov. xix. 20. Hear Counsel, and receive Instruction, that thou mayest be wise in thy latter End.

Hos. vi. 3. Then shall we know, if we follow on to know the Lord.

2 *Chron.* i. 11. And God said to Solomon, Because this was in thy Heart, and thou hast not asked Riches, Wealth, or Honour, nor the Life of thine Enemies, neither yet hast thou asked long Life; but hast asked Wisdom and Knowledge for thyself, that thou mayest judge my People, over whom I have made thee King:

Ver. 12. Wisdom and Knowledge is granted unto thee; and I will give thee Riches, and Wealth, and Honour.

Ps. xci. 14. I will set him on high, because he hath known my Name.

John xvii. 3. And this is Life eternal, that they may know thee the only true God, and Jesus Christ whom thou hast sent.

2 *Pet.* i. 2. Grace and Peace be multiplied unto you, through the Knowledge of God, and of Jesus our Lord.

Ver. 3. According as his divine Power hath given unto us all Things that pertain unto Life and Godliness, through the Knowledge of him that hath called us to Glory and Virtue.

Matt. xi. 29. Take my Yoke upon you, and learn of me, for I am meek and lowly in Heart; and ye shall find Rest unto your Souls.

X. *To a due* Regard *to the* Word *of* God.

Prov. viii. 34. Blessed is the Man that heareth me, watching daily at my Gates, waiting at the Posts of my Doors.

Is. ii. 3. Come ye, and let us go up to the Mountain of the Lord, to the House of the God of *Jacob,* and he will teach us of his Ways, and we will walk in his Paths.

Is. lv. 2. Hearken diligently unto me, and eat ye that which is good, and let your Soul delight itself in Fatness.

Ver. 3. Incline your Ear, and come unto me; hear, and your Soul shall live: And I will make an everlasting Covenant with you, even the sure Mercies of *David*.

Ver. 10. For as the Rain cometh down, and the Snow from Heaven, and returneth not thither, but watereth the Earth, and maketh it bring forth and bud that it may give Seed to the Sower, and Bread to the Eater;

Ver. 11. So shall my Word be, that goeth forth out of my Mouth; it shall not return unto me void, but it shall accomplish that which I please, and it shall prosper in the Thing whereto I sent it.

Ver. 12. For ye shall go out with Joy, and be led forth with Peace.

John v. 39. Search the Scriptures, for in them ye think ye have eternal Life; and they are they which testify of me.

Mark iv. 24. Unto you that hear, shall more be given.

Ver. 25. For he that hath, to him shall be given; and he that hath not, from him shall be taken even that which he hath.

Rom. i. 16. The Gospel of Christ is the Power of God unto Salvation, to every one that believeth.

Rom. x. 17. Faith cometh by Hearing, and Hearing by the Word of God.

1 *Cor.* i. 21. It pleased God, by the Foolishness of Preaching, to save them that believe.

Jam. i. 21. Wherefore lay apart all Filthiness, and Superfluity of Naughtiness, and receive with Meekness the ingrafted Word, which is able to save your Souls.

2 *Pet.* i. 19. We have also a more sure Word of Prophecy; whereunto ye do well that ye take heed, as unto a light shining in a dark Place, until the Day dawn, and the day star arise in your Hearts.

Rev. i. 3. Blessed is he that readeth, and they that hear the Words of this Prophecy, and keep those Things which are written therein.

2 *Tim.* iii. 15. The Holy Scriptures, which are able to make thee wise unto Salvation, through Faith which is in Christ Jesus.

Heb. iv. 12. For the Word of God is quick and powerful, and sharper than any two-edged Sword, piercing even to the dividing asunder of the Soul and Spirit, and of the Joints and Marrow, and is a Discerner of the Thoughts and Intents of the Heart.

Ps. xix. 7. The Law of the Lord is perfect, converting the Soul; the Testimony of the Lord is sure, making wise the Simple.

Ver. 8. The Statutes of the Lord are right, rejoicing the Heart; the Commandment of the Lord is pure, enlightening the Eyes.

Ver. 11. Moreover, by them is thy Servant warned; and in keeping of them there is great Reward.

Ps. cxix. 105. Thy Word is a Lamp unto my Feet, and a Light unto my Path.

Ver. 130. The Entrance of thy Words giveth Light, it giveth Understanding unto the Simple.

Prov. vi. 23. The Commandment is a Lamp, and the Law is a Light, and Reproofs of Instruction are the Way of Life.

Ps. cxix. 165. Great Peace have they which love thy Law, and nothing shall offend them.

Ps. cxii. 1. Blessed is the Man that feareth the Lord, that delighteth greatly in his Commandments.

I *Pet.* ii. 2. As new-born Babes desire the sincere Milk of the Word, that ye may grow thereby.

Prov. xiii. 13. He that feareth the Commandment, shall be rewarded.

Is. lxvi. 2. To this Man will I look, even to him that is poor, and of a contrite Spirit, and trembleth at my Word.

XI. To Meditation.

Deut. xi. 18. Ye shall lay up these Words in your Heart, and in your Soul, and bind them for a Sign upon your Hand, that they may be as Frontlets between your Eyes.

Ver. 21. That your Days may be multiplied, and the Days of your Children in the Land which the Lord sware unto your Fathers to give them, as the Days of Heaven upon the Earth.

Josh. i. 8. This Book of the Law shall not depart out of thy Mouth, but thou shalt meditate therein Day and Night, that thou mayest observe to do according to all that is written therein: For then shalt thou make thy Way prosperous, and then thou shalt have good Success.

Ps. cxix. 9. Wherewith shall a young Man cleanse his Way? By taking heed thereto, according to thy Word.

Ps. xxxvii. 31. The Law of God is in his Heart; none of his Steps shall slide.

Ps. i. 2. His delight is in the Law of the Lord, and in his Law doth he meditate Day and Night.

Ver. 3. And he shall be like a Tree planted by the Rivers of Water, that bringeth forth his Fruit in his Season: His Leaf also shall not wither, and whatsoever he doth shall prosper.

Ps. lxiii. 5. My Soul shall be satisfied as with Marrow and Fatness, and my Mouth shall praise thee with joyful Lips;

Ver. 6. When I remember thee upon my Bed, and meditate on thee in the Nightwatches.

Ps. ciii. 17. The Mercy of the Lord is from Everlasting to Everlasting, upon them that fear him; and his Righteousness to Children's Children:

Ver. 18. To such as keep his Covenant, and to those that remember his Commandments to do them.

Prov. lv. 26. Ponder the Path of thy Feet, and let all thy Ways be established [*or*, All thy Ways shall be ordered aright]

Prov. xiv. 22. Mercy and Truth shall be to them that devise Good.

Is. lxiv. 5. Thou meetest him that rejoiceth and worketh Righteousness, those that remember thee in thy Ways.

XII. *To* Fasting.

Joel. ii. 15. Blow the Trumpet in *Sion,* sanctify a Fast, call a solemn Assembly.

Ver. 16, Gather the People, sanctify the Congregation; assemble the Elders; gather the Children, and those that suck the Breasts; let the Bridegroom go forth of his Chamber, and the Bride out of her Closet.

Ver. 17. Let the Priests, the Ministers of the Lord, weep between the Porch and the Altar, and let them say. Spare thy People, O Lord, &c.

Ver. 18. Then will the Lord be jealous for his Land, and pity his People.

Matt. vi. 17. Thou, when thou fastest, anoint thine Head, and wash thy Face.

Ver. 18. That thou appear not to Men to fast, but unto thy Father which is in secret; and thy Father which seeth in secret, shall reward thee openly.

XIII. *To* Baptism.

Mark xvi. 16. He that believeth, and is baptized, shall be saved.

Acts ii. 38. Repent, and be baptized, every one of you, in the Name of Jesus Christ, for the Remission of Sins, and ye shall receive the Gift of the Holy Ghost.

Acts xxii. 16. Arise, and be baptized, and wash away thy Sins, calling upon the Name of the Lord.

Rom. vi. 3. Know ye not, that as many of us as were Baptized into Jesus Christ, were baptized into his Death?

Ver. 4. Therefore we are buried with him by Baptism into Death; that like as Christ was raised up from the Dead by the Glory of the Father, even so we also should walk in Newness of Life.

I *Cor.* xii. 13. By one Spirit we are all baptized into one Body, whether we be *Jews* or *Gentiles,* whether we be bond or free.

Gal. iii. 27. For as many of you as have been baptized into Christ, have put on Christ.

Col. ii. 12. Buried with him in Baptism, wherein also you are risen with him through the Faith of the Operation of God, who hath raised him from the Dead.

I *Pet.* iii. 20. Wherein [*i.e.* the Ark] few, that is, Eight Souls, were saved by Water.

Ver. 21. The like Figure whereunto even Baptism doth also now save us (not the putting away of the Filth of the Flesh, but the Answer of a good Conscience towards God) by the Resurrection of Jesus Christ.

XIV. *To the* Lord's Supper.

Matt. xxvi. 26. Jesus took Bread and blessed it, and brake it, and gave it to the Disciples, and said. Take, eat: this is my Body.

Ver. 27. And he took the Cup, and gave Thanks, and gave it to them, saying. Drink ye all of it:

Ver. 28. For this is my Blood of the New Testament, which is shed for many, for the Remission of Sins.

I *Cor.* x. 16. The Cup of Blessing, which we bless, is it not the Communion of the Blood of Christ? The Bread which we break, is it not the Communion of the Body of Christ?

I *Cor.* xii. 13. We have been all made to drink into one Spirit.

John vi. 54. [1] Whoso eateth my Flesh, and drinketh my Blood, hath eternal Life, and I will raise him up at the last Day.

Ver. 55. For my Flesh is Meat indeed, and my Blood is Drink indeed.

Ver. 56. He that eateth my Flesh, and drinketh my Blood, dwelleth in me, and I in him.

Ver. 57. As the living Father hath sent me, and I live by the Father; so he that eateth me, even he shall live by me.

Ver. 63. It is the Spirit that quickeneth, the Flesh profiteth nothing: The Words that I speak unto you, they are Spirit, and they are Life.

Cant. ii. 3. I sat under his Shadow with great Delight, and his Fruit was sweet to my Taste.

Ver. 4. He brought me to the Banqueting House, and his Banner over me was Love.

Cant. v. 1. Eat, O Friends; drink, yea, drink abundantly, O Beloved.

Is. xxv. 6. And in this Mountain shall the Lord of Hosts make unto all People a Feast of fat Things, a Feast of Wines on the Lees, of fat Things full of Marrow, of Wines on the Lees well refined.

XV. *To* Good Discourse.

Prov. xii. 6. The Mouth of the Upright shall deliver them.

Ver. 14. A Man shall be satisfied with Good by the Fruit of his Mouth, and the Recompence of a Man's Hands shall be rendered unto him.

Ver. 18. The Tongue of the Wise is Health.

Prov. xiii. 2. And Man shall eat good by the Fruit of his Mouth.

Prov. xv. 4. A wholesome Tongue is a Tree of Life.

Ver. 23. A Man hath Joy by the Answer of his Mouth, and a Word spoken in due Season, how good is it?

Prov. xvi, 24. Pleasant Words are as an Honey-Comb, sweet to the Soul, and Health to the Bones.

Prov. xviii. 20. A Man's Belly shall be satisfied with the Fruit of his Mouth; and with the Increase of his Lips shall he be filled.

Ver. 21. Death and Life are in the Power of the Tongue; and they that love it shall eat the Fruit thereof.

Mal. iii. 16. Then they that feared the Lord spake often one to another, and the Lord hearkened and heard it; and a Book of Remembrance was written before him, for them that feared the Lord, and that thought upon his Name.

Ver. 17. And they shall be mine, saith the Lord of Hosts, in that Day when I make up my Jewels; and I will spare them as a Man spareth his own Son, that serveth him.

Prov. xiii. 3. He that keepeth his Mouth, keepeth his Life.

Prov. xiv. 3. The Lips of the Wise shall preserve them.

Prov. xxi. 23. Whoso keepeth his Mouth and his Tongue, keepeth his Soul from Trouble.

Matt. xii. 37. By thy Words thou shalt be justified, and by thy Words thou shalt be condemned.

I *Pet.* iii. 10. He that will love Life, and see good Days, let him refrain his Tongue from Evil; and his Lips, that they speak no Guile.

XVI. *To* Watchfulness.

Luke xii. 37. Blessed are those Servants, whom the Lord when he cometh shall find watching: Verily I say unto you, that he shall gird himself, and make them to sit down to Meat, and will come forth and serve them.

Ver. 38. And if he shall come in the second Watch, or come in the third Watch, and find them so, blessed are those Servants.

Rev. xvi. 15. Behold, I come as a Thief; Blessed is he that watcheth, and keepeth his Garments, lest he walk naked, and they see his Shame.

Prov. xxii. 5. Thorns and Snares are in the Way of the Froward: He that doth keep his Soul, shall be far from them,

Prov. xxviii. 14. Happy is the Man that feareth alway; but he that hardeneth his Heart, shall fall into Mischief.

XVII. *To them that keep* Good Company.

Prov. xiii. 20. He that walketh with wise Men, shall be wise: But a Companion of Fools shall be destroyed.

Prov. xxvii, 17. Iron sharpeneth Iron; so a Man sharpeneth the Countenance of his Friend.

Ps. i. 1. Blessed is the Man that walketh not in the Counsel of the Ungodly, nor standeth in the Way of Sinners, nor sitteth in the Seat of the Scornful.

Prov. ix. 6. Forsake the Foolish, and live; and go in the Way of Understanding.

2 *Cor.* vi. 17. Come ye out from among them, and be ye separate, saith the Lord, and touch not the unclean Thing, and I will receive you.

XVIII. *To them that* Perform *their* Oaths.

Ps. xv. 1. Lord, who shall abide in thy Tabernacle? Who shall dwell in thy holy Hill?

Ver. 4. He that sweareth to his own Hurt, and changeth not.

Ps. xxiv. 4. He who hath not lift up his Soul to Vanity, nor sworn deceitfully;
Ver. 5. He shall receive the Blessing from the Lord, and Righteousness from the God of his Salvation.

XIX. *To the* Keeping *of the* Sabbath.

Exod. xx. 11. The Lord blessed the Sabbath-day, and hallowed it.
Is. lvi. 2. Blessed is the Man that doeth this, and the Son of Man that layeth hold on it: that keepeth the Sabbath from polluting it, and keepeth his Hand from doing any Evil.
Ver. 6. The Sons of the Stranger that join themselves to the Lord, to serve him, and to love the Name of the Lord, to be his Servants; every one that keepeth the Sabbath from polluting it, and taketh hold of my Covenant:
Ver. 7. Even them will I bring to my holy Mountain, and make them joyful in my House of Prayer; their Burnt-offerings and their Sacrifices shall be accepted upon mine Altar: For mine House shall be called a House of Prayer unto all People.
Is. lviii. 13. If thou turn away thy P'oot from the Sabbath, from doing thy Pleasure on my holy Day, and call the Sabbath a Delight, the Holy of the Lord, honourable, and shalt honour him, not doing thine own Ways, nor finding thine own Pleasure, nor speaking thine own Words:
Ver. 14. Then shalt thou delight thyself in the Lord, and I will cause thee to ride upon the high Places of the Earth, and feed thee with the Heritage of Jacob thy Father: For the Mouth of the Lord hath spoken it.
Ezek. xx. 20. Hallow my Sabbaths, and they shall be a Sign between me and you, that ye may know that I am the Lord your God.

[1] *Though this be a figurative Expression of Faith in Christ's Death, yet it is applicable to the particular Exercise of it at the Lord's Table.*

Chapter Two - Promises *to* Duties *of the* Second Table

I. *To* Obedience *to* Parents.

EPH. vi. I. Children obey your Parents in the Lord; for this is right.
Ver. 2. Honour thy Father and thy Mother (which is the First Commandment with Promise).
Ver. 3. That it may be well with thee, and that thou mayest live long on the Earth.
Col. iii. 20. Children, obey your Parents in all Things; for this is well pleasing unto the Lord.
I *Tim.* v. 4, But if any Widow have Children, or Nephews, [*Grand-Children*] let them learn to shew Piety at home, and to requite their Parents; for that is good and acceptable before God,

Prov. i. 8, My Son, hear the Instruction of thy Father; and forsake not the Law of thy Mother.

Ver. 9. For they shall be an Ornament of Grace unto thy Head, and Chains about thy Neck.

Prov. vi. 20. My Son, keep thy Father's Commandment, and forsake not the Law of thy Mother.

Ver. 21. Bind them continually upon thine Heart, and tie them about thy Neck.

Ver. 22. When thou goest, it shall lead thee; when thou sleepest it shall keep thee; and when thou wakest, it shall talk with thee.

Jer. xxxv. 18. Thus saith the Lord of Hosts, the God of Israel, Because ye have obeyed the Commandment of *Jonadab* your Father, and kept all his Precepts, and done according to all that he hath commanded you;

Ver. 19. Therefore thus saith the Lord of Hosts, the God of *Israel, Jonadab* shall not want a Man to stand before me for ever.

II. *To* Good Education.

Deut. xi. 19. And ye shall teach them your Children, speaking of them when thou sittest in thine House, and when thou walkest by the Way; when thou liest down, and when thou risest up.

Ver. 20. And thou shalt write them upon the Door-Posts of thine House, and upon thy Gates:

Ver. 21. That your Days may be multiplied, and the Days of your Children in the Land which the Lord sware unto your Fathers to give them, as the Days of Heaven upon the Earth.

Gen. xviii. 19. For I know him [*Abraham*] that he will command his Children and his Household after him, and they shall keep the Way of the Lord, to do Justice and Judgment, that the Lord may bring upon *Abraham* that which he hath spoken of him.

Prov. xxii. 6. Train up a Child in the Way he should go; and when he is old, he will not depart from it.

Prov. xxii. 15. Foolishness is bound in the Heart of a Child; but the Rod of correction shall drive it far from him.

Prov. xxiii. 13. Withhold not Correction from the Child; for if thou beatest him with the Rod, he shall not die.

Ver. 14. Thou shalt beat him with the Rod, and shalt deliver his Soul from Hell.

Prov. xxix. 15. The Rod and Reproof give Wisdom; but a Child left to himself, bringeth his Mother to Shame.

Ver. 17. Correct thy Son, and he shall give thee Rest: Yea, he shall give Delight unto thy Soul.

III. To a Good Wife.

Prov. xi. 16. A gracious Woman retaineth Honour, and strong Men retain Riches.

Prov. xii. 4. A virtuous Woman is a Crown to her Husband; but she that maketh ashamed, is as Rottenness in his Bones.

Prov. xiv. I. Every wise Woman buildeth her House.

Prov. xxxi. 10. Who can find a virtuous Woman? For her Price is far above Rubies.

Ver. 25. Strength and Honour are her Clothing, and she shall rejoice in Time to come.

Ver. 28. Her Children arise up, and call her Blessed; her Husband also, and he praiseth her.

Ver. 30. Favour is deceitful, and Beauty is vain; but a Woman that feareth the Lord, she shall be praised.

Ver. 31. Give her of the Fruit of her Hands, and let her own Works praise her in the Gates.

IV. *To* Faithful Servants.

Prov. xvii. 2. A wise Servant shall have Rule over a Son that causeth Shame; and shall have Part of the Inheritance among the Brethren.

Prov. xiv. 35. The King's Favour is toward a wise Servant.

Prov. xxvii. 18. Whoso keepeth the Fig-tree, shall eat the Fruit thereof: So he that waiteth on his Master, shall be honoured.

Eph. vi. 5. Servants, be obedient to them that are your Masters according to the Flesh, with Fear and Trembling, in Singleness of your Heart, as unto Christ:

Ver. 6. Not with Eye Service, as Menpleasers; but as Servants of Christ, doing the Will of God from the Heart.

Ver. 7. With Good will doing Service, as to the Lord, and not unto Men:

Ver. 8. Knowing, that whatsoever good Thing any Man doeth, the same shall he receive of the Lord, whether he be bond or free.

Col. iii. 22. Servants, obey in all Things your Masters according to the Flesh, &c.

Ver. 24. Knowing that of the Lord ye shall receive the Reward of the Inheritance: For ye serve the Lord Christ.

V. *To* Good Kings *and* Magistrates.

Deut. xvii. 18. And it shall be, when he sitteth upon the Throne of his Kingdom, that he shall write him a Copy of this Law, in a Book out of that which is before the Priests the Levites.

Ver. 19. And it shall be with him, and he shall read therein all the Days of his Life; that he may learn to fear the Lord his God, to keep all the Words of this Law, and these Statutes to do them:

Ver. 20. That his Heart be not lifted up above his Brethren, and that he turn not aside from the Commandment, to the Right Hand, or to the Left; to the End that he may prolong his Days in his Kingdom, he and his Children, in the Midst of Israel.

Prov. xvi. 12. The Throne is established by Righteousness.

Prov. xx. 28. Mercy and Truth preserve the King, and his Throne is upholden by Mercy.

Prov. xxix. 14. The King that faithfully judges the Poor, his Throne shall be established for ever.

Is. xxviii. 6. In that Day shall the Lord of Hosts be for a Spirit of Judgment to them that sit in Judgment, and for Strength to them that turn the Battle at the Gate.

VI. *To* Obedient Subjects.

I *Pet.* ii. 13. Submit yourselves to every Ordinance of Man for the Lord's sake; whether it be to the King, as supreme;

Ver. 14. Or unto Governors, as unto them that are sent by him for the Punishment of Evil-doers, and for the Praise of them that do well.

Ver. 15. For so is the Will of God, that with Well-doing you may put to Silence the Ignorance of Foolish Men.

Eccl. viii. 5. Whoso keepeth the Commandment [*the King's*] shall feel no evil Thing; and a wise Man's Heart discerneth both Time and Judgment.

VII. *To* Faithful Ministers.

Luke xii. 42. Who is that faithful and wise Steward whom his Lord shall make Ruler over his Household, to give them their Portion of Meat in due Season?

Ver. 43. Blessed is that Servant whom his Lord, when he cometh, shall find so doing.

Ver. 44. Of a Truth I say unto you, that he will make him Ruler over all that he hath.

Matt. xxviii. 20. Teaching them to observe all Things whatsoever I have commanded you: And, lo, I am with you alway, even to the End of the World.

I *Tim.* iv. 16. Take heed unto thyself, and to thy Doctrine; continue in them: For in doing this, thou shalt both save thyself, and them that hear thee.

I *Pet.* v. 2. The Elders which are among you, I exhort, Feed the Flock of God which is among you, taking the Oversight thereof, not by Constraint, but willingly; not for filthy Lucre, but of a ready Mind.

Ver. 3. Neither as being Lords over God's Heritage, but being Ensamples to the Flock:

Ver. 4. And when the chief Shepherd shall appear, ye shall receive a Crown of Glory that fadeth not away.

Dan. xii. 3. And they that be wise, shall shine as the Brightness of the Firmament: and they that turn many to Righteousness, as the Stars, for ever and ever.

Is. xxxii. 20. Blessed are ye that sow beside all Waters, that sendeth forth thither the Feet of the Ox and the Ass.

Is. xlix. 4. Then said I, I have laboured in vain, I have spent my Strength for nought, and in vain; yet surely my Judgment is with the Lord, and my Work with my God.

John iv. 36. And he that reapeth, receiveth Wages, and gathereth Fruit unto Life eternal; that both he that soweth, and he that reapeth may rejoice together.

Rev. ii. 1. These Things, saith he that holdeth the Seven Stars in his Right Hand.

Ps. cxxxii. 16. I will cloathe her Priests with Salvation; and her Saints shall shout aloud for Joy.

Jer. xxxi. 14. And I will satiate the Soul of the Priests with Fatness, and my People shall be satisfied with my Goodness, saith the Lord.

Jer. i. 7. The Lord said unto me, Say not, I am a Child: For thou shalt go to all that I send thee; and whatsoever I command thee, thou shalt speak.

Ver. 8. Be not afraid of their Faces, for I am with thee to deliver thee, saith the Lord.

Ver. 19. They shall fight against thee, but shall not prevail against thee; for I am with thee, saith the Lord, to deliver thee.

Jer. xv. 19. Thus saith the Lord: If thou return, then will I bring thee again, and thou shalt stand before me: And if thou take forth the Precious from the Vile, thou shalt be as my Mouth: Let them return unto thee, but return not thou unto them.

Ver. 20. And I will make thee unto this People a fenced brazen Wall, and they shall fight against thee, but they shall not prevail against thee, &c.

Ver. 21. And I will deliver thee out of the Hand of the Wicked; and I will redeem thee out of the Hand of the Terrible.

Jer. xx. 11. The Lord is with me as a mighty terrible one: Therefore my Persecutors shall stumble, and they shall not prevail: They shall be greatly ashamed, for they shall not prosper: Their everlasting Confusion shall never be forgotten.

Ezek. iii. 8. Behold, I have made thy Face strong against their Faces, and thy Forehead strong" against their Foreheads.

Ver. 9. As an Adamant harder than Flint, have I made thy Forehead: Fear them not, neither be dismayed at their Looks, though they be a rebellious House.

Matt. x. 19. And when they shall deliver you up, take no Thought how or what you shall speak; for it shall be given you in that same Hour what ye shall speak.

Ver. 20. For it is not ye that speak, but the Spirit of your Father which speaketh in you.

Luke xxi. 15. I will give you a Mouth, and Wisdom, which all your Adversaries shall not resist.

Deut. x. 9. *Levi* hath no Part nor Inheritance with his Brethren, the Lord is his Inheritance, according as the Lord thy God promised him.

Deut. xxxiii. 11. Bless, Lord, his [*Levi's*] Substance, and accept the Work of his Hands: Smite through the Loins of them that rise against him, and of them that hate him, that they rise not again.

VIII. To them that Receive and Hearken to Ministers.

Matt. x. 40. He that receiveth you, receiveth me; and he that receiveth me, receiveth him that sent me. [So John xiii. 20.]

Ver. 41. He that receiveth a Prophet in the Name of a Prophet, shall receive a Prophet's Reward: And he that receiveth a righteous Man in the Name of a righteous Man, shall receive a righteous Man's Reward.

Luke xi. 16. He that heareth you, heareth me.

2 *Chron.* xx. 20. Believe in the Lord your God, so shall you be established; believe his Prophets, so shall you prosper.

IX. To Love and Unity.

Ps. cxxxiii. 1. Behold, how good and pleasant it is for Brethren to dwell together in Unity!

Ver. 2. It is like the precious Ointment upon the Head, that ran down upon the Beard, even *Aaron's* Beard, that went down to the Skirts of his Garments.

Ver. 3. As the Dew of *Hermon*, and as the Dew that descended upon the Mountains of *Zion*: For there the Lord commanded the Blessing, even Life for evermore.

1 *John* ii. 10. He that loveth his Brother, abideth in the Light, and there is none Occasion of Stumbling in him.

John xiii. 35. By this shall all Men know that ye are my Disciples, if ye have Love one to another.

2 *Cor.* xiii. 11. Be perfect, be of good Comfort, be of one Mind; live in Peace; and the God of Love and Peace shall be with you.

Matt. v. 9. Blessed are the Peace-makers; for they makers. shall be called the Children of God.

Prov. xii. 20. To the Counsellors of Peace is Joy.

I *Pet.* iii. 10. He that will love Life, and seek good Days —

Ver. 11. Let him seek Peace, and ensue it.

I *John* iii. 14. We know that we have passed from Death to Life, because we love the Brethren: He that loveth not his Brother, abideth in Death.

Ver. 18. My little Children, let us not love in Word, neither in Tongue, but in Deed and in Truth.

Ver. 19. And hereby we know that we are of the Truth, and shall assure our Hearts before him.

1 *John* iv. 12. If we love one another, God dwelleth in us, and his Love is perfected in us.

Ps. xv. 1. Lord, who shall abide in thy Tabernacle? Who shall dwell in thy holy Hill?

Ver. 4. He in whose Eyes a vile Person is contemned: But he honoureth them that fear the Lord.

Ps. cxxii. 6. Pray for the Peace of *Jerusalem*: They shall prosper that love thee.

Heb. vi. 10. God is not unrighteous to forget your Work and Labour of Love, which ye have shewed towards his Name, in that ye have ministered to the Saints, and do minister.

Numb. xxiv. 9. Blessed is he that blesseth thee; and cursed is he that curseth thee.

X. *To the* Charitable, *the* Merciful, *and the* Liberal, *to* God's Ministers.

Deut. xv. 10. Thou shalt surely give him [*thy poor Brother*]: And thine Heart shall not be grieved, when thou givest unto him; because that for this Thing the Lord thy God shall bless thee in all thy Works, and in all that thou puttest thine Hand unto.

Ps. xli. 1. Blessed is he that considereth the Poor; the Lord will deliver him in Time of Trouble.

Ver. 2. The Lord will preserve him, and keep him alive, and he shall be blessed upon the Earth; and thou wilt not deliver him unto the Will of his Enemies.

Ver. 3. The Lord will strengthen him upon the Bed of Languishing; thou wilt make all his Bed in his Sickness.

Ps. cxii. 9. He hath dispersed, he hath given to the Poor; his Righteousness endureth for ever; his Horn shall be exalted with Honour.

Ver. 5. A good Man sheweth Favour, and lendeth; he will guide his Affairs with Discretion.

Ver. 6. Surely, he shall not be moved for ever: The Righteous shall be in everlasting Remembrance.

Ps. xxxvii. 25. I have been young, and now am old; yet have I not seen the Righteous forsaken, nor his Seed begging Bread.

Ver. 26. He is ever merciful, and lendeth; and his Seed is blessed.

Prov. xi. 24. There is that scattereth, and yet increaseth; and there is that withholdeth more than is meet, but it tendeth to Poverty.

Ver. 25. The liberal Soul shall be made fat; and he that watereth, shall be watered also himself.

Ver. 27. He that diligently seeketh Good, procureth Favour.

Prov. xiv. 21. He that hath Mercy on the Poor, happy is he.

Prov. xix. 17. He that hath Pity on the Poor, lendeth unto the Lord; and that which he hath given, will He pay him again.

Prov. xxii. 9. He that hath a bountiful Eye, shall be blessed; for he giveth of his Bread to the Poor.

Prov. xxviii. 8. He that by Usury and unjust Gain increaseth his Substance, he shall gather it for him that will pity the Poor.

Prov. xxviii. 27. He that giveth unto the Poor, shall not lack.

Eccl. xi. 1. Cast thy Bread upon the Waters; for thou shalt find it after many Days.

Ver. 2. Give a Portion to seven, and also to Eight; for thou knowest not what Evil shall be upon the Earth.

Is. xxxii. 8. The Liberal deviseth liberal Things, and by liberal Things he shall stand.

Is. lviii. 7. Is it not [*the Fast that I have chosen*] to deal thy Bread to the Hungry, and that thou bring the Poor that are cast out to thy House? When thou seest the Naked, that thou cover him; and that thou hide not thyself from thine own Flesh?

Ver. 8. Then shall thy Light break forth as the Morning, and thine Health shall spring forth speedily: And thy Righteousness shall go before thee; the Glory of the Lord shall be thy Reward.

Ver. 10. If thou draw out thy Soul to the Hungry, and satisfy the afflicted Soul; then shall thy Light rise in Obscurity, and thy Darkness be as the Noonday.

Ver. 11. And the Lord shall guide thee continually, and satisfy thy Soul in Drought, and make fat thy Bones; and thou shalt be like a watered Garden, and like a Spring of Water, whose Waters fail not.

Matt. x. 42. And whosoever shall give to drink unto one of these little ones a Cup of cold Water only, in the Name of a Disciple; verily I say unto you, he shall in no wise lose his Reward.

Matt. xxv. 34. Then shall the King say unto them on his Right Hand, Come ye Blessed of my Father, inherit the Kingdom prepared for you from the Foundation of the World:

Ver. 35. For I was an hungered, and ye gave me Meat: I was thirsty, and ye gave me Drink: I was a Stranger, and ye took me in:

Ver. 36. Naked, and ye cloathed me: I was sick, and ye visited me: I was in Prison, and ye came unto me.

Ver. 40. Verily, I say unto you, Inasmuch as ye have done it unto one of the least of these my Brethren, ye have done it unto me.

Mark x. 21. Go thy Way. sell whatsoever thou hast, and give to the Poor, and thou shalt have Treasure in Heaven.

Luke vi. 38. Give, and it shall be given unto you; good Measure, pressed down, and shaken together, and running over, shall Men give into your Bosom: For with the same Measure that ye mete withal, it shall be measured unto you again.

Luke xi. 41. Give Alms of such Things as ye have; and behold all Things are clean unto you.

Luke xii. 33. Sell that ye have, and give Alms; provide yourselves Bags which wax not old, a Treasure in the Heavens that faileth not, where no Thief approacheth, neither Moth corrupteth.

Luke xvi. 9. And I say unto you, Make to yourselves Friends of the Mammon of Unrighteousness; that when ye fail, they may receive you into everlasting Habitations.

Luke xiv. 13. When thou makest a Feast, call the Poor, the Maimed, the Lame, the Blind;

Ver. 14. And thou shalt be blessed: For they cannot recompense thee; for thou shalt be recompensed at the Resurrection of the Just.

2 *Cor.* ix. 6. He which soweth sparingly, shall reap also sparingly; and he which soweth bountifully, shall reap also bountifully.

Ver. 7. — God loveth a cheerful giver.

2 *Cor.* viii, 12. If there be first a willing Mind, it is accepted according to what a Man hath, and not according to what he hath not.

I *Tim.* vi. 17, 18. Charge them that are rich in this World — that they do good, that they be rich in good Works, ready to distribute, willing to communicate;

Ver. 19. Laying up in store for themselves a good Foundation against the Time to come, that they may lay hold on eternal Life.

Heb. xiii. 16. To do good, and to communicate forget not; for with such Sacrifices God is well pleased.

2 *Cor.* ix. 8. God is able to make ail Grace to abound towards you, that ye always having All-sufficiency in all Things, may abound to every good Work.

Ver. 10. Now he that ministereth Seed to the Sower, both minister Bread for your Food, and multiply your Seed sown, and increase the Fruits of your Righteousness.

Matt. vi. 3. When thou doest Alms, let not thy Left Hand know what thy Right Hand doth:

Ver. 4. That thine Alms may be in secret; and thy Father which seeth in secret, will reward thee openly.

Gal. vi. 6. Let him that is taught in the Word, communicate unto him that teacheth in all good Things.

Ver. 7. Be not deceived; God is not mocked: For whatsoever a Man soweth, that shall he also reap.

Ver. 8. For he that soweth to his Flesh, shall of the Flesh reap Corruption: But he that soweth to the Spirit, shall of the Spirit reap Life everlasting.

Mal. iii. 10. Bring ye all the Tithes into the Store-house, that there may be Meat in my House, and prove me now herewith, saith the Lord of Hosts, if I will not open to you the Windows of Heaven, and pour you out a Blessing, that there shall not be room enough to receive it.

Ver. 11. And I will rebuke the Devourer for your sakes, and he shall not destroy the Fruits of your Ground; neither shall your Vine cast her Fruit before the Time in the Field, saith the Lord of Hosts,

Ver. 12. And all Nations shall call you Blessed; for ye shall be a delightsome Land, saith the Lord of Hosts.

Phil. iv. 17. Not because I desire a Gift; but I desire Fruit that may abound to your Account.

Ver. 18. But I have all, and abound; I am full, having received of *Epaphroditus* the Things which were sent from you, an Odour of a sweet Smell, a Sacrifice acceptable, well pleasing to God.

Ver. 19, But my God shall supply all your Need, according to his Riches in Glory, by Christ Jesus.

Deut. xiv. 29. And the *Levite,* (because he hath no Part nor Inheritance with thee) and the Stranger, and the Fatherless, and the Widow, which are within thy Gates, shall come, and shall eat, and be satisfied, that the Lord thy God may bless thee in all the Work of thine Hand which thou doest.

Prov. iii. 9. Honour the Lord with thy Substance, and with the First Fruits of all thine Increase.

Ver. 10. So shall thy Barns be filled with Plenty, and thy Presses shall burst out with new Wine.

Matt. v. 7. Blessed are the Merciful, for they shall obtain Mercy.

Ps. xviii. 25. With the Merciful thou wilt shew thyself merciful.

Prov. iii. 3. Let not Mercy and Truth forsake thee; bind them about thy Neck, write them upon the Table of thine Heart.

Ver. 4. So shalt thou find Favour and good Understanding in the Sight of God and Man.

Prov. xi. 17. The merciful Man doeth good to his own Soul; but he that is cruel, troubleth his own Flesh.

Deut. xxiv. 12. If the Man be poor, thou shalt not sleep with his Pledge.

Ver. 13. In any Case thou shalt deliver him the Pledge again when the Sun goeth down, that he may sleep in his own Raiment, and bless thee; and it shall be Righteousness unto thee before the Lord thy God.

XI. *To the Giving and Receiving of* Reproofs.

Prov. xxiv. 25. To them that rebuke him [*the Wicked*] shall be Delight, and a good Blessing shall come upon them.

Prov. xxviii. 23. He that rebuketh a Man, afterwards shall find more Favour than he that flattereth with his Tongue.

Prov. xiii. 18. Poverty and shame shall be to him that refuseth Instruction; but he that regardeth Reproof, shall be honoured.

Prov. xv. 31. The Ear that heareth the Reproof of Life, abideth among the wise.

Ver. 32. He that refuseth Instruction, despiseth his own Soul; but he that heareth Reproof, getteth Understanding.

Prov. xxv. 12. As an Ear-ring of Gold, and an Ornament of fine Gold, so is a wise Reprover upon an obedient Ear.

XII. To Forgiving Injuries.

Prov. xx. 22. Say not thou, I will recompense Evil; but wait on the Lord, and he shall save thee.

Prov. xxv. 21. If thine Enemy be hungry, give him Bread to eat; and if he be thirsty, give him Water to drink:

Ver. 22. For thou shalt heap Coals of Fire upon his Head, and the Lord shall reward thee. *Rom.* xii. 20.

Matt. v. 44. Love your Enemies; bless them that curse you; do good to them that hate you; and pray for them which despitefully use you, and persecute you:

Ver. 45. That ye may be the Children of your Father which is in Heaven; for he maketh his Sun to rise on the Evil and on the Good, and sendeth Rain on the Just and on the Unjust.

Matt. vi. 14. If ye forgive Men their Trespasses, your heavenly Father will also forgive you.

Mark xi. 25. And when ye stand praying, forgive, if ye have ought against any; that your Father also which is in Heaven, may forgive your Trespasses.

Luke vi. 35. Love ye your Enemies, and do good, and lend, hoping for nothing again; and your Reward shall be great, and ye shall be the Children of the Highest: For he is kind unto the Unthankful, and to the Evil.

Ver. 37. Forgive, and ye shall be forgiven.

I *Pet.* iii. 9. Not rendering Evil for Evil, or Railing for Railing; but contrariwise. Blessing: Knowing that ye are thereunto called, that ye should inherit a Blessing.

XIII. To Chastity *and* Purity.

Ezek. xviii. 5. If a Man be just, and do that which is lawful and Right;

Ver. 6. — And hath not defiled his Neighbour's Wife, neither hath come near to a menstruous Woman;

Ver. 9. Hath walked in my Statutes, and hath kept my Judgments, to deal truly; He is just, he shall surely live, saith the Lord.

Matt. v. 8. Blessed are the Pure in Heart; for they shall see God.

Ps. xxiv. 3. Who shall ascend into the Hill of the Lord? and who shall stand in his holy Place?

Ver. 4. He that hath clean Hands, and a pure Heart.

Ps. xviii. 26. With the Pure thou wilt shew thyself pure.

Ps. lxxiii. 1. Truly God is good to *Israel,* even to such as are of a clean Heart.

2 *Tim.* ii. 21. If a Man therefore purge himself from these, he shall be a Vessel unto Honour, sanctified and meet for the Master's Use, and prepared unto every good Work.

Tit i. 15. Unto the Pure all Things are pure.

XIV. *To* Diligence.

Prov. x. 4. The Hand of the Diligent maketh rich.

Prov. xii. 24. The Hand of the Diligent shall bear Rule; but the Slothful shall be under Tribute.

Ver. 27. The Substance of a diligent Man is precious.

Ver. 11. He that tilleth his Land shall be satisfied with Bread.

Prov. xiii. 4. The Soul of the Sluggard desireth, and hath nothing; but the Soul of the Diligent shall be made fat.

Ver. 11. Wealth gotten by Vanity shall be diminished; but he that gathereth by Labour shall increase.

Prov. xiv. 23. In all Labour there is Profit; but the Talk of the Lips tendeth only to Penury.

Prov. xxi. 5. The Thoughts of the Diligent tend only to Plenteousness; but of every one that is hasty, only to Want.

Prov. xxii. 29. Seest thou a Man diligent in his Business; he shall stand before Kings, he shall not stand before mean Men.

Prov. xxviii. 19. He that tilleth his Land, shall have Plenty of Bread; but he that followeth after vain Persons, shall have Poverty enough.

Matt. xxv. 23. Well done, good and faithful Servant; thou hast been faithful over a few Things, I will make thee Ruler over many Things: Enter thou into the Joy of thy Lord.

Ver. 29. Unto every one that hath, shall be given, and he shall have abundance. *Matt.* xiii. 12.

Prov. xx. 13. Love not Sleep, lest thou come to Poverty; open thine eyes, and thou shalt be satisfied with Bread.

XV. *To the* Just *and* Honest.

Deut. xvi. 20. That which is altogether just shalt thou follow, that thou mayest live, and inherit the Land which the Lord thy God giveth thee.

Deut. xxv. 15. Thou shalt have a perfect and just Weight; a perfect and just Measure shalt thou have; that thy Days may be lengthened in the Land which the Lord thy God giveth thee.

Prov. xi. 1. A false Balance is an Abomination unto the Lord; but a just Weight is his Delight.

Prov. xv. 27. He that is greedy of Gain, troubleth his own House; but he that hateth Gifts, shall live.

Prov. xvi. 8. Better is a little with Righteousness, than great Revenues without Right.

Prov. xxviii. 20. A faithful Man abounds with Blessings; but he that maketh haste to be rich, shall not be innocent.

Prov. xxi. 3. To do Justice and Judgment, is more acceptable to the Lord, than Sacrifice.

Prov. xii. 21. There shall no Evil happen to the Just; but the Wicked shall be filled with Mischief.

Is. xxxiii. 15. He that walketh righteously, and speaketh uprightly; he that despiseth the gain of Oppressions, that shaketh his Hands from holding of Bribes, that stoppeth his Ears from hearing of Blood, and shutteth his Eyes from seeing Evil:

Ver. 16. He shall dwell on high; his Place of Defence shall be the Munition of Rocks: Bread shall be given him, his Waters shall be sure.

Is. lvi. 1. Thus saith the Lord, Keep ye Judgment, and do Justice; for my Salvation is near to come, and my Righteousness to be revealed.

Ver. 2. Blessed is the Man that doth this, and the Son of Man that layeth hold on it.

Ezek. xviii. 5. If a Man be just, and do that which is lawful and rig-ht;

Ver. 7. And hath not oppressed any, but hath restored to the Debtor his Pledge; hath spoiled none by Violence; hath given his Bread to the Hungry, and hath covered the Naked with a Garment:

Ver. 8. He that hath not given forth upon Usury, neither hath taken any Increase; that hath withdrawn his Hand from Iniquity; hath executed true Judgment between Man and Man;

Ver. 9. Hath walked in my Statutes, and hath kept my Judgments, to deal truly: He is just, he shall surely live, saith the Lord.

Ps. xv. 5. He that putteth not out his Money to Usury, nor taketh a Reward against the Innocent: He that doth these Things, shall never be moved.

XVI. *To* Truth.

Ps. xv. 1. Lord, who shall abide in thy Tabernacle? Who shall dwell in thy holy Hill?

Ver. 2. — He that speaketh the Truth in his Heart.

Prov. xii. 19. The Lip of Truth shall be established for ever; but a lying Tongue is but for a Moment.

Ver. 22. Lying Lips are Abomination to the Lord; but they that deal truly, are his Delight.

I *Pet.* iii. 10. He that will love Life, and see good Days, let him refrain his Tongue from Evil, and his Lips that they speak no Guile. *Ps.* xxxiv. 12, 13.

XVII. *To* Candour.

Matt. vii. 1. Judge not, that ye be not judged.

Ver. 2. For with what Judgment ye judge, ye shall be judged; and with what Measure ye mete, it shall be measured to you again.

Ps. xv. 1. Lord, who shall dwell, &c.

Ver. 3. He that backbiteth not with his Tongue, nor doth Evil to his Neighbour, nor taketh up a Reproach against his Neighbour.

XVIII. To Contentment and Mortification.

Prov. xiv. 30. A sound Heart is the Life of the Flesh, but Envy the Rottenness of the Bones.

Prov. xv. 15. All the Days of the Afflicted are evil; but he that is of a merry Heart hath a continual Feast.

Prov. xvii. 22. A merry Heart doeth good like a Medicine; but a broken Spirit drieth the Bones.

Prov. xxiii. 17. Let not thine Heart envy Sinners; but be thou in the Fear of the Lord all the Day long.

Ver. 18. For surely there is an End, and thine Expectation shall not be cut off.

I *Tim.* vi. 6. Godliness with Contentment is great Gain.

Heb. xiii. 5. Let your Conversation be without Covetousness, and be content with such Things as you have: For he hath said, I will never leave thee nor forsake thee.

Rom. viii. 13. If ye, through the Spirit, do mortify the Deeds of the Body, ye shall live.

Matt. v. 29. If thy Right Eye offend thee, pluck it out, and cast it from thee; for it is profitable for thee, that one of thy Members should perish, and not that thy whole Body should be cast into Hell.

Ver. 20. And if thy Right Hand offend thee, cut it off, and cast it from thee; for it is profitable for thee, that one of thy Members should perish, and not that thy whole Body should be cast into Hell.

Rom. viii. 6. To be carnally-minded, is Death; but to be spiritually-minded, is Life and Peace.

Chapter Three - Promises *to* Duties *belonging to* Both Tables

I. *To the* Meek, Humble, Contrite.

Psalm xxii. 26. The Meek shall eat, and be satisfied: They shall praise the Lord that seek him; your Heart shall live for ever.

Ps. xxv. 9. The Meek will he guide in Judgment, and the Meek will he teach his Way.

Ps. xxxvii. 11. The Meek shall inherit the Earth, and shall delight themselves in the Abundance of Peace.

Matt. v. 5. Blessed are the Meek, for they shall inherit the Earth.

Ps. cxlvii. 6. The Lord lifteth up the Meek: He casteth the Wicked down to the Ground.

Ps. cxlix. 4. The Lord taketh Pleasure in his People; he will beautify the Meek with his Salvation.

Zeph. ii. 3. Seek ye the Lord, all ye Meek of the Earth, which have wrought his Judgment; seek Righteousness, seek Meekness: It may be ye shall be hid in the Day of the Lord's Anger.

Is. xi. 4. With Righteousness shall he judge the Poor, and reprove with Equity for the Meek of the Earth.

Is. xxix. 19. The Meek shall increase their Joy in the Lord, and the Poor among Men shall rejoice in the Holy One of *Israel*.

I *Pet.* iii. 3. Whose adorning, let it not be that outward adorning of plaiting the Hair, and of wearing the Gold, or of putting on of Apparel:

Ver. 4. But let it be the hidden Man of the Heart, in that which is not corruptible; even the Ornament of a meek and quiet Spirit, which is in the Sight of God of great Price.

Prov. xiv. 29. He that is slow to Wrath, is of great Understanding.

Prov. xv. 18. He that is slow to Anger, appeaseth Strife.

Ver. 1. A soft Answer turneth away Wrath.

Prov. xvi. 32. He that is slow to Anger, is better than the Mighty; and he that ruleth his Spirit, than he that taketh a City.

Prov. xix. 11. The Discretion of a Man deferreth his Anger, and it is his Glory to pass over a Transgression.

Prov. xx. 3. It is an Honour to a Man to cease from Strife.

Job xxii. 29. He shall save the humble Person.

Ps. ix. 12. He forgetteth not the Cry of the Humble.

Ps. x. 17. Lord, thou hast heard the Desire of the Humble.

Ps. cxxxviii. 6. Though the Lord be high, yet hath he Respect unto the Lowly: But the Proud he knoweth afar off

Prov. iii. 34. Surely, he scorneth the Scorners; but he giveth Grace to the Humble.

Jam. iv. 6. Wherefore he saith, He resisteth the Proud, but giveth Grace unto the Humble, i *Pet.* v. 5.

Prov. xi. 2. When Pride cometh, then cometh Shame; but with the Lowly is Wisdom.

Prov. xv. 33. The Fear of the Lord is the Instruction of Wisdom; and before Honour is Humility.

Prov. xviii. 12. Before Destruction, the Heart of Man is haughty; and before Honour is Humility.

Prov. xxix. 23. A Man's Pride shall bring him low; but Honour shall uphold the Humble in Spirit.

Prov. xvi. 19. Better is it to be of an humble Spirit with the Lowly; than to divide the Spoil with the Proud.

Prov. xxii. 4. By Humility, and the Fear of the Lord, are Riches, Honour, and Life.

Matt, xxiii. 12. Whosoever shall exalt himself, shall be abased; and he that shall humble himself, shall be exalted. Luke xviii. 14.

Matt. xviii. 4. Whosoever shall humble himself as this little Child, the same is greatest in the Kingdom of Heaven.

Ps. xxxiv. 18. The Lord is nigh unto them that are of a broken Heart, and saveth such as be of a contrite Spirit.

Ps. li. 17. The Sacrifices of God are a broken Spirit; a broken and a contrite Heart, O God, thou wilt not despise.

Ps. xlvii. 3. He healeth the broken in Heart, and bindeth up their Wounds,

Eccl. vii. 3. Sorrow is better than Laughter; for by the Sadness of the Countenance the Heart is made better.

Is. lvii. 15. Thus saith the High and Lofty One that inhabiteth Eternity, whose Name is HOLY, I dwell in the high and holy Place; with him also that is of a contrite and humble Spirit; to revive the Spirit of the Humble, and to revive the Heart of the Contrite ones.

Is. lxvi. 2. To this Man will I look, even to him that is of a poor and contrite Spirit, and trembleth at my Word.

Matt. v. 3. Blessed are the Poor in Spirit: for theirs is the Kingdom of Heaven.

Ver. 4. Blessed are they that mourn: for they shall be comforted.

II. *To them that* Suffer *for* Righteousness' *Sake.*

Matt. v. 10. Blessed are they which are persecuted for Righteousness' sake: for theirs is the Kingdom of Heaven.

Ver. 11. Blessed are ye when Men shall revile you, and persecute you, and shall say all manner of Evil against you falsely, for my sake.

Ver. 12. Rejoice, and be exceeding glad, for great is your Reward in Heaven: For so persecuted they the Prophets which were before you.

Matt. x. 39. He that findeth his Life, shall lose it; and he that loseth his Life for my sake, shall find it.

Matt. xix. 29. Every one that hath forsaken Houses, or Brethren, or Sisters, or Father, or Mother, or Wife, or Children, or Lands, for my Name's sake, shall receive an hundred-fold, and shall inherit everlasting Life.

2 *Cor.* iv, 9. Persecuted, but not forsaken.

2 *Tim.* ii. 12. If we suffer, we shall also reign with him.

Rom. viii. 17. If so be that we suffer with him, that we may be also glorified together.

Ver. 35. Who shall separate us from the Love of Christ? Shall Tribulation, or Distress, or Persecution, or Famine, or Nakedness, or Peril, or the Sword?

Ver. 36. (As it is written, For thy Sake we are killed all the Day long; we are accounted as Sheep for the Slaughter).

Ver. 37, Nay, in all these Things we are more than Conquerors through him that loved us.

Heb. x. 34. For ye had Compassion of me in my Bonds, and took joyfully the spoiling of your Goods, knowing in yourselves, that ye have a better and an enduring Substance.

Ver. 35. Cast not away therefore your Confidence, which hath great Recompense of Reward.

I *Pet.* iii. 14. If ye suffer for Righteousness' sake, happy are ye: And be not afraid of their Terror, neither be troubled;

Ver. 17. For it is better, if the Will of God be so, that ye suffer for Welldoing, than for Evil-doing.

I *Pet.* iv. 12. Beloved, think it not strange concerning the fiery Trial, which is to try you, as though some strange Thing happened unto you:

Ver. 13. But rejoice, inasmuch as ye are Partakers of Christ's Sufferings; that when his Glory shall be revealed, ye may be glad also with exceeding Joy.

Ver. 14. If ye be reproached for the Name of Christ, happy are ye; for the Spirit of Glory and of God resteth upon you: On their Part he is evil spoken of, but on your Part he is glorified.

Is. lxvi. 5. Hear the Word of the Lord, ye that tremble at his Word: Your Brethren that hated you, that cast you out for my Name's sake, said, Let the Lord be glorified: But ye shall appear to your Joy, and they shall be ashamed.

Luke vi, 22. Blessed are ye, when Men shall hate you, and when they shall separate you from their Company, and shall reproach you, and cast out your Name as evil, for the Son of Man's sake.

Ver. 23. Rejoice ye in that Day, and leap for Joy, for behold, your Reward is great in Heaven.

III. *To* Patience *and* Submission.

Lam. iii. 26. It is good that a Man should both hope, and quietly wait for the Salvation of the Lord.

Ver. 27. It is good for a Man that he bear the Yoke in his Youth.

Ver. 28. He sitteth alone and keepeth Silence, because he hath borne it upon him.

Ver. 29. He putteth his Mouth in the Dust, if so be there may be Hope.

Ver. 31. For the Lord will not cast off for ever.

Heb. x. 35. Cast not away your Confidence, which hath great Recompence of Reward.

Ver. 36. For ye have need of Patience, that after ye have done the Will of God, ye might receive the Promise.

Ver. 37. For yet a little while, and he that shall come will come, and will not tarry.

Heb. vi. 12. That ye be not slothful, but Followers of them, who through Faith and Patience inherit the Promises.

Jam. i. 2. My Brethren, count it all Joy when ye fall into divers Temptations:

Ver. 3. Knowing this, that the Trying of your Faith worketh Patience.

Ver. 4. But let Patience have her perfect Work, that ye may be perfect and entire, wanting nothing.

Ver. 12. Blessed is the Man that endureth Temptation; for when he is tried, he shall receive the Crown of Life, which the Lord hath promised to them that love him.

Rom. v. 3. We glory in Tribulation, knowing that Tribulation worketh Patience;

Ver. 4. And Patience worketh Experience; and Experience, Hope.

Prov. x. 28. The Hope of the Righteous shall be Gladness.

I *Pet.* v. 6. Humble yourselves under the mighty Hand of God, that ye may be exalted in due Time.

Jam. iv. 10. Humble yourselves in the Sight of the Lord, and he shall lift you up. *Jam.* v. 7. Be patient. Brethren, unto the Coming of the Lord. Behold, the Husbandman waiteth for the precious Fruit of the Earth, and hath long Patience for it, until he receive the early and the latter Rain.

Ver. 8. Be ye also patient; stablish your Hearts: For the Coming of the Lord draweth nigh.

Ver. 11. Behold, we count them happy which endure. Ye have heard of the Patience of *Job*, and have seen the End of the Lord, that the Lord is very pitiful, and of tender Mercy.

I *Pet.* ii. 20. If when ye do well, and suffer for it, ye take it patiently, this is acceptable with God.

IV. *To* Perseverance.

Matt. x. 22. He that endureth to the End shall be saved. *Chap.* xxiv. 13.

John viii. 31, If ye continue in my Word, then are ye my Disciples indeed.

Ver. 32. And ye shall know the Truth, and the Truth shall make you free.

John xv. 7. If ye abide in me, and my Words abide in you, ye shall ask what ye will, and it shall be done unto you.

I *Cor.* xv. 58. My beloved Brethren, be ye stedfast, unmoveable, always abounding in the Work of the Lord, forasmuch as ye know that your Labour is not in vain in the Lord.

Gal. vi. 9. Let us not be weary in Welldoing; for in due Season we shall reap, if we faint not.

Heb. iii. 14. We are made Partakers of Christ, if we hold the Beginning of our Confidence stedfast unto the End.

Heb. x. 23. Let us hold fast the Profession of our Faith without wavering, for he is faithful that promised.

Ver. 35. Cast not away your Confidence, which hath great Recompence of Reward.

1 *John* ii. 24. Let that abide in you which ye have heard from the Beginning. If that which ye have heard from the Beginning shall remain in you, ye shall also continue in the Son, and in the Father.

Ver. 28. And now, little Children, abide in him, that when he shall appear, we may have Confidence, and not be ashamed before him at his Coming.

2 *John* 8. Look to yourselves, that we lose not the Things which we have wrought, but that we receive a full Reward.

Ver. 9. Whosoever transgresseth, and abideth not in the Doctrine of Christ, hath not God: He that abideth in the Doctrine of Christ, he hath both the Father and the Son.

Rev. ii. 10. Be thou faithful unto Death, and I will give thee a Crown of Life.

Rev. ii. 7. To him that overcometh, will I give to eat of the Tree of Life, which is in the midst of the Paradise of God.

Ver. 11. He that overcometh, shall not be hurt of the second Death.

Ver. 17. To him that overcometh, will I give to eat of the hidden Manna; and will give him a white Stone, and in the Stone a new Name written, which no Man knoweth, saving he that receiveth it.

Ver. 26. And he that overcometh, and keepeth my Words unto the End, to him will I give Power over the Nations.

Ver. 27. And he shall rule them with a Rod of Iron: As the Vessels of a Potter shall they be broken to shivers (even as I received of my Father.)

Ver. 28. And I will give him the Morning Star.

Rev. iii. 5. He that overcometh, the same shall be cloathed in white Raiment, and I will not blot out his Name out of the Book of Life; but I will confess his Name before my Father, and before his Angels.

Ver. 12. Him that overcometh will I make a Pillar in the Temple of my God, and he shall go no more out: And I will write upon him the Name of my God, and the Name of the City of my God, which is *New Jerusalem,* which cometh down out of Heaven from my God; and I will write upon him my New Name.

Ver. 21. To him that overcometh, will I grant to sit with me in my Throne; even as I also overcame, and am set down with my Father in his Throne.

Rev. xxi. 7. He that overcometh, shall inherit all Things; and I will be his God, and he shall be my Son.

An Appendix of Promises Relating to the State *of the* Church

I. *Of the* Enlargement of the Church, *and the* Spreading *of the* Gospel, *and* Kingdom *of* CHRIST *through the World*

Psal. ii. 8. Ask of me, and I will give thee the Heathen for thine Inheritance, and the uttermost Parts of the Earth for thy Possession.

Ver. 9. Thou shalt break them with a Rod of Iron; thou shalt dash them in pieces like a Potter's Vessel.

Ps. xxii. 27. All the Ends of the Earth shall remember, and turn unto the Lord; and all the Kindreds of the Nations shall worship before him.

Ver. 28. For the Kingdom is the Lord's, and he is the governor among the Nations.

Ps. lxvii. 2. That thy Way may be known upon Earth, thy saving Health among all Nations.

Ver. 7. God shall bless us, and all the Ends of the Earth shall fear him.

Ps. lxviii. 31. Princes shall come out of *Egypt; Ethiopia* shall soon stretch out her Hands unto God.

Ps. lxxii. 8. He shall have Dominion from Sea to Sea, and from the River unto the Ends of the Earth.

Ver. 11. Yea, all Kings shall fall down before him; all Nations shall serve him.

Ver. 17. His name shall endure for ever; his Name shall be continued as long as the Sun; and Men shall be blessed in him; all Nations shall call him blessed.

Ver. 19. Let the whole Earth be filled with his Glory.

Ps. lxxxvi. 9. All Nations whom thou hast made, shall come and worship before thee, O Lord, and shall glorify thy Name.

Ps. cii. 15. The Heathen shall fear the Name of the Lord, and all the Kings of the Earth thy Glory.

Ver. 16. When the Lord shall build up *Zion,* he shall appear in his Glory.

Ps. cx. 3. Thy People shall be willing in the Day of thy Power, in the Beauties of Holiness from the Womb of the Morning: thou hast the Dew of thy Youth.

Is. ii. 2. And it shall come to pass in the last Days that the Mountain of the Lord's House shall be established in the Top of the Mountains, and shall be exalted above the Hills; and all Nations shall flow unto it.

Ver. 3. And many People shall go and say, Come ye, and let us go up to the Mountain of the Lord, to the House of the God of *Jacob;* and he will teach us of his Ways, and we will walk in his Paths: For out of *Zion* shall go forth the Law, and the Word of the Lord from *Jerusalem*. *Mic.* iv. 1, 2,

Is. xi. 10. In that Day there shall be a Root of *Jesse,* which shall stand for an Ensign of the People; to it shall the *Gentiles* seek, and his rest shall be glorious.

Is. xix. 21. And the Lord shall be known to *Egypt,* and the *Egyptians* shall know the Lord in that Day, and shall do Sacrifice and Oblation; yea, they shall vow a Vow unto the Lord, and perform it.

Ver. 24. In that Day shall *Israel* be the Third with *Egypt,* and with *Assyria,* even a Blessing in the midst of the Land.

Ver. 25. Whom the Lord of Hosts shall bless, saying, Blessed be *Egypt* my People, and *Assyria* the Work of mine Hands, and *Israel* mine Inheritance. See *Ver.* 18, 19, 20, 22, 23.

Is. xxiii. 18. And her [*Tyre's*] Merchandize and her Hire, shall be Holiness unto the Lord: It shall not be treasured nor laid up; for her Merchandize shall be for them that dwell before the Lord, to eat sufficiently, and for durable Cloathing.

Is. xxvii. 6. He shall cause them that come to *Jacob* to take Root; *Israel* shall blossom and bud, and fill the Face of the World with Fruit.

Is. xl. 3. The Voice of him that crieth in the Wilderness, Prepare ye the Way of the Lord, make straight in the Desert a Highway for our God.

Ver. 4. Every Valley shall be exalted, and every Mountain and Hill shall be brought low; and the Crooked shall be made straight, and the rough Places plain. *Ver.* 5. And the Glory of the Lord shall be revealed, and all Flesh shall see it together: For the Mouth of the Lord hath spoken it.

Is. xlii. 1. Behold my Servant, whom I uphold; mine Elect, in whom my Soul delighteth: I have put my Spirit upon him; he shall bring forth Judgment to the *Gentiles.*

Ver. 4. He shall not fail, nor be discouraged, till he have set Judgment in the Earth; and the Isles shall wait for his Law.

Ver. 6. I, the Lord, have called thee in Righteousness, and will hold thine Hand, and will keep thee, and give thee for a Covenant of the People, for a Light of the Gentiles.

Ver. 7. To open the blind Eyes, to bring out the Prisoners from the Prison, and them that sit in Darkness out of the Prison-house.

Is. xlv. 23. I have sworn by myself, the Word is gone forth out of my Mouth in Righteousness, and shall not return. That unto me every Knee shall bow, every Tongue shall swear.

Ver. 24. Surely, shall one say, in the Lord have I Righteousness and Strength: Even to him shall men come, and all that are incensed against him shall be ashamed. *See Ver.* 14.

Is. xlix. 6. And he said, It is a light Thing that thou shouldst be my Servant, to raise up the Tribes of *Jacob,* and to restore the Preserved of *Israel:* I will also give thee a Light to the *Gentiles,* that thou mayest be my Salvation unto the Ends of the Earth.

Ver. 12. Behold, these shall come from far; and lo, these from the North, and from the West, and these from the Land of *Sinim.*

Ver. 18. Lift up thine Eyes round about, and behold, all these gather themselves together, and come to thee: As I live, saith the Lord, thou shalt surely cloath thee with them all, as with an Ornament, and bind them on thee as a Bride doth.

Ver. 20. The Children which thou shalt have after thou hast lost the other, shall say again in thine Ears, The Place is too strait for me; give place, that I may dwell. *See Ver.* 8, 9, 11, 19, 21, 22. And *Chap.* lx. 4.

Is. li. 4. Hearken unto me, my People, and give Ear unto me, O my Nation; for a Law shall proceed from me, and I will make my Judgment to rest for a Light of the People.

Ver. 5. My Righteousness is near, my Salvation is gone forth, and mine Arms shall judge the People: The Isles shall wait upon me, and on mine Arm shall they trust.

Ver. 16. I have put my Words in thy Mouth, and have covered thee in the Shadow of mine Hand, that I may plant the Heavens, and lay the Foundations of the Earth, and say to *Zion,* Thou art my People.

Is. lii. 10. The Lord hath made bare his holy Arm in the Eyes of all Nations, and all the Ends of the Earth shall see the Salvation of our God.

Is. liii. 10. When thou shah make his Soul an Offering for Sin, he shall see his Seed, he shall prolong his Days, and the Pleasure of the Lord shall prosper in his Hand.

Ver. 11. He shall see of the Travail of his Soul, and shall be satisfied: By his Knowledge shall my righteous Servant justify many; for he shall bear their Iniquities.

Ver. 12, Therefore will I divide him a Portion with the Great, and he shall divide the Spoil with the Strong.

Is. liv. 1. Sing, O Barren, thou that didst not bear; break forth into Singing, and cry aloud, thou that didst not travail with Child; for more are the Children of the Desolate, than the Children of the married Wife, saith the Lord.

Ver. 2. Enlarge the Place of thy Tent, and let them stretch forth the Curtains of thine Habitations; spare not, lengthen thy Cords, and strengthen thy Stakes.

Ver. 3. For thou shalt break forth on the Right Hand and on the Left, and thy Seed shall inherit the *Gentiles,* and make the desolate Cities to be inhabited.

Is. lv. 4. Behold I have given him for a Witness to the People; a Leader and Commander to the People.

Ver. 5. Behold, thou shalt call a Nation that thou knowest not: and Nations that knew not thee, shall run unto thee, because of the Lord thy God, and for the Holy One of *Israel;* for he hath glorified thee.

Is. lix. 19. So shall they fear the Name of the Lord from the West, and his Glory from the Rising of the Sun: When the Enemy shall come in like a Flood, the Spirit of the Lord shall lift up a Standard against him.

Ver. 20. And the Redeemer shall come to *Zion,* and unto them that turn from Transgression in *Jacob,* saith the Lord.

Is. ix. 3. The *Gentiles* shall come to thy Light, and Kings to the Brightness of thy Rising.

Ver. 8. Who are these that fly as a Cloud, and as the Doves to their Windows?

Ver. 9. Surely the Isles shall wait for me, and the Ships of *Tarshish* first, to bring thy Sons from far, their Silver and their Gold with them, unto the Name of the Lord thy God, and unto the Holy One of *Israel,* because he hath glorified thee.

Ver. 10. And the Sons of Strangers shall build thy Walls, &c. See *Ver.* 4, 5, 6, 7, 11, 16.

Is. lxv. 17. Behold, I create New Heavens and a New Earth, and the former shall not be remembered, nor come into mind.

Is. lxvi. 8. Who hath heard such a Thing? Who hath seen such Things? Shall the Earth be made to bring forth in one Day? Or shall a Nation be born at once? for as soon as *Zion* travailed, she brought forth her Children.

Ver. 9. Shall I bring to the Birth, and not cause to bring forth, saith the Lord: Shall I cause to bring forth, and shut the Womb? saith thy God.

Ver. 18. It shall come, that I will gather all Nations and Tongues, and they shall see my Glory.

Ver. 19. And I will set a Sign among them, and I will send those that escape of them unto the Nations, to *Tarshish, Pul,* and *Lud,* that draw the Bow, to *Tubal,* and *Javan,* to the Isles afar off, that have not heard my Fame, neither have seen my Glory; and they shall declare my Glory among the *Gentiles.*

Ver. 20. And they shall bring all your Brethren for an Offering unto the Lord out of all Nations —

Ver. 21. And I will also take of them for Priests and for *Levites,* saith the Lord.

Ver. 23. And it shall come to pass, that from one New Moon to another, and from one Sabbath to another, shall all Flesh come to worship before me, saith the Lord.

Dan. ii. 44. And in the Days of these Kings shall the God of Heaven set up a Kingdom, which shall never be destroyed: And the Kingdom shall not be left to other People; but it shall break in pieces and consume all these Kingdoms, and it shall stand for ever.

Dan. vii. 13. And I saw in the Night Visions, and behold, one like the Son of Man came with the Clouds of Heaven, and came to the Ancient of Days, and they brought him near before him.

Ver. 14. And there was given him Dominion and Glory, and a Kingdom, that all People, Nations, and Languages, should serve him.

Ver. 27. And the Kingdom, and Dominion, and the Greatness of the Kingdom under the whole Heaven, shall be given to the People of the Saints of the Most High, whose Kingdom is an everlasting Kingdom, and all Dominions shall serve and obey him.

Amos ix. 11. In that Day will I raise up the Tabernacle of *David* that is fallen, and close up the Breaches thereof; and I will raise up his Ruins, and I will build it as in the Days of old:

Ver. 12. That they may possess the Remnant of *Edom* [*or*, That the Residue of Men might seek after the Lord, *Acts* xv. 17,] and of all the Heathen which are called by my Name, saith the Lord that doth this.

Zech. ii. 10. Sing and rejoice, O Daughter of Zion; for lo I come, and I will dwell in the midst of thee, saith the Lord.

Ver. 11. And many Nations shall be joined to the Lord in that Day, and shall be my People; and I will dwell in the midst of thee, and thou shalt know that the Lord of Hosts hath sent me unto thee.

Zech. vi. 15. And they that are far off, shall come and build in the Temple of the Lord.

Zech. viii. 21. And the Inhabitants of one City shall go to another, saying, Let us go speedily to pray before the Lord, and to seek the Lord of Hosts; I will go also.

Ver. 22. Yea, many People, and strong Nations shall come to seek the Lord of Hosts in *Jerusalem*, and to pray before the Lord.

Ver. 23. Thus saith the Lord of Hosts, In those Days it shall come to pass, that Ten Men shall take hold out of all Languages of the Nations, even shall take hold of the Skirt of him that is a *Jew*, saying, We will go with you; for we have heard that God is with you.

Zech. xiv. 9. And the Lord shall be King over all the Earth: In that Day shall there be one Lord, and his Name one.

Mal. i. 11. From the Rising of the Sun, even to the Going down of the same, my Name shall be great among the *Gentiles,* and in every Place Incense shall be offered unto my Name, and a pure Offering; for my Name shall be great among the *Heathen,* saith the Lord of Hosts.

Matt. viii. 11. I say unto you, that many shall come from the East and West, and shall sit down with *Abraham,* and *Isaac,* and *Jacob,* in the Kingdom of Heaven.

Matt. xxiv. 14. This Gospel of the Kingdom shall be preached in all the World, for a Witness unto all Nations; and then shall the End come.

John xii. 32. And I, if I be lifted up, will draw all Men after me.

Rev. xi. 15. And the seventh Angel sounded, and there were great Voices in Heaven, saying, The Kingdoms of this World are become the Kingdoms of our Lord, and of his Christ; and he shall reign for ever and ever. *See Rev.* vii. 9, 10. *Rev.* xii. 10.

II. *The* **Glory** *of the* **Church.**

Ps. xlv. 13. The King's Daughter is all glorious within; her Cloathing is of wrought Gold.

Ps. xlviii. 2. Beautiful for Situation, the Joy of the whole Earth is Mount *Zion*, on the Sides of the North, the City of the Great King.

Ver. 12. Walk about *Zion,* and go round about her; tell the Towers thereof:

Ver. 13. Mark ye well her Bulwarks, consider her Palaces, that ye may tell it to the Generations following.

Ps. lxxxvii. 3. Glorious Things are spoken of thee, O City of God.

Is. xlvi. 13. I will bring near my Righteousness; it shall not be far off, and my Salvation shall not tarry; and I will place Salvation in *Zion* for *Israel* my Glory.

Is. liv. 11. O thou afflicted, tossed with Tempest, and not comforted, behold, I will lay thy Stones with fair Colours, and lay thy Foundations with Sapphires.

Ver. 12. And I will make thy Windows of Agates, and thy Gates of Carbuncles, and all thy Borders of pleasant Stones.

Is. lx. 1. Arise, shine, for thy Light is come, and the Glory of the Lord is risen upon thee.

Ver. 2. For behold Darkness shall cover the Earth, and gross Darkness the People: but the Lord shall arise upon thee, and his Glory shall be seen upon thee.

Ver. 13. The Glory of *Lebanon* shall come unto thee, the Fir-tree, the Pine-tree, and the Box together, to beautify the Place of my Sanctuary; and I will make the Place of my Feet glorious,

Ver. 14. Whereas thou hast been forsaken and hated, so that no Man went through thee; I will make thee an eternal Excellency, a Joy of many Generations.

Ver. 19. The Sun shall be no more thy Light by Day, neither for Brightness shall the Moon give Light unto thee; but the Lord shall be unto thee an everlasting Light, and thy God thy Glory.

Ver. 20. Thy Sun shall no more go down, neither shall thy Moon withdraw itself; for the Lord shall be thine everlasting Light, and the Days of thy Mourning shall be ended.

Is. lxii. 2, The *Gentiles* shall see thy Righteousness, and all Kings thy Glory; and thou shalt be called by a new Name, which the Mouth of the Lord shall name.

Ver. 3. Thou shalt also be a Crown of Glory in the Hand of the Lord, and a royal Diadem in the Hand of thy God.

Rev. xxi. 10. And he carried me away in the Spirit, to a great and high Mountain, and shewed me that great City, the holy Jerusalem, descending out of Heaven from God.

Ver. 11. Having the Glory of God: And her Light was like unto a Stone most precious; even like a Jasper-stone, clear as Crystal. See *Ver.* 18, 21.

Ver. 22. And I saw no Temple therein; for the Lord God Almighty, and the Lamb, are the Temple of it,

Ver. 23. And the City had no need of the Sun, neither of the Moon to shine in it; for the Glory of God did lighten it, and the Lamb is the Light thereof.

Ver. 24. And the Nations of them which are saved, shall walk in the Light of it; and the Kings of the Earth do bring their Glory and Honour into it.

Ver. 25. And the Gates of it shall not be shut at all by Day; for there shall be no Night there.

Ver. 26. And they shall bring the Glory and Honour of the Nations into it.

III. *Promises of the Increase of* Light *and* Knowledge, *and of the* Means *of* Grace.

Is. xi. 4. The Earth shall be full of the Knowledge of the Lord, as the Waters cover the Sea.

Is. xxv. 6. And in this Mountain shall the Lord of Hosts make unto all People a Feast of fat Things, a Feast of Wines on the Lees, of fat Things full of Marrow, of Wines on the Lees well refined.

Ver. 7, And he will destroy in this Mountain the Face of the Covering cast over all People, and the Veil that is spread over all Nations.

Is. xxix. 18. In that Day shall the Deaf hear the Words of the Book, and the Eyes of the Blind shall see out of Obscurity, and out of Darkness.

Ver. 24. They also that erred in Spirit, shall come to Understanding; and they that murmured, shall learn Doctrine.

Is. xli. 18. I will open Rivers in high Places, and Fountains in the midst of the Valleys: I will make the Wilderness a Pool of Water, and the dry Land Springs of Water.

Ver. 19. I will plant in the Wilderness the Cedar, the Shittah Tree, and the Myrtle, and the Oil-Tree; I will set in the Desert the Fir-Tree, and the Pine, and the Box Tree together. See *Chap.* xxxv, 6, 7, 8.

Is. lii. 7. How beautiful upon the Mountains are the Feet of him that bringeth good Tidings, that publisheth Peace, that bringeth good Tidings of Good, that publisheth Salvation, that saith unto *Zion,* Thy God reigneth.

Ver. 8. Thy Watchman shall lift up the Voice; with the Voice together shall they sing: For they shall see Eye to Eye, when the Lord shall bring again *Zion.*

Is. liv. 13. And all thy Children shall be taught of the Lord.

Dan. xii. 4. Many shall run to and fro, and Knowledge shall be increased.

IV. *Promises of* Purity, Holiness, *and* Righteousness *in the* Church.

Is. iv. 3. And it shall come to pass, that he that is left in *Zion,* and he that remaineth in *Jerusalem,* shall be called Holy; even every one that is written among the Living in *Jerusalem.*

Ver. 4. When the Lord shall have washed away the Filth of the Daughters of *Zion,* and shall have purged the Blood of *Jerusalem* from the midst thereof, by the Spirit of Judgment, and by the Spirit of Burning.

Is. xxxii. 15. Until the Spirit be poured upon us from on high, and the Wilderness be a fruitful Field, and the fruitful Field be counted for a Forest:

Ver. 16. Then Judgment shall dwell in the Wilderness, and Righteousness remain in the fruitful Field.

Is. xxxiii. 5. The Lord is exalted, for he dwelleth on high: He hath filled *Zion* with Judgment and Righteousness.

Ver. 6. And Wisdom and Knowledge shall be the Stability of thy Times, and Strength of Salvation: The Fear of the Lord is his Treasure.

Is. xlv. 8. Drop down, ye Heavens from above, and let the Skies pour down Righteousness; let the Earth open, and let them bring forth Salvation, and let Righteousness spring up together: I the Lord have created it.

Ps. lxxxv. 10. Mercy and Truth are met together: Righteousness and Peace have kissed each other.

Ver. 11. Truth shall spring out of the Earth; and Righteousness shall look down from Heaven.

Ver. 13. Righteousness shall go before him, and shall set us in the Way of his Steps.

Is. lx. 21. Thy People shall be all righteous; they shall inherit the Land for ever, the Branch of my planting, the Work of my Hands, that I may be glorified.

Is. lxi. 11. As the Earth bringeth forth her Bud, and as the Garden causeth the Things that are sown in it to spring forth; so the Lord God will cause Righteousness and Praise to spring forth before all the Nations.

Mal. iii. 43. He shall sit as a Refiner and Purifier of Silver, and he shall purify the Sons of *Levi,* and purge them as Gold and Silver, that they may offer unto the Lord an Offering in Righteousness.

Ver. 4. Then shall the Offering of *Judah* and *Jerusalem* be pleasant unto the Lord, as in the Days of old, and as in former Years.

Ps. lxxii. 5. They shall fear thee as long as the Sun and Moon endure throughout all Generations.

Zech. xiv. 20. In that Day shall there be upon the Bells of the Horses, Holiness unto the Lord; and the Pots in the Lord's House shall be like the Bowls before the Altar.

Ver. 21. Yea, every Pot in *Jerusalem,* and in *Judah,* shall be Holiness unto the Lord of Hosts; and all they that sacrifice shall come and take of them, and seethe therein: And in that Day there shall be no more the *Canaanite* in the House of the Lord of Hosts.

Rev. xix. 8. And to her [*the Lamb's Wife*] was granted, that she should be arrayed in fine Linen, clean and white: For the fine Linen is the Righteousness of the Saints.

V. *Promises of* Peace, Love, *and* Unity.

Is. ii. 4. And they shall beat their Swords into Plow-shares, and their Spears into Pruning-hooks: Nation shall not lift up Sword against Nation, neither shall they learn War any more.

Is. xi. 6. The Wolf also shall dwell with the Lamb, and the Leopard shall lie down with the Kid; and the Calf, and the young Lion, and the Fatling together, and a little Child shall lead them.

Ver. 7. And the Cow and the Bear shall feed; their young ones shall lie down together; and the Lion shall eat Straw like the Ox.

Ver. 8. And the sucking Child shall play on the Hole of the Asp, and the weaned Child shall put his Hand on the Cockatrice Den.

Ver. 9. They shall not hurt nor destroy in all my holy Mountain.

Ver. 13. The Envy also of *Ephraim* shall depart, and the Adversaries of *Judah* shall be cut off: *Ephraim* shall not envy *Judah*, said *Judah* shall not vex *Ephraim*.

Ps. lxxii. 3. The Mountains shall bring Peace to the People, and the little Hills, by Righteousness.

Ver. 7. In his Days shall the Righteous flourish; and abundance of Peace, so long as the Moon endureth.

John xvii. 20. Neither pray I for these alone, but for them also which shall believe on me through their Word:

Ver. 21. That they all may be one, as Thou, Father, art in me, and I in Thee; that they also may be one in Us, that the World may believe thou hast sent me.

Ver. 22. And the Glory which thou gavest me, I have given them, that they may be one, even as we are one.

Ver. 23. I in them, and thou in me, that they may be made perfect in one, and that the World may know that thou hast sent me, and hast loved them, as thou hast loved me.

Eph. iv. 16. From whom [*Christ*] the whole Body fitly joined together, and compacted by that which every Joint supplieth, according to the effectual working in the Measure of every Part, maketh Increase of the Body, unto the Edifying of itself in Love.

VI. *Promises of the* Submission *and the* Destruction *of the* Enemies *of the* Church.

Ps. Ex. 2. The Lord shall send the Rod of thy Strength out of *Zion:* Rule thou in the midst of thy Enemies.

Ver. 5. The Lord at thy Right Hand shall strike through Kings, in the Day of his Wrath.

Ver. 6. He shall judge among the Heathen: He shall fill the Places with dead Bodies: He shall wound the Heads over many Countries.

Is. xi. 4. He shall smite the Earth with the Rod of his Mouth; and with the Breath of his Lips shall he slay the Wicked.

Is. xxvii. 1. In that Day the Lord with his sore and great and strong Sword shall punish Leviathan, the piercing Serpent; even Leviathan, that crooked Serpent; And he shall slay the Dragon that is in the Sea.

Is. xli. 11. Behold all they that were incensed against thee, shall be ashamed and confounded; they shall be as nothing: And they that strive with thee, shall perish.

Ver. 12. Thou shalt seek them, and shalt not find them, even them that contended with thee: They that war against thee shall be as nothing, and as a Thing of nought. *See Ver.* 15, 16.

Is. xlix. 24. Shall the Prey be taken from the Mighty, or the lawful Captive delivered?

Ver. 25. But thus saith the Lord, Even the Captives of the Mighty shall be taken away, and the Prey of the Terrible shall be delivered; for I will contend with him that contendeth with thee, and I will save thy Children.

Ver. 26. And I will feed them that oppress thee with their own Flesh, and they shall be drunken with their own Blood, as with sweet Wine; and all Flesh shall know that I the Lord am thy Saviour, and thy Redeemer the Mighty One of *Jacob*.

Is. lix. 19. When the Enemy shall come in like a Flood, the Spirit of the Lord shall lift up a Standard against him.

Is. ix. 14. The Sons also of them that afflicted thee, shall come bending unto thee; and all they that despised thee, shall bow themselves down at the Soles of thy Feet; and they shall call thee, The City of the Lord, The Zion of the Holy One of Israel.

2 Thes. ii. 8. Then shall the Wicked by revealed, whom the Lord shall consume with the Spirit of his Mouth, and destroy with the Brightness of his Coming. See *Dan.* vii. 24, 25, 26.

Rev. xiv. 9. If any Man worship the Beast and his Image, and receive his Mark in his Forehead, or in his Hand;

Ver. 10. The same shall drink of the Wine of the Wrath of God, which is poured out without Mixture, into the Cup of his Indignation.

Rev. xvii. 1. Come hither, I will shew thee the Judgment of the great Whore, that sitteth upon many Waters, &c.

Ver. 16. And the Ten Horns which thou sawest upon the Beast, these shall hate the Whore, and shall make her desolate and naked, and shall eat her Flesh, and burn her with Fire.

Rev. xviii. 2. *Babylon* the great is fallen, is fallen, and is become the Habitation of Devils, and the Hold of every foul Spirit, and the Cage of every unclean and hateful Bird. *And so to the End of the Chapter.*

Rev. xix. 19. And I saw the Beast, and the Kings of the Earth, and their Armies gathered together, to make War against him that sat on the Horse, and against his Army.

Ver. 20. And the Beast was taken, and with him the false Prophet that wrought Miracles before him, with which he deceived them that had received the Mark of the Beast, and them that worshipped his Image: These both were cast alive into a Lake of Fire burning with Brimstone.

Rev. xx. 7. And when the Thousand Years are expired, Satan shall be loosed out of Prison.

Ver. 8. And shall go out to deceive the Nations which are in the four Quarters of the Earth, *Gog* and *Magog*, to gather them together to Battle; the Number of whom is as the Sand of the Sea.

Ver. 9. And they went up on the Breadth of the Earth, and compassed the Camp of Saints about, and the beloved City; and Fire came down from God out of Heaven, and devoured them. *See Ezek.* xxxviii. *and* xxxix.

VII. *Promises to the* Favour *and* Submission *of* Kings *to the* Kingdom *of* Christ.

Is. xlix. 7. Thus saith the Lord, the Redeemer of *Israel*, and his Holy One, to Him whom Men despiseth, to Him whom the Nation abhorreth, to a Servant of Rulers, Kings shall see and arise. Princes also shall worship, because of the Lord that is faithful, and the Holy One of *Israel*, and he shall choose thee.

Ver. 23. And Kings shall be thy Nursing Fathers, and their Queens thy Nursing Mothers: They shall bow down to thee with their Face toward the Earth, and lick up the Dust of thy Feet, and thou shalt know that I am the Lord; for they shall not be ashamed that wait for me.

Is. lii. 15. So shall he sprinkle many Nations; the Kings shall shut their Mouths at him: For that which had not been told them, shall they see; and that which they had not heard, shall they consider.

Is. lx. 3. And the *Gentiles* shall come to thy Light, and Kings to the Brightness of thy Rising.

Ver. 10. And the Sons of Strangers shall build up thy Walls, and their Kings shall minister unto thee; for in my Wrath I smote thee, but in my Favour have I had Mercy on thee.

Ver. 11. Therefore thy Gates shall be open continually; they shall not be shut Day nor Night, that Men may bring unto thee the Forces of the *Gentiles*, and that their Kings may be brought.

Ver. 16. Thou shalt suck the Milk of the Gentiles, and shalt suck the Breast of Kings, and shalt know that I the Lord am thy Saviour and thy Redeemer, the Mighty One of *Jacob*.

VIII. *Promises of the* Security, Tranquility, *and* Prosperity *of the* Church.

Is. iv. 5. And the Lord will create upon every Dwelling-place of Mount *Zion*, and upon her Assemblies, a Cloud and Smoke by Day, and the shining of a flaming Fire by Night: For upon all the Glory shall be a Defence.

Ver. 6. And there shall be a Tabernacle for a Shadow in the Day-time from the Heat, and for a Place of Refuge, and for a Covert from Storm and from Rain.

Is. xxvii. 2. In that Day sing ye unto her, A Vineyard of red Wine.

Ver. 3. I the Lord do keep it; I will water it every Moment: Lest any hurt it, I will keep it Night and Day.

Is. xxxiii. 20, Look upon *Zion* the City of our Solemnities; thine Eyes shall see *Jerusalem* a quiet Habitation, a Tabernacle that shall not be taken down; not one of the Stakes thereof shall ever be removed, neither shall any of the Cords thereof be broken.

Ver. 21. For there the glorious Lord will be unto us a Place of broad Rivers and Streams, wherein shall go no Galley with Oars, neither shall gallant Ship pass thereby:

Ver. 22. For the Lord is our Judge, the Lord is our Lawgiver, the Lord is our King; He will save us.

Is. liv, 14. In Righteousness shalt thou be established: Thou shalt be far from Oppression, for thou shalt not fear; and from Terror, for it shall not come near thee.

Ver. 15. Behold, they shall surely gather together, but not by me: Whosoever shall gather together against thee, shall fall for thy sake.

Ver. 17. No Weapon that is formed against thee shall prosper; and every Tongue that shall rise against thee in Judgment thou shalt condemn. This is the Heritage of the Servants of the Lord, and their Righteousness is of me, saith the Lord.

Is. lxv. 18. Be you glad, and rejoice for ever in that which I create; for, behold, I create *Jerusalem* a Rejoicing, and her People a Joy.

Ver. 19. And I will rejoice in *Jerusalem,* and joy in my People; and the Voice of Weeping shall be no more heard in her, nor the Voice of Crying.

Is. li. 3. The Lord will comfort *Zion:* He will comfort all her waste Places, and he will make her Wilderness like *Eden,* and her Desert like the Garden of the Lord; Joy and Gladness shall be found therein, Thanksgiving, and the Voice of Melody.

Ps. cii. 13. Thou shalt arise, and have Mercy upon *Zion;* for the Time to favour her, yea, the set Time is come:

Ver. 14. For thy Servants take Pleasure in her Stones, and favour the Dust thereof.

Ver. 16. When the Lord shall build up *Zion,* he shall appear in his Glory.

Is. lxvi. 10. Rejoice ye with *Jerusalem,* and be glad with her, all ye that love her; rejoice for Joy with her, all ye that mourn for her:

Ver. 11. That ye may suck and be satisfied with the Breasts of her Consolations; that ye may milk out and be delighted with the Abundance of her Glory.

Ver. 12. For thus saith the Lord, Behold, I will extend Peace to her like a River, and the Glory of the *Gentiles* like a flowing Stream: Then shall ye suck, ye shall be borne upon her Sides, and be dandled upon her Knees. See *Ver.* 13, 14.

Jer. xxxiii. 6. In his Days *Judah* shall be saved, and *Israel* shall dwell safely.

Matt. xvi. 18. Upon this Rock will I build my Church, and the Gates of Hell shall not prevail against it.

Dan. vii. 27. And the Kingdom and Dominion, and the Greatness of the Kingdom under the whole Heaven, shall be given to the People of the Saints of the Most High, whose Kingdom is an everlasting Kingdom, and all Dominions shall serve and obey him.

IX. *Promises of the* Perpetual Continuance *of the* Church.

Is. lix. 21. As for me, this is my Covenant with them, saith the Lord, My Spirit that is upon me, and my Words which I have put into thy Mouth, shall not depart out of thy Mouth, nor out of the Mouth of thy Seed, nor out of the Mouth of thy Seed's Seed, saith the Lord, from henceforth and for ever.

Is. lxvi. 22. For as the new Heavens and the new Earth which I will make shall remain before me, saith the Lord, so shall your Seed and your Name remain.

Jer. xxxi. 35. Thus saith the Lord, which giveth the Sun for a Light by Day, and the Ordinances of the Moon and of the Stars for a Light by Night, which divideth the Sea when the Waves thereof roar; the Lord of Hosts is his Name:

Ver. 36. If those Ordinances depart from before me, saith the Lord, then the Seed of *Israel* also shall cease from being a Nation before me for ever.

Ver. 37. Thus saith the Lord, If Heaven above can be measured, and the Foundations of the Earth searched out beneath; I will also cast off all the Seed of *Israel,* for all that they have done, saith the Lord. *See also Chap,* xxxiii. 20, 21, 22, 25, 26.

Dan. vii. 14. His Dominion is an everlasting Dominion, which shall not pass away, and his Kingdom that which shall not be destroyed.

Matt, xxviii. 20. Lo, I am with you alway, even unto the End of the World.

X. *Promises of the* Conversion *and* Restoration *of the* Jews.

Jer. xxx. 9. They shall serve the Lord their God, and *David* their King, whom I will raise up unto them.

Ver. 10. Therefore fear thou not, O my Servant *Jacob,* saith the Lord, neither be thou dismayed, O *Israel;* for lo, I will save thee from afar, and thy Seed from the Land of their Captivity; and *Jacob* shall return, and shall be in Rest and Quiet, and none shall make him afraid. *See to the End of the Chapter.*

Jer. xxxi. 1. At the same Time, saith the Lord, will I be the God of all the Families of *Israel,* and they shall be my People.

Ver. 4. Again I will build thee, and thou shalt be built, O Virgin of *Israel;* thou shalt again be adorned with thy Tabrets, and shalt go forth in the Dances of them that make merry.

Ver. 10. Hear the Word of the Lord, O Nations, and declare it in the Isles afar off, and say, He that scattered *Israel* will gather him, and keep him, as a Shepherd doth his Flock.

Ver. 17. There is Hope in thine End, that thy Children shall come again to their own Border.

Ver. 31. Behold, the Days come, saith the Lord, that I will make a new Covenant with the House of *Israel,* and with the House of *Judah.*

Ver. 32. Not according to the Covenant that I made with their Fathers, &c.

Ver. 33. But this shall be the Covenant that I will make with the House of *Israel:* After those Days, saith the Lord, I will put my Law in their inward Parts, and write it in their Hearts; and I will be their God, and they shall be my People.

Ver. 38. Behold, the Days come, saith the Lord, that the City shall be built to the Lord, from the Tower of *Hananeel* unto the Gate of the Corner. *See the whole Chapter.*

Jer. xxxii. 41. Yea, I will rejoice over them to do them good, and I will plant them in this Land assuredly, with my whole Heart, and with my whole Soul. *See from Ver. 37 to the End.*

Jer. xxxiii. 7. And I will cause the Captivity of *Judah* and the Captivity of *Israel* to return, and will build them as at the first.

Ver. 8. And I will cleanse them from all their Iniquities, &c.

Ver. 9. And it shall be to me a Name of Joy, a Praise and an Honour before all the Nations of the Earth, which shall hear all the Good that I do unto them, &c.

Ver. 15. In those Days, and at that Time, will I cause the Branch of Righteousness to grow up unto *David,* and he shall execute Judgment and Justice in the Land.

Ver. 16. In those Days shall *Judah* be saved, and *Jerusalem* shall dwell safely; and this is the Name wherewith she shall be called, The Lord our Righteousness.

Ver. 24. Considerest thou not, what this People have spoken, saying, The two Families which the Lord hath chosen, he will even cast them off? &c.

Ver. 25. Thus saith the Lord, If my Covenant be not with Day and Night, and if I have not appointed the Ordinances of Heaven and Earth:

Ver. 26. Then will I cast away the Seed of *Jacob* and *David* my Servant, so that I will not take any of his Seed to be Rulers over the Seed of *Abraham, Isaac,* and *Jacob:* for I will cause their Captivity to return, and have Mercy on them. *To the same purpose see the whole Chapter. See also Chap.* l. 4, 5, 19, 20.

Ezek. xvi. 60. Nevertheless, I will remember my Covenant with thee in the Days of thy Youth, and I will establish unto thee an everlasting Covenant.

Ver. 61. Thou shalt remember thy Ways, and be ashamed, when thou shalt receive thy Sisters, thine Elder and thy Younger [*Sodom* and *Samaria, Ver.* 55] and I will give them unto thee for Daughters, but not by thy Covenant. *Ver.* 62, 63.

Ezek. xx. 34. I will bring you out from the People, and will gather you out of the Countries, wherein ye are scattered, with a mighty Hand. —

Ver. 35. And I will bring you into the Wilderness of the People, and there will I plead with you Face to Face.

Ver. 37. And I will cause you to pass under the Rod, and I will bring you into the Bond of the Covenant.

Ver. 38. And I will purge out from among you the Rebels, and them that transgress against me.

Ver. 40. In my holy Mountain, in the Mountain of the Height of *Israel,* saith the Lord God, there shall all the House of *Israel,* all of them in the Land, serve me; and there will I accept them, and there will I require your Offerings, and the First-fruits of your Oblations, with all your Holy Things. *See also Ver.* 41, 44.

Ezek. xxxiv. 23. And I will set one Shepherd over them, and he shall feed them, even my Servant *David;* he shall feed them and be their Shepherd.

Ver. 24. And I the Lord will be their God, and my Servant *David* a Prince among them: I the Lord have spoken it.

Ver. 28. And they shall no more be a Prey among the Heathen, neither shall the Beasts of the Land devour them; but they shall dwell safely, and none shall make them afraid.

Ver. 29. And I will raise up for them a Plant of Renown. *See also Ver.* 11, 16, *and from Ver.* 22 *to the End of the Chapter.*

Ezek. xxxvi. 11. I will multiply upon you [the Mountains of *Israel*] Man and Beast, and they shall increase, and bring Fruit; and will settle you after your old Estates, and I will do better unto you than at your Beginnings, and ye shall know that I am the Lord.

Ver. 24. I will take you from among the Heathen, and gather you out of all Countries, and will bring you into your own Land.

Ver. 25. Then will I sprinkle clean Water upon you, and ye shall be clean; from all your Filthiness, and from all your Idols, will I cleanse you.

Ver. 26. A new Heart also will I give you, &c.

Ver. 33. In the Day that I shall have cleansed you from all your Iniquities, I will also cause you to dwell in the Cities, and the Wastes shall be builded. *See the whole Chapter; as also Chap.* xxxvii.

Ezek. xxxvii. 25. And they shall dwell in the Land that I have given unto Jacob my Servant, wherein your Fathers have dwelt; and they shall dwell therein, even they, and their Children, and their Children's Children, for ever, and my Servant David shall be their Prince for ever.

Hos. i. 10. Yet the Number of the Children of *Israel* shall be as the Sand of the Sea, which cannot be measured nor numbered; and it shall come to pass, that in the Place where it was said unto them. Ye are not my People, there it shall be said unto them, Ye are the Sons of the living God.

Ver. 11. Then shall the Children of *Judah,* and the Children of *Israel,* be gathered together, and appoint themselves one Head, and they shall come up out of the Land; great shall be the Day of *Jezreel.*

Hos. ii. 14. Behold, I will allure her, and bring her into the Wilderness, and speak comfortably unto her.

Ver. 15. And I will give her Vineyards from thence, and the Valley of *Achor* for a Door of Hope; and she shall sing there, as in the Days of her Youth, and as in the Day when she came up out of the Land of *Egypt.*

Ver. 19. And I will betroth thee unto me for ever, &c. *See from Ver.* 16 *to the End.*

Hos. iii. 4. The Children of *Israel* shall abide many Days without a King, and without a Prince, and without a Sacrifice, and without an Image, and without an Ephod, and without Teraphim.

Ver. 5. Afterwards shall the Children of *Israel* return, and seek the Lord their God, and *David* their King, and shall fear the Lord and his Goodness in the latter Days. *See also Chap.* xiv.

Joel m. I. Behold, in those Days, and in that Time, when I shall bring again the Captivity of *Judah* and of *Jerusalem*;

Ver. 2. I will also gather all Nations, and will bring them down into the Valley of *Jehoshaphat,* and will plead with them for my People, &c.

Ver. 17. So shall ye know that I am the Lord your God, dwelling in *Zion,* my holy Mountain: Then shall *Jerusalem* be holy, and there shall be no more Strangers pass through her any more.

Ver. 20. *Judah* shall dwell for ever, and *Jerusalem* from Generation to Generation. *See also Ver.* 7, 14, 16, 18, 21.

Amos. ix. 14. And I will bring again the Captivity of my People *Israel,* and they shall build the waste Cities, and inhabit them. —

Ver. 15. And I will plant them upon their Land, and they shall be no more pulled up out of their Land, which I have given them, saith the Lord thy God.

Obad. Ver. 17. Upon Mount *Zion* shall be Deliverance, and there shall be Holiness, and the House of Jacob shall possess their Possessions.

Ver. 21. And Saviours shall come upon Mount *Zion* to judge the Mount of *Esau,* and the Kingdom shall be the Lord's.

Mic. ii. 12. I will surely assemble, O *Jacob,* all of thee; I will surely gather the Remnant of Israel, I will put them together as the Sheep of *Bozrah,* as the Flock in the midst of their Fold; they shall make great Noise by reason of the Multitude of Men.

Ver. 13. The Breaker is come up before them; they have broken up, and have passed through the Gate, and are gone out by it; and their King shall pass before them, and the Lord on the Head of them.

Mic. v. 3. Therefore will he give them up, until the Time that she which travaileth, hath brought forth; then the Remnant of his Brethren shall return unto the Children of *Israel.*

Ver. 4. And he shall stand and feed in the Strength of the Lord, in the Majesty of the Name of the Lord his God, and they shall abide, for now shall he be great unto the Ends of the Earth.

Ver. 7. And the Remnant of *Jacob* shall be in the midst of many People, as a Dew from the Lord, as the Showers upon the Grass that tarrieth not for Man, nor waiteth for the Sons of Men.

Ver. 13. Thy graven Images also will I cut off, and thy standing Images out of the midst of thee, and thou shalt no more worship the Work of thine Hands. *See the whole Chapter, and Chap.* iv. *and Chap.* vii. 14, 17. *See also* Zeph. iii. 9. *to the End.*

Zech. ii. 10. Sing and rejoice, O Daughter of Zion; for lo I come, and I will dwell in the midst of thee, saith the Lord.

Ver. 12. And the Lord shall inherit *Judah,* his Portion in the Holy Land, and shall choose *Jerusalem* again.

Zech. x. 6. And I will strengthen the House of *Judah,* and I will save the House of *Joseph,* and I will bring them again to place them; for I have Mercy upon them, and they shall be as though I had not cast them off; for I am the Lord their God, and will hear them.

Ver. 8. I will hiss for them, and gather them, for I have redeemed them; and they shall increase, as they have increased.

Ver. 9. And I will sow them among the People, and they shall remember me in far Countries, and they shall live with their Children, and turn again. *See the whole Chapter.*

Zech. xii. 6. In that Day will I make the Governors of *Judah* like a Hearth of Fire among the Wood, and like a Torch of Fire in a Sheaf; and they shall devour all the People round about, on the Right Hand and on the Left; and *Jerusalem* shall be inhabited again, in her own Place, even in *Jerusalem.*

Ver. 10. And I will pour upon the House of *David,* and upon the Inhabitants of *Jerusalem,* the Spirit of Grace and Supplications; and they shall look upon me, whom they have pierced, &c. *See the whole Chapter.*

Zech. xiv. 11. And Men shall dwell in it [*i.e., all the Land*] and there shall be no more utter Destruction; but *Jerusalem* shall be safely inhabited. *See the whole Chapter.*

Luke xxi. 24. *Jerusalem* shall be trodden down of the *Gentiles,* until the Times of the *Gentiles* be fulfilled.

2 *Cor.* iii. 15. Even unto this Day, when Moses is read, the Veil is upon their Heart.

Ver. 16. Nevertheless, when it shall turn unto the Lord, the Veil shall be taken away.

Rom. xi. 2. God hath not cast away his People, which he foreknew.

Ver. 12. If the Fall of them be the Riches of the World, and the Diminishing of them the Riches of the *Gentiles;* how much more their Fulness?

Ver. 15. For if the Casting away of them be the Reconciling of the World, what shall the receiving of them be but Life from the Dead?

Ver. 23. And they also, if they abide not still in Unbelief, shall be graffed in; for God is able to graff them in again.

Ver. 24. — How much more shall these, which be the natural Branches, be graffed in their own Olive-tree?

Ver. 25. For I would not, Brethren, that ye should be ignorant of this Mystery (lest ye should be wise in your own Conceit) that Blindness in part is happened unto *Israel,* until the Fulness of the *Gentiles* be come in.

Ver. 26. Then all *Israel* shall be saved; as it is written, There shall come out of *Zion* the Deliverer, and shall turn away the Ungodliness from *Jacob.*

Ver. 27. For this is my Covenant unto them, when I shall take away their Sins.

Ver. 28. As concerning the Gospel, they are Enemies for your sakes; but as touching the Election, they are beloved for the Father's sake.

Ver. 29. For the Gifts and Calling of God are without Repentance. *See also Ver.* 30, 31.

Ver. 32. God hath concluded them all in Unbelief, that he might have Mercy upon all.

Ver. 33. O the Depth of the Riches both of the Wisdom and Knowledge of God! How unsearchable are his Judgments, and his Ways past finding out!

Conclusion - *That* God *will perform all His* Promises

Deut. vii. 9. Know that the Lord thy God, he is God, the faithful God, which keepeth Covenant and Mercy with them love him, and keep his Commandments, to a thousand Generations.

Numb. xxiii. 19. God is not a Man, that he should lie; neither the Son of Man, that he should repent: Hath he said, and shall he not do it? Or hath he spoken, and shall not he make it good?

Josh. xxiii. 14. Ye know in all your Hearts, and in all your Souls, that not one Thing hath failed, of all the good Things which the Lord your God spake concerning you; all are come to pass unto you, and not one thing hath failed thereof. I Kings viii. 56.

Ps. xviii. 30. The Word of the Lord is tried.

Ps. lxxxix. 34. My Covenant will I not break, nor alter the Thing that is gone out of my Lips.

Ps. cv. 8. He hath remembered his Covenant for ever, which he commanded to a thousand Generations.

Ps. cxix. 89. For ever, O Lord, thy Word is settled in Heaven.

Ver. 90. Thy Faithfulness is unto all Generations.

Ver. 160. Thy Word is true from the Beginning.

Ps. cxlvi. 6. Which keepeth Truth for ever.

Is. xxv. 1. Thy Counsels of old are Faithfulness and Truth.

Is. xlvi. 11. I have spoken it, I will also bring it to pass: I have purposed it, I will also do it.

Is. lv. 10. As the Rain cometh down, and the Snow from Heaven, and returneth not thither, but watereth the Earth, and maketh it bring forth and bud, that it may give Seed to the Sower, and Bread to the Eater:

Ver. 11. So shall my Word be, that goeth forth out of my Mouth; it shall not return unto me void, but it shall accomplish that which I please; and it shall prosper in the Thing whereunto I sent it.

Rom. xv. 8. Jesus Christ was a Minister of the Circumcision for the Truth of God, to confirm the Promises made unto the Fathers.

2 *Cor.* i. 20. All the Promises of God in him [*Christ*] are Yea, and in him Amen, unto the Glory of God by us.

2 *Tim.* ii. 13. If we believe not, yet he abideth faithful; he cannot deny himself.

2 *Pet.* iii. 9. The Lord is not slack concerning his Promise (as some Men count Slackness).

Heb. vi. 17. God, willing more abundantly to shew unto the Heirs of Promise the Immutability of his Counsel, confirmed it by an Oath.

Ver. 18, That by two immutable Things, in which it was impossible for God to lie, we might have strong Consolation, who have fled for Refuge, to lay hold upon the Hope set before us.

Heb. x. 23. He is faithful that promised.

www.ingramcontent.com/pod-product-compliance
Lightning Source LLC
LaVergne TN
LVHW091302080426
835510LV00007B/363